D1626988

# THE MUNCHKIN DIARY

Munchkin Hugs,
Betty Ann Bruno

# THE MUNCHKIN DIARY

*my personal*
*yellow brick road*

BETTY ANN BRUNO

Library of Congress Cataloging-in-Publication Data

ISBN: 9781736205600 (Print Edition)
ISBN: 9781736205617 (EPUB Edition)

Editing by David Bolling
Book design by Kara Adanalian | www.acmegraphics.net

To contact the author, visit www.TheMunchkinDiary.org

# DEDICATION

For my sons Daniel *Liloa*, Michael *Kalani*,
and Steven *Keali`ipu`uwaialoha* —
a few stories about the world I grew up in.
Times and struggles — lost and won.

# TABLE *of* CONTENTS

# FOREWORD

A Few Words About the Magic of Oz

*by* Bob Baum

When Betty Ann Bruno asked me to write a few words for her book, I felt genuinely honored. My wife and I have known Betty Ann for many years through our mutual relationship with Oz. Knowing the story of how Betty Ann became a Munchkin, I was immediately struck by a series of what I feel are coincidences. At once, I pictured Betty Ann and her mother reading a notice on a bulletin board calling for girls who could sing, dance and act terrified. At that moment in time, Betty Ann Bruno had no idea that her life would be changed by an event that happened many years earlier.

That event was when L. Frank Baum, my great grandfather, wrote the final chapter of his new children's book in 1898. His hope then was that it would bring some success to him as an author. He had no way of realizing just how much of a lasting impact *The Wonderful Wizard of Oz* would have on his life, and the lives of so many others.

When the main actors first came together to film MGM's *The Wizard of Oz*, they had no idea that their performances would be the benchmark by which their future careers would be measured. MGM had hopes that the film would not only make back the money it cost to produce, but also be profitable. They had no idea that *The Wizard of Oz* would become a classic by which films would be judged. Nor did any of the 124 Little People, who were assembled to make a film in Hollywood, know that their performances in *The Wizard of Oz* would forever change their lives. When my wife Clare and I began our life together, neither of us had any inkling of the wonderful chain of events we would become part of.

*The Wonderful Wizard of Oz* not only became a worldwide literary success, it ultimately led to my great grandfather receiving the title of the first "American Fairy Tale Author." Since its publication, the book has weathered the test of time, and is as popular and new to its readers today as it was in 1900.

I am often asked two questions about L. Frank Baum. First, where did he come up with the name "Oz." And second, where did he get his imagination?

The answer to the first question comes from a family story that was often related to me. Frank loved to try out his new story ideas on the neighborhood children, and on his four sons. On one such evening, a group of children had gathered to hear the continuing story of Dorothy and her friends as they traveled down a road made of yellow bricks. Frank was sitting on the edge of his chair and intently telling the story to the boys and girls before him. "Remember, last time when we stopped, Dorothy, the Scarecrow, the man made of Tin and the Lion were about to enter a dark and scary forest? As we join them tonight, they are slowly walking down the road of yellow bricks, arm in arm because they are afraid. The big trees looked as if they were following them. The further they traveled into the forest, the darker and more frightening it became." Just at this moment a little girl asked, "Mr. Baum, where is this magic land?"

"You mean the land that Dorothy flew to on a tornado?" Frank asked.

"Yes." replied the girl with a bright, questioning face.

Frank didn't have a name for this magic land yet, as he was still developing the details of his new story. With a big smile, he said, "I'm glad you asked. I was just about to get to that part."

As he was answering the girl, he was also looking around the room in hopes something would give him an idea for a name. Nothing helped, until he looked into his office next to the front room. He caught a glimpse of his desk and the filing cabinet next to it. He looked at the top drawer, which was labeled A–N.

Frank, pleased with himself, continued on with the story, "The trees seemed to be coming alive and following Dorothy and her comrades as they walked along. This made Dorothy very afraid. She had no way of knowing this could only happen in the magic land that the tornado had brought her to. You see, she was in the Land of Oz."

The assembled group let out an audible sigh. Oz! The children's reaction and the wonderment showing on their faces told Frank he had found the perfect name for his new land. He continued with the tale and chuckled to himself, not bad for a filing cabinet drawer labeled O-Z.

The answer to the second question could fill a book, but I always like to tell people it was simply because he became an adult with his childhood imagination intact. My great grandfather had the uncanny ability to understand how a child's mind worked. He could find characters in anyone or anything, and bring them to life. He would give just enough description to tell the story, but leave some things to be filled in by the reader's imagination. *The Wonderful Wizard of Oz* is a perfect example of this and, combined with all the line drawings on most pages, and the 24 color plates by W. W. Denslow, the book became a child's gateway into a new world of fantasy and imagination. The reader could not only become friends with the characters, but also interact with the story whenever they wanted to.

This magic that is Oz has lived on since it was written. The actors who played the main characters not only captured this magic in their performances, but carried it throughout their lives. They immediately became synonymous with Dorothy, the Scarecrow,

Tin Woodman and the Cowardly Lion, wherever they went. Their performances gave them a permanent place in history and made the film a treasured classic.

So I hope you now see how Betty Ann Bruno's life was changed so many years before she ever got the part of a Munchkin in the MGM film, *The Wizard of Oz*. As you read about her life, you will see that not only was she a Munchkin in Oz, but much like Dorothy, she is now traveling down her own Yellow Brick Road with all of its own adventures.

My wife, Clare, and I are grateful to be a part of Betty Ann Bruno's journey. Betty Ann Bruno *is* a living part of history. She *is* a Munchkin ambassador from Oz, and she has helped make Oz a *real* place, not *just* a dream.

*Robert A. Baum is a great-grandson of L. Frank Baum, and has maintained and built upon the author's own private collection. Bob Baum contributed information and material for the L. Frank Baum display at the Frances Goldwyn Library in Hollywood. He assisted the producers of the BBC's production,* In Search of Oz, *as well as Radio City Entertainment's version of* The Wizard of Oz, *and other theatrical productions. His support of the television movie* The Dreamer of Oz, *included loaning L. Frank Baum's own copies of books and other materials for use in sets and as props.*

*As a teacher, Bob used* The Wizard of Oz *as a teaching tool, and Baum's life as a model of perseverance and courage. Since retiring from formal education, Bob and his wife Clare have made appearances all over the country dressed in character as Frank and Maud Baum.*

# PREFACE

ONE OF THE LAST LIVING LINKS TO OZ
*by* STEVE COX

My relationship with Betty Ann Bruno goes back to 1988 when I was fresh out of college and writing a book about the Munchkins who worked in the MGM favorite, *The Wizard of Oz,* 50 years earlier. Some of the Munchkin actors told me they recalled a few children were in their scene as well, but they didn't know much about them, who they were, or where they might be today. And MGM Studios (at that time owned by Turner Broadcasting) had not saved vintage files or documents to support my research with regard to these children.

But I had an idea: Why not let newspapers around the country do some of the legwork for me? Through a local Associated Press office in St. Louis, I pitched a story about my search for the Munchkins in The Wizard of Oz, all these decades later. The article they promptly ran was printed across the nation, many times with the headline, "Come Out, Come Out, Wherever You Are."

Well, it worked. And not long after the story ran, an editor at AP called me with a message from "a Betty Ann Bruno … she says she was a Munchkin in the movie." I think Betty Ann was one of the first to approach me, and we've been friends ever since.

I'm so thankful that she was open to my interrogations (I had tons of questions) and I even had the pleasure of speaking with her mother, who provided her own memories of escorting her young daughter to the studio every day for work on what would become the grandpappy of all classic films.

Despite the fact she was all of seven years old during the filming, Betty Ann had a great memory of the events, as did several additional "Munchkids," as they're affectionately called. Today, as I write this, there are six of the dozen or so young girls from the film surviving. They are the just about the last living links we fans have to that magical movie. I'm so glad Betty Ann has put her memories in print because I'm still learning things from and about her. After all, she was in *Oz*, and for me, it doesn't get any better than that.

*Steve Cox, shown here to the left of Munchkin Jerry Maren of The Lollipop Guild, is the author of more than 20 books covering television, film and popular culture, including books on* The Three Stooges, The Munsters *and* The Addams Family. *He has written for numerous national publications and spurred the public's inexhaustible interest in all things Oz with his 1989 book,* The Munchkins Remember – The Wizard of Oz and Beyond.

# INTRODUCTION

BETTY ANN BRUNO'S LONG ROAD HOME
*by* DAVID BOLLING

Betty Ann Bruno is a treasure. Formally and officially. It says so on the certificate she received early in 2020 from the Cultural and Fine Arts Commission of the City of Sonoma, California.

Sonoma Treasure Artist of the Year is the whole title, and it's shared by previous honorees that include famed food writer M.F.K. Fisher, cartoonist Linus Maurer, harmonica virtuoso Norton Buffalo, nationally-collected fine artists Keith Wicks, Dennis Ziemienski and Chester Arnold, along with famed sculptor Jim Callahan and too many more to list.

It's a small town honor, to be sure, but it carries a lot of weight, partly because Sonoma is not your average small town. Besides some of the world's best wine, culture and art are strung through its DNA. Creative people, free thinkers, dreamers and builders have come here since long before Jack London arrived. Perhaps the most popular author on Earth in his time, London settled in the surrounding Valley of the Moon to live, work and die.

Among that uncommon company, Betty Ann fits right in, but defining precisely why takes a little explaining. You have to start with the Munchkin Period, which, for her, lasted all of three weeks, although it was one of the most important periods in the history of Hollywood.

That's because, in 1938, Betty Ann was one of about a dozen normal-sized children hired by MGM Studios to join 124 Little People (that's the politically correct term, but everyone called them midgets) to populate Munchkin Country in the Land of Oz, in the act of making perhaps the most beloved movie of all time. Because they couldn't find enough midgets to act as Munchkins in *The Wizard of Oz*, MGM hired a few kids, including Betty Ann.

Becoming a Munchkin was a glorious escapade, if only briefly, but she was just a kid and she wasn't conscious of it coloring her life. She had already been in other films, and what she actually dreamed of was having a horse.

Still, the Munchkin imprint stuck to her like a birthmark on the back of her neck, invisible to her but always there. And, as she would later discover, an international following would never let her forget it. That was in part because the film's special magic has continued to touch a global audience, generation after generation, a source of comfort and inspiration. Even as erudite a writer as Salman Rushdie would confide that, seeing *The Wizard of Oz* at the age of 10, "made a writer of me."

And it must be said that, as a metaphorical child of Oz, in a very real-world sense she has followed her own Yellow Brick Road through a series of adventures, trials, challenges, tests and triumphs easily as dramatic as the events that transpired somewhere over the rainbow.

If Oz were the sum total of Betty Ann's memorable experiences, you might find her as a footnote in someone else's book, but you wouldn't be reading hers. So, no, *The Wizard of Oz* was not the end of an interesting but brief story, it is the beginning of a fascinating and often deeply inspiring life.

A child of Hollywood, at age 8 she was transplanted by her parents to a small farm in the California outback, 100 miles east of the Twentieth Century Fox Studios, where several life lessons led her through an inventory of issues that in so many ways define the times we live in now.

Living in the San Jacinto Valley of Southern California could have been every horse-loving girl's dream. If you once were a girl who read *Misty of Chincoteague*, *Black Beauty*, *My Friend Flicka* or *The Black Stallion*, you can imagine how little Betty Ann Cain (her maiden name) felt about the opportunity to have her own horse. But you would never have imagined that a tiny pig (named, of course, Tiny) would displace a horse in her heart.

Sure, that's warm and fuzzy kid content and not a story worth a book, but what follows is Betty Ann's induction into the initially enchanting world of orthodox religion, wherein she became the local church's daily organist at the age of 12, shortly after a lapsed seminarian (and her Catholic mentor) attempted to seduce her, foreshadowing the polar opposite impulses too often rooted and harbored inside the Catholic Church. And that is a story as relevant now as then.

As is the often-buried, deeply-conflicted relationship she had with her mother, who struggled with her mixed-race Hawaiian heritage and instilled in her daughter both a fascination with island culture and a denial of her multiracial identity that shadowed her for years.

Sandwich that with a loving father whose early suicide plunged her into an abyss of sorrow and guilt, and you have the makings of a Shakespearean tragedy.

But Betty Ann's life has been far from tragic.

An outstanding student, and an astute witness of contemporary life, Betty Ann dragged her cultural ambivalence with her through a Stanford University education, a job with the CIA, a period of civic activism in Oakland, California where she ultimately ran for City Council and then launched a 22-year career in television news, one of the first broadcast positions for an Asian-American woman.

Along the way she broke stories of national importance, interviewed notorious drug dealers, crossed paths with the Mafia and, in what had to be a television first, produced a show on women's health that featured actual on-air images of a vagina.

Betty Ann found drama in her life even when she wasn't looking for it. In 1991, the precursor of California's current string of wildfires erupted in the Oakland hills and Betty Ann had a front-row seat, until it burned down around her.

Seeing her house erupt in flames, Betty Ann escaped with her life, then reported the experience live on CNN as the world watched 3,000 homes incinerated.

That catastrophe was followed by another, as California insurance agencies stonewalled and lowballed the claims of fire victims in a business pattern that resumed too often during the next round of fires, beginning in 2017, when Betty Ann's new hometown, Sonoma, came perilously close to going up in flames, forcing her and her husband to evacuate their house. It all felt horribly familiar.

That the fire didn't reach them should not be surprising. There seems to be a halo of some sort parked over her head, an openness to guidance beyond her understanding that has flavored her life with insights, mysteries and some extraordinary, almost mystical experiences.

That said, there is nothing flighty or New Agey about the woman. And the only obvious thing about her that might be deemed remotely mystical is her age. When you meet her, and see the spark in her deep brown eyes or hear her throaty laugh, your first thought may well be, "There's no way she can be 89 years old." She looks, acts and sounds 20 years younger. At least.

She might tell you that's partly because of the hula, a piece of her Hawaiian heritage she has reclaimed, embraced and turned into a local movement. For 10 years she has been teaching classes to a devoted, ever-growing throng, who dance for joy, and for the joy of others, all over the San Francisco Bay Area.

It is the gift of hula, bestowed on an entire community, that inspired her selection as Sonoma's Treasure Artist. Who knew the hula was over the rainbow and at the end of the Yellow Brick Road? In the truest sense, Betty Ann Bruno has come home, and this is her story.

It's a really good read.

*David Bolling is a veteran journalist, newspaper and magazine editor and publisher, author and documentary filmmaker, grateful and privileged to live in Jack London's Valley of the Moon, not very far from Betty Ann Bruno. That proximity has become a source of joy.*

# HOLLYWOOD

# CHAPTER 1

# A MUNCHKIN *for* LIFE

## My Personal Yellow Brick Road

It's true. I'm a Munchkin. Or I was for three weeks when I was seven years old.

Three weeks as a Munchkin does not define a life. Or so I thought. I had no idea when I played the part that I would become permanently embedded in one of the most magical, beloved and enduring film fantasies in all movie history. Who knew? I was a kid and three weeks is not a lifetime.

But it turns out, once a Munchkin, always a Munchkin. I mean, there's a whole book about Munchkins, and I'm in it.

But there's very much more to my life story than having been a movie Munchkin, much as I loved doing it and as much as I will always love the film.

I was never going to write a book about it, but I thought my kids would like the real story — on set with Judy Garland and Bert Lahr and Ray Bolger and a whole bunch of midgets. So I wrote about that.

And that led to other stories — like the one about my Uncle Ace who ran a nightclub in Hollywood, right across the street from Twentieth Century Fox, where he posted dramatic posters of himself from bit parts in movies and carried on with chorus girls (one of them was named Jibouti) while living with his wife in a one-bedroom apartment in the back of his nightclub.

There's a story about Auntie Berdie, the enormous entrepreneur, literally larger-than-life, who lived next door and made a very good living as "the lei lady." Not for any clumsy, sexual, double entendre, but because she made crepe-paper leis by the hundreds while catering Hawaiian luaus in 1930s Los Angeles when all of California seemed to be enchanted by the South Seas.

My show business career was brief but memorable, both before and after visiting the Land of Oz. The legendary director John Ford directed my first (and only) nude scene when I was five, hunkered down in a dugout canoe during a hurricane.

I had small parts in other films too, but before I could become a star my parents left Hollywood for a more sublime life, with cleaner air, in the country 100 miles away.

The small farm we settled on was everything Hollywood wasn't. It had fruit trees, an actual outhouse, and room for a horse — my life-long dream. It also had room for a pig, named Tiny, who became one of the early loves of my life.

Another love, for a time, became the Catholic Church, where the ritual of the mass and the promise of the reward of heaven fired my longing for something beyond myself. Equally fired up was the young seminarian and distant cousin who came to live with us after dropping out of a cloistered life in Belgium. He had discovered that, while he was devout, he was not meant for the priesthood. So he began to mentor me in the mysteries of the church, and tried to teach me other mysteries as well. That, of course, did not go well.

But it did lead to a gig as church organist — seven days a week — when I was all of 12. Why I got fired — and rehired — makes for another good story.

Buried in all these earthy anecdotes is the thread of an identity crisis that originated with my Chinese-Hawaiian mother who clearly suffered from some form of systemic insecurity despite being attractive, vivacious, musically talented and very smart. But she not only denied her Chinese ancestry, she turned her own children against it as well. My brother and I were taught to dislike and distrust Chinese, especially Chinese men.

On the other hand, being Hawaiian was good (except when it wasn't). Although she frequently insisted "we should be proud of our Hawaiian blood," she never taught us to speak Hawaiian and openly denigrated Hawaiian relatives and friends.

That may be why, growing up, I felt increasingly disconnected from other people. I realize now I was not alone in feeling that way, but at the time I believed I was the only person in the world who had been born to the wrong family, in the wrong place, at the wrong time. It was a full-blown identity crisis without an identifiable focus. I wasn't sure *who* I was, *what* I was, or *how* I was supposed to act. I never felt on the inside of either friends or family — always on the outside, set apart somehow.

Perhaps a big part of my problem was being multiracial before it became fashionable to have almond-shaped eyes and nut-brown skin. I grew up confused about whether my various nationalities were good or bad. It was a crisis born from my own attitude toward myself, rather than from being victimized by others. And it wasn't helped when, early on, my mother opened an emotional chasm between us she never really closed.

Maybe that's why I grew so close to my father, why I loved to watch him expertly shave with a straight razor, why I loved our fishing trips, his willingness to indulge me with both a horse and a pig.

And yet I was never neglected, ignored or abused. My parents provided a stable environment. I was well-fed, well-clothed, well-educated. Just not very clear about who I really was.

In the stories that follow I skip over some periods and some details to spare you more information than you need. I speed past my first marriage, which gave me three wonderful sons and a wonderful ex-husband, and I won't share details about my post-Stanford stint in Washington D.C. working for the CIA, where I met that first husband.

There is a wealth of stories to tell when I return to California and the City of Oakland, where I joined the Oakland League of Women Voters, became their president, relentlessly lobbied KTVU, the local TV station, to produce more public affairs programming, became actively engaged in local politics and ran for city council.

I was shocked when, during a period of public activism against TV stations that didn't honor the FCC's fairness doctrine and equal time provisions, the KTVU leadership turned around 180 degrees, asked my group what we wanted and promptly gave it to us.

That open door led to a lot of good community programming, but I never dreamed that I would ever be on the other side and have a career in television. But that's exactly what happened.

I spent 22 years in TV-land covering stories with more variety than Oz-land. I crossed paths with the Mafia while blundering into an FBI witness protection program; I interviewed every manner of human being, including the leader of a notorious Oakland drug gang who, amazingly, consented to a multi-part series and then threatened to kill me. I also covered a snail race, and an earthquake in Idaho.

I did a five-part series on para-psychology and was both reporter and subject in a past-life regression. The program broke a lot of commercial TV rules, including an 11-minute segment in a news slot where nothing had ever run longer than four minutes. The series won an Emmy.

And that subject matter reflected a growing interest of mine in things you might call supernatural, including a number of life events ranging from unexplainable to practically miraculous. When you read them you'll see what I mean.

One other time I was both reporter and subject, in what might have been the biggest story I ever covered — the 1991 Oakland Hills Firestorm. That holocaust destroyed 3,000 homes in the Oakland/Berkeley hills, including mine, and helped change the direction of my life. I almost didn't escape from the flames, and when I did, recovering from the structural, financial and emotional ashes took a very long time.

Ultimately, of course, a fire is just a fire, a house is just a house and things that burn up in a house fire are just things. So much more important than all that was my struggle to accept myself for who and what I am. That's probably the most important story in this book, and it happened in increments as I closed in on my true Hawaiian identity. In the end it was all a dance, literally a hula dance, and I'm still dancing.

There's more, as you'll discover in these pages, but I think you may be getting the picture already. A lot has happened in my 89 years, one life chapter flowing into the next. I never intended to write a book, just a series of short memories for my boys, and certainly not an autobiography, which this, emphatically, is not. But people who have read my stories, including friends who are serious writers, kept telling me, "Betty Ann, it's a book."

And finally, I believed them.

So here it is, *The Munchkin Diary*, chapters of a life that went so very far beyond Oz that I could never have dreamed where it would take me. I'm far from done with this life, but the Munchkin magic is forever branded on my soul even though I long ago left The Yellow Brick Road.

CHAPTER 2

# IN THE MOVIES

HOLLYWOOD WAS ACROSS THE STREET

M y brother Everett and I could hardly have avoided being in the movies. We lived across the street from 20th Century Fox Studios in Hollywood, and show biz was on both sides of our family. My mother was a singer, and my dad's brother, Uncle Ace, was playing bit parts in Westerns and owned a nightclub that featured three floorshows every evening. Performing seemed *normal*. Just about everybody we knew was either in or connected to show business.

Everett and I took dancing and singing lessons even before we were in kindergarten. First we went to Franchin & Marco Studios, and later enrolled at Bud Murray's Studio. Bud specialized in stage dancing, while his brother Arthur parlayed ballroom dancing lessons into a nationwide empire. Auditions for children's roles in movies were regularly posted on the bulletin boards at the dance studios, and stage moms swapped the latest news about which film studios were auditioning for kids. We all had professional photographs made at the couple of photo studios that specialized in pictures that would appeal to casting directors. Everyone was into the next audition or role. I mean, hey, it was HOLLYWOOD!

Shirley Temple was our idol. We all wanted to look and dance like she did. One mother bleached her daughter's brown hair and put it up in "Shirley Temple curls." With my Hawaiian features and very dark brown hair, there was no way my mother was going to try to turn me into a Shirley Temple look-alike, but I really, really, *really* wanted a Shirley Temple doll — the kind with "real hair" and eyes that blinked. I had to wait until my seventh birthday, but she was worth it.

My other dolls had painted-on-hair, but the Shirley Temple doll had the real stuff — or at least it looked like real hair. I was so thrilled. The first thing I did was comb through those beautiful curls and, of course, that was the end of the curls. That "real hair" was just for looking, not for combing. My beautiful Shirley Temple lost her glamor, but I loved her anyway — her eyes still blinked.

Everett and I did have one advantage over other young movie hopefuls — our Hawaiian heritage. It was the 1930s and Hollywood was in love with all things Hawaiian. A radio show called *Hawaii Calls* filled California's airwaves with the sounds of ukuleles and steel guitars. Our mother was not a dancer, but she knew enough basic hula steps to create a couple of simple routines for us. By today's standards, it was pretty corny. "Moon," "croon" and "swoon" were in all the lyrics, girls were flirty and guys were romantic. One number we did had me in a little cellophane hula skirt and Everett in a sailor suit. I don't remember the song we sang, but we were such a hit. I liked that number a lot better than our tap dance, "buck and wing" routine, for which we wore farm outfits. Not nearly as glamorous as my cellophane hula skirt.

My first movie role was in *The Hurricane*, starring Dorothy Lamour and Jon Hall. I was five years old. Everett and I were part of the gaggle of native kids ubiquitous in the South Seas film genre; our roles were usually limited to running around in the background of a thatched hut village. *The Hurricane*, directed by soon-to-be Hollywood legend John Ford, takes place on the fictitious Isle of Manakoora. It was exceptionally well produced, and its story line of forbidden love and racism has stood the test of time. Dorothy

Lamour popularized two things from this film: the sarong, which was her staple costume and with which she became identified, and the song, "The Moon of Manakoora," which she sang in the film and later recorded as a hit single. The song also launched the careers of Frank Loesser, who wrote the lyrics, and Alfred Newman, who composed the music.

During lunch breaks, Dorothy Lamour would invite all of us children to listen to stories as she read aloud. She seemed genuinely fond of children and apparently, especially liked me, because she always invited me to sit on her lap while the other kids just gathered around or sat on the floor. One day, when John Ford needed a child to appear alone in a scene depicting the height of the storm, Dorothy Lamour told him I'd be perfect. Well, I was perfect all right — a perfect nightmare. It wasn't that I didn't want to cooperate, but what they wanted me to do created a moral dilemma for me, and I couldn't explain it to them. There was a communication gap. After all, I was only five.

In the scene they wanted me to do, high winds are blasting across the island, sweeping away everything in the village — people, houses, trees, even the church. All of this is on a sound stage in Hollywood. Director Ford wanted a series of vignettes of people coping with the storm. One scene shows the high drama of a woman giving birth while the storm rages all around. Another sequence shows people screaming and running for the doors as waves flood the sanctuary of their church. In my scene, I was adrift in a canoe. My instructions were to start out in the middle of the canoe and, as the storm howls, crawl toward the bow away from the camera. Easy? Sure. No problem. The only trouble was that, to heighten the interest, they wanted my *pareau* (a little wrap-around skirt) to blow off and reveal my little bare buns as I crawled into the bow of the canoe. Isn't that just like Hollywood?

My mother had always impressed on me the importance of being modest, of never dropping my panties in public, of keeping my private parts covered except in the bathtub. So, although I knew I wasn't going to do what Director Ford told me to do, I was much too polite (or shy) to tell him. I just kept sabotaging take-after-expensive-take.

I was on a fake beach by a fake ocean in a big fake storm. An army's worth of storm-making equipment was aimed at my little outrigger canoe: the wind machines, the rain machines, the lightning and thunder machines, and the entire production crew. I was placed in the boat and a stagehand nailed a corner of my *pareau* to the side of the canoe.

Ford cued everyone on the set. "Waves! … Wind! … Rain! … Action!" When I heard my cue, I started moving but of course my *pareau* didn't. I felt it slipping off me. To understand the full impact of what I was being asked to do, you should know that an innocently provocative dance I had recently performed sans underwear, for my Uncle Ace, my mother and other family members, ended badly. My alarmed mother had made it extremely clear: People were never — NEVER, EVER — to see me without my panties. That message was now tattooed on my psyche. I wasn't about to invite *that* humiliation again. So when I felt my *pareau* slipping, I ripped it off the nail and clutched it to my loins with one hand as I used the other to crawl into the bow. The unscripted action was not appreciated.

Ford's voice broke through the storm. "CUT!!" he bellowed. The wind and rain ceased. I sat up in the canoe, still holding on to my *pareau*. Ford ran toward me. I think the rest of the film crew did too. They were all exclaiming, all explaining. I guess they thought I hadn't understood their instructions. They didn't know I had a moral conflict.

The next couple of tries weren't any more successful from Ford's point of view. And I must say, he showed more patience with me than other directors might have with a five-year-old, in take-after-take. Again and again, he explained what he wanted me to do. He even told my mother he'd pay me a bonus of $100 if *she* could get me to leave my *pareau* on the nail. She gave me a pep talk about how "this time it's okay," but I didn't understand *why* it was. Besides, I had no idea what $100 meant. A nickel, yes. A dime, yes. But $100? No. Not in my five-year-old lexicon.

Finally, Dorothy Lamour said she had an idea she'd like to try. An exasperated Ford turned me over to her. She came to the canoe and talked to me, and we tried the scene again. This time, I left my *pareau* on the nail and let the camera catch my little bare butt as I crawled into the bow of the boat. The scene lasts about two seconds in the finished film. If you blink slowly you'll miss it. I look very small, very vulnerable and very naked.

What persuasion had Dorothy Lamour used? She talked to me in language any little girl could understand. She offered me a reward any little girl would want. There was a wind-up, dancing hula doll that was a major prop in the movie. Dorothy Lamour merely whispered to me it would be mine if I would just leave my *pareau* on the nail. As far as I know, that *pareau* may still be on that nail.

My best souvenir from *The Hurricane* was a lovely autograph album in which I collected many signatures throughout the years. It was a very fancy album — fitting for the Hollywood of the '30s — with padded and embossed maroon (probably fake) leather covers, with "Autographs" spelled in gilt letters in the lower right corner. The inside pages were satiny, tinted in pastels and edged with gold. Dorothy Lamour wrote a lovely greeting on the very first page. I can still close my eyes and see her beautiful handwriting. The only problem was, she either had a very light hand or wrote with a very hard pencil. I could barely make out her message.

I wanted to be able to read her writing easily, so I re-traced it with a softer pencil of my own. I could now clearly read what she said, but after that it never looked quite right. At age five, I didn't have the same flowing hand Ms. Lamour did, so yes, I ruined it. It was my best autograph too. Not the most famous perhaps, but it was the most personal message and a real treasure — just a little tarnished by childish enthusiasm.

*The Hurricane* was followed by several other movies in which my brother and I had bit parts. Sometimes we just did the "kids in the village" thing and ran around in the background (as in *The Tuttles of Tahiti*). But other times, if the movie had a luau scene, we danced (*Hawaii Calls*, and *Aloma of the South Seas*). In a movie called *No Greater Love*, about the sanctified priest Father Damien who cared for lepers in Molokai`i, I was in a little skit. In the scene, my movie mother and I are walking along the village street, and I am looking at my rag doll when suddenly a leper staggers toward us. I look up, am startled and drop my doll. The leper collapses on it. Father Damien comes along, helps the leper to his feet, recovers my doll and starts to hand it back to me. My movie mother — in horror and repulsion — grabs me and rejects the doll. At this point, I reach out because I want my doll back, but my mother pulls me away. End of scene.

One time, a part was actually created for me. The story didn't have anything to do with Hawai`i, and I don't remember the reason they wanted me in it, but they did. The film was a privately-sponsored movie for children based on the book *Snickerty Nick*, who was a dwarf living in Fairyland. Snickerty Nick was the court jester for the Queen of the Butterflies. The girl who played the Fairy Queen was a tallish blond who got to wear a costume with long flowing gossamer wings — all shiny and covered with glitter. Her throne was a plastic mushroom in a glade of huge artificial flowers, and she carried a magic wand.

I remember wishing I could be the Fairy Queen — if only for a little while. I wanted to be a willowy blue-eyed blond. It seemed to me they always got picked for all the best parts. They got to dance in the center of the line, which was definitely the best spot, but I was always at one end or the other because I was so short.

Apparently, the producers of *Snickerty Nick* had seen me in a kiddy revue and decided the Fairy Court needed a Hawaiian butterfly. They rigged me up in a multi-colored cellophane skirt, some short wings and a couple of silver antennae coming out of the top of my cap. My job was to flirt with Snickerty Nick. (See, there's the stereotype again.) The director told me to put both hands behind my head, shake my hips and roll my eyes. That was certainly more acceptable than dropping my pants, but I wonder if those adult filmmakers ever thought about the kinds of lessons they were teaching a little girl.

There are only two movies in which I wasn't cast as an Island girl; one was *Girl from God's Country*, in which I was an Eskimo child. It was also my big chance for a speaking part, but I blew it because I answered the interview questions too honestly. My mother was pretty upset when she debriefed me and found out what I had said. The audition call was for little girls about nine or ten years old — brunettes who could *pass* for Eskimos. We were ushered into a room away from our mothers, where the casting director could look us over free of maternal interference. I guess I looked more like an Eskimo than the other little girls, because the casting director came right over to me and started asking questions. They were all easy: Name? Age? School? Did I take acting lessons? *(Yes)* Had I ever been in a movie before? *(Yes)* Had I ever had a speaking part? *(No)*.

That ended the interview, but he had someone write my name down in a notebook and went on to talk to the other little girls in the room.

Afterwards my mother grilled me. "Exactly what did he ask you and exactly what did you tell him." I told her all the questions and repeated all my answers. "Why did you tell him you've never had a speaking part?" She asked with a distinct edge to her voice.

"Because I haven't had one." The answer seemed obvious. I thought she should have known better, but then she explained the advantages of telling *white lies,* although I don't think she called them that at the time. What she told me was, I should have told the casting director I *had* had speaking parts, because then I would have gotten one. And how was I ever to get a speaking part if I kept telling people I had never had one? It was pretty simple to me. I told the truth because I had been taught to — by her. That was the first time I heard about any exceptions.

I was hired for the movie anyway, but didn't get the speaking part. When the scene was shot, I remember thinking I could have easily done the lines. There were only about three of them. It would have been so simple. I remember being jealous and wishing I had been sophisticated enough to know when I should have lied.

All the movies I was in have faded in my memory and are largely forgotten by the public, except for one. And that movie has been seen by more people all over the world than any other film. That, of course, is *The Wizard of Oz,* with Judy Garland. I was one of the 135 or so Munchkins, the tiny people who lived in the land of Oz, precisely where Dorothy's house landed after a tornado carried it away from Kansas.

Most of the actors hired to be Munchkins were adult midgets — well-proportioned people no taller than four and a half feet. The height was specified in a contract between MGM and a German producer named Leo Singer. Years earlier, he had combed Europe and recruited all the midgets he could find for his vaudeville troupe. For 40 years, his show had travelled all over Europe, Asia, South

America and Australia. He brought his midgets to the United States hoping to make it big in Hollywood. The timing was serendipitous. But despite his connections with the midget network, Singer wasn't able to find as many midgets as MGM needed. Even by letting a couple of dwarfs into the cast, they still didn't have as many as Director Victor Fleming wanted, so an audition call went out for little girls the same size as the midgets.

I had just turned seven, and the notice on Bud Murray Studio's bulletin board was for little girls under four and a half feet tall, who could sing, dance and act terrified. My mother took me to the audition, and I made the cut. A dozen of us little girls rehearsed together in one of the studios on the MGM lot. There were no midgets in our view at this point. We practiced in a rehearsal studio by ourselves, dancing up some stairs, over an arch and down the other side. Going up and down those stairs seemed pretty important, although we didn't understand why until a week or so later when we actually got onto the set of Munchkinland and saw that the little village had stairs going up and through it.

Oh, that set! What a miracle it was to my seven-year-old eyes. It had no equal anywhere in the world — not even in the universe — not in 1938 anyway. Disneyland and television were not yet on the horizon. There weren't even a lot of Technicolor movies. When you think about it, our lives were quite drab compared to the colorful world kids live in today. Hundreds of giant plastic flowers of every hue and color, playhouse-sized thatched huts and a road of bright yellow bricks made the set a wonderland.

Plus, there were all the other Munchkins. One hundred twenty-four of them. Adults. No taller than we were. I could hardly believe my eyes. As one of the shortest kids in my class at school, I was ecstatic when I saw all those adults who were my size. It was so amazing, I had to keep proving it was really true. I would sidle up to one of the midgets and run the flat of my hand from the top of their head to mine. "Oh! Ah! It *is* true. This adult is shorter than I am. Delirium."

But part of the Munchkin experience was super boring. That was getting fitted for our costumes. Every single part of every single costume was custom-made, which meant you had to stand still on a table for what seemed like hours while very serious-looking old ladies with straight pins in their pursed lips measured and muttered to themselves as they wrote your measurements down in their notebooks. "Stand still. On both legs, please. Don't move. Stand straight." I hated having to stand still and not move almost as much as I hated my drab little costume. It was all gray felt. I mean, why couldn't I have a bright blue, green or purple one? Any color except drab gray. But I had nothing to say about that at all. I did like the full skirt and petticoats that made it stick out all around, and I liked my shoes with the up-turned pointy toes. And I *loved* my hat. A little cloth bonnet with a ruffle around my face, and a red and white bud vase fastened on top, with a little rose sticking out of it. That was all cute. I just hated the grayness of the skirt and bodice.

The Munchkin scene is one of the most alluring in the whole of filmdom. The beautiful little village — full of perfect little people in wonderfully zany costumes, singing and talking in such squeaky charming voices, poetically thanking Dorothy for killing the wicked witch — is when the magic of the land of Oz really begins. It was the only scene of its kind in the entire world.

We children were just part of the background, which was pretty much the same place I was in other movies, too, except more so in *The Wizard of Oz*. Director Fleming made it very clear, "Kids are to stay in the back!" His casting crew had worked too hard to find adult actors to play the other Munchkins, and they did not want to see children's faces popping up in the crowd scenes. He didn't want to spoil the illusion of Munchkinland as a community of grownups. And as far as I'm concerned, he was a complete success. We have looked and looked, frame-by-frame, and have not been able to pick me out in any of the scenes. I'm just part of the crowd, way in the back, just like Fleming ordered, but that didn't keep me from feeling the thrill and excitement of it.

On the set between takes, we children were segregated from the midgets; mixing was strictly prohibited. Nevertheless, one of the midgets kept coming over to my mother and asking if I could go to lunch with him. Every time he asked her she would put her arms around me as though to protect me. I didn't see any need for protection because I didn't see any implications in an invitation to lunch. But my mother obviously saw something sinister in an adult male asking to take her seven-year-old daughter out to lunch. All I knew about lunch was my mother brought it in a brown paper bag and it didn't seem like a big deal until my male admirer, having failed in his plans for a luncheon date, sought another means to get close to me.

"What's your favorite candy bar?" he asked me one day. I quickly responded, "The Oh Henry! Bar." I didn't see anything sinister in the question and thought it was nice anybody would want to know that about me. I loved that chocolate-covered, nutty, caramel/nougat candy bar, but it wasn't long before I began to sense something fishy was going on — or trying to go on.

As we arrived at MGM in the morning, children were ushered to one of the offices to wait until the studio was ready to take us to the sound stage. The office walls had glass panels facing the hallway so we could see the midgets going by on their way to the set. Every morning, my admirer would break from the group for a minute and stand at one of the glass panels. He would scan the group of little girls until he spotted me, and then would reach into his jacket breast pocket and pull out — yes — an Oh Henry! candy bar. I thought the prospects of the candy bar were very pleasant, but there was something I didn't like about the smile he wore while he held the candy bar up to the window. Anyway, I never went to lunch with him, and I don't think I ever even got one of those Oh Henry! bars. At least I can't remember getting one, although I can still see him at the window leering and holding one up.

Lunch, as I said, was something Mom brought for us from home. Sometimes sandwiches, but more likely leftovers from dinner the night before. One of my favorites was cold-baked yams; they were so sweet and tasty. Most of the time, Mom and I ate our lunch in a nearby set where the flying monkeys practiced in their trapeze harnesses, doing touch-and-goes for the scene where they trash the Scarecrow and the Tin Woodman, and pick up Dorothy and carry her to the Wicked Witch's castle. They didn't wear their monkey costumes for those practices, so they weren't scary looking, they were just an immensely entertaining diversion. I mean, how many kids got to watch live aerialists during their brown-bag lunch hour?

As had happened in other movies, I got picked for a little extra part — this time, to be one of the Munchkin Sleepytime hatchlings in a nest on one of the thatched rooftops. On cue, we popped out of our shells, rubbed our eyes, stretched and yawned. It was another two-second scene, but get enough of those and pretty soon you have a career. We were outfitted with baby clothes, rehearsed the scene and shot it. But then the midgets' agent lowered the boom. He pointed out to the director that the contract with the midgets stipulated *all feature parts* would go to them — we kids were only to be *in the back*. Our nest scene ended up on the cutting room floor, and the scene was re-shot using adult midgets for the hatchlings. I think children's faces would have been totally appropriate here, but the contract was binding and that's the biz of show biz.

*The Wizard of Oz* set was a gold mine for autographs. Billie Burke (Glinda the Good Witch) and Margaret Hamilton (the Wicked Witch of the West) were in the Munchkin scene, of course, and very available on the set. Ray Bolger (the Scarecrow), Jack Haley (the Tin Woodman) and Bert Lahr (the Cowardly Lion) dropped in once or twice, so I easily collected signatures in my book. The Wizard, of course, was not around Munchkinland, and as far as I know, Frank Morgan, who played that part, didn't visit the set. But a couple of years later, after we had moved to the country, I heard he had a ranch in the same little town where we lived. My mother drove us by it once, but we didn't have the nerve to stop and introduce ourselves, so I never got his autograph. I also missed the most important one, but not for a lack of trying.

The story circulated that Judy Garland had given some of the midgets an autographed photograph of herself. That was the brass ring! All the children were lusting for one too. The problem was, Judy Garland was kept sequestered in her trailer, so getting her autograph was not easy. To reach her, you first had to cross the set to a kind of out-of-bounds area where her trailer was parked. Once you made it that far, you had to knock on the door, wait for her to answer and then ask for the picture.

Doing all that seemed a very big deal to me at the time, and I remember having to screw up all my courage to make the trip to her trailer door. It was a big scary adventure because children were not supposed to be wandering around the sound stages unescorted. Mothers were supposed to be with us all the time, but my mother apparently thought getting my own autograph would be a character-building exercise, and she wouldn't come with me. So, I did it by myself — not just once, but day after day.

And every day, Judy Garland would say, "Oh, I'm so sorry, I don't have a picture today. Maybe you could come back tomorrow ..."

Oh, agony! Did she have any idea how disappointing it was to hear that? But I really wanted her autographed picture, so I kept making the long, lonely trip across the sound stage to her trailer, and every day she told me to come back "tomorrow."

I wish this part of the story had a happy ending, but sadly I never did get her autographed picture. Nevertheless, what a great experience and wonderful childhood memory to have been part of one of the world's greatest films. Yes, that's pretty special.

My movie career ended when I was 10 years old. We had moved to the clean air of the Hemet-San Jacinto Valley two years earlier, because of my father's health. For a couple of years, my mother drove us the 100 miles to Hollywood whenever the movie studios called, but World War II changed all that. Gas rationing and tire shortages made it impossible to continue trips to Hollywood for dancing lessons, auditions or bit parts in the movies.

I especially missed the dancing lessons. Maybe our little farming town had a dance studio, but my mother told us there wasn't a teacher *good enough*. Our consolation prizes were piano lessons for me and violin lessons for my brother. I enjoyed playing the piano and singing in the choruses at school. There was a lot of music in the curriculum in that little country school — lots of opportunities to perform — and I had many speaking and even lead roles in elementary and high school plays. But San Jacinto and Hemet weren't Hollywood, and, no matter how many school plays, spring concerts or marching bands I was in, no matter how many solos I performed, there was never anything that equaled *the movies* and especially *The Wizard of Oz*. That point, however, was not clear to me until *much* later.

In the 1960s, when my own children were young, our family always watched the annual showing of *The Wizard of Oz* on television, with the family of one of my life-long friends, Mary Hudson. Her two daughters were very close in age to two of my sons, and our two families celebrated most holidays together. On Oz nights, Mary brought what became known as the Wizard of Oz cake — an orange cake with half-congealed Jello poured into it, which made it very moist and yummy. I don't think any of the kids were impressed with the fact I was in the movie, mainly because they couldn't *see* me in it. Mary had grown up in Beverly Hills and had been around the biggest and brightest movie stars, so why should she be impressed with my invisible bit part? And for me, being in that movie, or any other movie, was part of my childhood — certainly a cherished part, but it didn't have a practical effect on my life. Being a Munchkin was just a wonderful memory, until one day in 1977, in the newsroom at Channel 2 KTVU.

It was my first year as a news reporter, and I was at my desk typing out my story when two editors who were about to leave for vacation strolled through the newsroom saying goodbye to everyone. "Where are you going for vacation?" I asked out of idle curiosity.

"We're going to an Oz convention. This year it's in Winkieland," one replied. Their faces were aglow with happy anticipation. Surprised to hear of such a thing, I asked them to explain what an Oz *convention* was. They told me it was like a big fair where people could dress up in costumes and relive their favorite characters in the film. So I mentioned to them that I had been a Munchkin. As soon as I said it, the noise in the newsroom suddenly stopped. I thought the world was going to stand still. The two editors were electrified. With eyes popping and mouths agape they asked for details.

I played it down and reminded them, "I was just a little girl. It was only about three weeks of my life, when I was seven years old." I tried to keep it in perspective for them — and for me too. After all, now I was a news reporter and doing work I thought was really important. But, it seemed, that was just *my* point of view. Within 30 seconds, everybody in the building seemed to have heard there was a Munchkin in the house. The next day, a radio reporter did a feature story on me and, after that, everywhere I went people asked about *The Wizard of Oz* and "what it was like being in it." Everyone seemed more impressed with my *Munchkinism* than my journalism. One evening, several years later, as I was leaving the building and heading for my car in the parking lot, an intern hailed me. "Mrs. Bruno, Mrs. Bruno, may I ask you a personal question, please?"

"Of course," I replied, thinking she probably wanted to know how I got all the tips for my inside-City Hall stories, or how I got people to tell me things they wouldn't tell anybody else.

As I pondered my possible reply, the truth came out. "I hope you don't mind my asking you," she said, "but were you *really* a Munchkin in *The Wizard of Oz*, Mrs. Bruno?" Call it a lesson in perspective. As one wiseacre friend cracked, "It must be a problem to have peaked so early in life."

By that time — the late '80s — *The Wizard of Oz* had become a legend, and everybody connected with it was touched by its mythical status. For its 50th anniversary, author Steve Cox located about 30 former Munchkins and wrote a book about them, called, *The Munchkins Remember*. In his profile about me, he noted I was a reporter at Channel 2, and I began receiving a steady stream of fan letters from all over the United States and Europe. I started to realize just how big a following *The Wizard of Oz* actually had and how devoted the fans were.

People sent letters telling me how much they loved the movie, they enclosed pictures to autograph, cardboard yellow bricks to autograph, and gobs of 3x5 cards to swap with other Oz fans. Throughout 1989, 50th anniversary Oz celebrations sprang up all over the country. Any town with a real or imagined connection to Oz author Frank Baum, Judy Garland or any part of the story, had an Oz festival and wanted former Munchkins to attend. Because

I was still working, I didn't go to any that year, but after I retired I accepted an invitation to one of the largest Oz festivals in the country, in Chesterton, Indiana.

Chesterton is a small town on Lake Michigan's southeastern shore, an hour from Chicago. It claims no direct connection to Baum or Garland, but it had some energetic Oz fans who turned one Oz week a year into a money-making proposition for their town. The Chesterton Oz festival was so successful, the town officially took it over. During festival week, downtown streets bore names from Oz: Emerald Way, Ruby Slipper Lane, and so forth, and the town invited every Munchkin and Oz celebrity they could find.

Since it was my first time there, they asked me to be the Grand Marshall of the Parade, with floats, marching bands and all the trimmings. It was the early 1990s, I was the only *Child Munchkin* there, but eight elderly midgets were still well enough to take part in the events. I really enjoyed getting acquainted with them; they were the sweetest people, plucky show biz folks with ready smiles. Some wore costumes made to look like the ones they had worn in the movie, and the dean of Oz Munchkins, Jerry Maren, carried a huge, all-day sucker around — just like the one he danced with as a member of the *Lollipop Guild*.

The weekend was planned down to the minute. Throughout the days and evenings, we Munchkins were deployed here and there all over town, signing autographs for the 95,000 fans who flooded the town. People stood in line for hours to get us to sign their stuff — books, cards, photographs, posters, tee shirts and caps. I have never seen anything like it. I think I must have signed autographs for all 95,000 because, by the end of the weekend, I had writer's cramp all the way up to my right ear. It was quite an experience, but I've never gone to another one. In some ways it was actually a little scary, just that tiny taste of Hollywood-style celebrity. In the years I was on TV, lots of people would recognize me, but it wasn't the same thing as what those movie fans did, and I had a little difficulty relating.

I also had difficulty with what I saw as exploitation of the midgets. By the way, in this politically-correct age, midgets are now called Little People. That phrase was promoted in 1975 by Billy Barty, a well-known, three-foot, nine-inch dwarf actor who founded an organization to promote medical research and support scholarships for Little People. The former Munchkins I met referred to themselves as midgets. Also, in the credits to the movie, they are listed as The Singer Midgets. Personally, I also prefer the word midgets and don't think it's pejorative.

Anyway, at these events, the midgets got paid a few hundred dollars for a weekend of signing autographs and being interviewed, but the organizers made thousands. The midgets apparently also got the same short end of the stick as Singer Midgets during that promoter's heyday. Under the contract with MGM, Singer got $100 a week for each midget. He paid them $50, and kept the other half. Of course, he paid expenses out of that, but in those days, hotel and dinner probably cost around $2 a day. Again, the midgets didn't mind. Fifty dollars a week was very big money in 1938.

In Chesterton, someone made a poster of all the midgets and sold them for $15 each. Then the people who bought those posters stood in line for *hours* to get all the midgets to autograph them — for nothing. Most of the midgets had their own souvenir pictures to sell too, but the fan who had just shelled out $15 for a poster with *everybody's* photograph on it wasn't likely to want to pay $5 for an individual picture. If the midgets resented these incursions into *their* market, they didn't show it. They were always charming and smiled through it all. I just hope the midgets got as much pleasure out of their celebrity as they gave to the fans who flocked to see them at the Oz conventions. I can understand it as an identity issue. That movie made the midgets into beloved icons. No other role on stage or in film has come close to doing that for them. So indeed — why not go for it full bore.

The Chesterton Oz festival ended in 2012, but plans have been announced for a new event, the "Wizard of Oz Days," to begin in May of 2021. Organizers have already announced there will be a "Breakfast with Characters," an afternoon "Celebration of the Munchkins," and an "Emerald City Gala."

As I write this in the year 2020, all the Oz midgets are gone; the last one was Jerry Maren, who died in 2018. There are still a few of us Child Munchkins around, but we are all now quite elderly. I'm still dancing, but not on the Yellow Brick Road. I have a wonderful life full of music in the little town of Sonoma, California, but *The Wizard of Oz* hasn't completely receded into the memory-only file of my life. A small but steady trickle of letters from Oz fans asking for autographs continues to arrive in the mail. There are still Oz festivals around the country, and the movie continues to attract good crowds. Last October, a full house enjoyed the film on the big screen of Sonoma's historic Sebastiani Theater, and the audience was dotted with little girls in blue and white gingham jumpers.

Thomas Wolfe famously wrote, "You can't go home again." Perhaps he was right. But I think Dorothy Gale might disagree, because she made it back to Kansas. And my journey, as you will read, has taken me all over the map, through uncharted emotional terrain and into professional domains I never could have imagined. It's been a long, often exciting journey, with more than one metaphorical tornado, but now I can truly say, with the fullness of 89 years, I'm home.

# CHAPTER 3

# UNCLE ACE

## Booze, Dice and Dancing Girls

Horace Truman Cain. Big tall Texan. Bit actor. Flamboyant, tough-as-nails businessman. Womanizer. Flirt. And the most fun uncle a little girl could ask for.

Uncle Ace's persona was fully expressed in his nightclub. A huge blinking neon sign on its roof hollered out the presence of Ace Cain's Cafe to surrounding blocks. Way up high, and all around on the walls of the main room, were gigantic blow-ups of Uncle Ace in his various movie roles. Uncle Ace in a white cowboy hat, Uncle Ace in a black cowboy hat, Uncle Ace as a boxer, Uncle Ace as a gangster, and on and on. The nightclub had other features too, but Uncle Ace was central.

Located on Western Avenue one block down from Sunset Boulevard, Ace Cain's Cafe was across the street from the old 20th Century Fox Studios. The studio took up the entire block to one side of his nightclub and two blocks across the street from it. Proximity to the big movie studio made Ace Cain's a convenient watering hole for the movie folks at 20th Century Fox, who in turn attracted other folks hoping to get a glimpse of a celebrity from the silver screen. As a result, during the 1930s and '40s, Ace Cain's Cafe was one of the most popular nightclubs in Hollywood. There were other big draws too — three floorshows every night and the Magic Mirror, with an unclothed occupant. Uncle Ace's was a slightly racy club with a down-home atmosphere. It also had a very good bar, presided over by cousin Walter. But I'm getting ahead of the story; let's go back to how it began.

Uncle Ace and my dad joined the Army Signal Corps as soon as they were old enough to enlist. The Army was their ticket out of Wichita Falls, Texas, and would take them halfway around the world. It was peacetime after World War I, and in the mid '20s they found themselves stationed at Schofield Barracks on Oahu, in Hawai`i. They had been successful gambling partners every payday since they had joined up, and by 1930 they had saved enough money that Uncle Ace decided to leave the Army and seek business opportunities on the mainland. Daddy, who was newly married, decided to stay in Honolulu and started a family.

First my brother Everett came along, and 18 months later I was born. In Southern California Uncle Ace found the business opportunity he was looking for — Hollywood — the perfect place to open a "distribution center." Prohibition was still the law of the land.

The building was on Western Avenue near Sunset Boulevard. The front part was a small restaurant and next to it was a ramp leading to a huge car repair shop in the back. That part of the building was cement, had no windows and smelled of axle grease. But Uncle Ace liked the spacious layout and it suited his purposes. The restaurant in the front was all that showed to the casual passer-by. Only if you looked carefully could you notice an entryway next to it, where cars entered the repair garage. That repair area in the back could — and would — hold hundreds of cases of bootleg liquor.

Uncle Ace had good contacts in the police department, who, for a price, would tip him off whenever a raid was planned. He said each "tip" cost him from $200 to $500 — a lot of money in those days — and he would also leave a few cases of cheap liquor so the police would have something to take with them. He was always warned in time to haul his inventory to safety if a raid was imminent. He would then bring it all back the next day and go on with business as usual, until the next raid a few months later.

That was the routine until 1933, when Congress passed the Volstead Act ending Prohibition. When liquor could be sold legally again, my dad came to California to help launch their new businesses. The restaurant became Jim Cain Liquors, and the "car repair shop" morphed into Ace Cain's Cafe. By draping the walls of the entrance ramp with dark velvets, and carpeting the ramp, they transformed the space into a glamorous, sloping approach to the big room, which now housed a bandstand, a stage and dance floor with tables all around, and a bar with a grill where customers could get hamburgers and toasted cheese sandwiches until 2 a.m.

My mother brought my brother and me to California a year later and soon we were living in a duplex right next to the liquor store. The nightclub was intriguing to me as a young child, and the fact my parents had put it off limits (except under very limited conditions) only made it more alluring. The nightclub was also a family enterprise, with Uncle Ace at the top and most of his siblings as employees. Uncle Earl worked the lights during the floorshows, and was the club's carpenter by day. He built everything inside, from the dance floor up to his own "crow's nest," where he worked the spotlights for the floorshows. Years earlier he had lost his right hand and forearm. My cousins and I once tried to get up enough nerve to ask him to let us touch his stump. It seemed like a very daring thing to do because, after all, who knew what risks we invited by running our curious fingers over his handless arm with the big scar that ran like a ditch across the end of it?

Henrietta, Uncle Earl's wife, flipped hamburgers at the little grill that was the cafe part of the business. If something could be fried, you could order it; if not, it wasn't on the menu. I never saw her use an oven or a pot — the grill was all she seemed to know or need. Their daughters, Mary Evelyn and Vera Helen, danced in the floorshow as soon as they developed boobs. Uncle Earl's twin brother, Uncle Carl, was a pretty hopeless alcoholic but, when he wasn't in jail or in the hospital drying out, he was part of the crew too. He and a wino named LeRoy, who lived in a packing box in the parking lot, picked up trash and empty bottles from the lot and surrounding sidewalks — that is, when my brother and I didn't beat them to it. My cousin Elena May was a cocktail waitress, and her husband Walter tended bar and was the bouncer when events called for one. He was very proud of his strength and loved to show how he could lie on the floor, put a cement block on his stomach and have someone smash it with a sledgehammer.

He and 'Lena May had three daughters. The middle one, Peggy Jo, was my age, and as kids we loved to play dress-up together. Fringed silk shawls became ball gowns when we draped them over our shoulders. Costume jewelry and our mothers' old purses were our accessories. Each of us had one prized dress-up possession: Peggy Jo's was a rhinestone tiara; mine was a pair of my mother's size 1½ high-heeled shoes that perfectly fit my 7-year-old feet.

All my Texas cousins had double names, which were always used complete and unabridged. I loved the sounds of the names — lots of syllables spoken as a single word with a lilt and twang you don't get in a single-word name. Imagine for a moment 'Lena May opening her back-screen door and calling: "RoseElla! PeggyJo! JimmyLou! Y'all come in now and warsh up for supper!"

The most cultured of my Texas cousins was William Glen, Auntie Hattie's son. As a teenager he trained to be a concert pianist, but after blistering his finger tips practicing for an important recital, he switched to ballet as a less painful profession and became a dancer for the Ballet Russe.

One sibling who did not follow Daddy and Uncle Ace to Hollywood was their sister Hughlemma. She remained in Texas with her husband and son, both of whom were named George. She always referred to her husband as Mr. Baker, only her son was George.

Hughlemma. What a wonderful name, Hughlemma. My favorite memory about her is that she wore a corset with whalebone stays and laces. I saw it when I was eight or nine because she visited us for a while. My eyes nearly popped out because my mother used to say, "I can't stand anything tight!" Mom's undies were panties and an undershirt. Once in a while, if she was going someplace special, Mom would forego the undershirt and put on a bra — but on a daily basis, her dress code was for comfort. When I saw Aunt Hughlemma's corset, I figured nothing could be tighter than that, nothing could be less comfortable, but she wore it every day.

Our one-bedroom duplex was next door to the former restaurant — now liquor store. On the other side of the duplex was a Union 76 station and across the street from that was Mae's Grocery Store. Some people will undoubtedly think our little neighborhood was not a good place to raise a family. But to my brother and me, it was just our home — with plenty of colorful and interesting characters around.

Like most other duplexes, ours consisted of two identical apartments that mirrored each other. The front porches differed in only one detail. Our neighbor Joe had a giant key hanging on his, signifying he was a locksmith. We called him Joe-the-Key Man. After he moved away, Auntie Berdie moved in and stayed the rest of her life. The double doors in the living rooms of the two units stayed locked on both sides when Joe-the-Key Man was our neighbor. But Auntie Berdie was like family, even though she wasn't really related, and the inside doors were always open, so the two small apartments seemed like one big house.

Mr. Murphy lived in a little cottage in back of our duplex and right next to the back doors of the nightclub. He had a loquat tree my brother and I used to climb to pick the fruit. On the other streets around the rest of the block there were other families with kids, so our neighborhood seemed perfectly normal to us. We played all the usual kid games of the time, including cops and robbers and tag, and we yelled ollie-ollie-oxen-free in hide 'n' seek, just like everybody else. While some might disagree, my brother and I thought our childhood was enriched by the presence of the nightclub. In one way quite literally; we were probably the only kids in the neighborhood who could walk around the sidewalk near our home and pick up empty bottles to turn in to our dad's liquor store and get pennies, or sometimes nickels, for return-deposits on them.

The differences in the businesses suited the personalities of the two brothers. My father — quiet and reserved — was comfortable in the liquor store, while my flamboyant uncle was the star in his own nightclub. What brought these two dirt-poor farm boys from Wichita Falls, Texas to property ownership in Hollywood? Certainly not something Grandma approved of. She had, in fact, condemned their path, but after Grandpa died she found herself totally dependent on Daddy and Uncle Ace. So she stopped complaining and concentrated on praying for their souls.

Grandma was a God-fearing woman whose radio dial was perpetually tuned to Christian evangelists. She truly believed fire and brimstone were the consequences for sin, and sin was the synonym for fun, especially for adolescent boys. At the top of her list of condemned activities were dancing, movies, cards, dice, smoking and drinking — everything it seemed except going to prayer meetings.

The inevitable result was that all her sons could hold their liquor, blow smoke rings and play cards like pros. They dealt cards by deftly sailing them through the air to land exactly where they wanted them. They learned how to count aces and face cards to figure the odds based on what was showing in a hand of poker. They learned how to control the number of times the dice rolled over after the throw. By skillfully placing the cubes in their fists just so, they could win consistently. They learned the parlance of gambling. Highly disciplined and self-trained, as long as they didn't have to roll the dice against a backboard, they kept on winning.

Thus armed, they enlisted in the U.S. Army Signal Corps and left Wichita Falls to seek their fortunes. It was the 1920s and times were good. The Army sent Uncle Ace and Daddy to bases all over the Pacific — the Philippines, Indonesia, Japan, the Hawaiian Islands — and everywhere they went they gambled, and every payday they won a big pile of money. By the time they mustered out of the Signal Corps in the late '20s, they had accumulated enough cash to buy a quarter of a Hollywood block. Although neither of them had a formal education beyond the fifth or sixth grades, they had keen minds that served them in business as well as in card and dice games.

I was too young to remember much about those early years. Instructions to my brother and me were to keep out of sight in the liquor store and keep out of the nightclub — period. My parents probably considered liquor store customers were average people engaged in average daytime activities and therefore were not a threat to us. But customers in the nightclub were drinking and therefore less trustworthy around little girls. Also, I might get a peek at the chorus girls if I hung around the nightclub, and they were considered unsuitable role models for me.

Uncle Ace's Cafe featured three floorshows every night. On very rare occasions my brother and I were allowed to see the early floorshow which started at 8:30. On those special occasions we sat at a table at the edge of the dance floor. When a cowboy entertainer and his horse were in the show, not only did I get to sit at a table right in front, but the horse always picked *me* from the audience, and I got to ride him for about 30 seconds. For a little city girl who dreamed nightly about owning her own horse, a 30-second ride around a dance floor was a bit of heaven.

Other kinds of shows we were allowed to see were the ones with magicians, ventriloquists, jugglers or clowns. My parents were apparently willing to overlook the fact that surrounding those *appropriate* acts were numbers with chorus girls in skimpy costumes, bumping and grinding to provocative rhythms. Although the costumes in the 8:30 show were less skimpy than those in the 10:30 or midnight shows (which I was not allowed to see), the overtones were quite clear.

I saw the "Magic Mirror" act only one time — it was activated only late at night. Most of the time, when the regular house lights were on, the Magic Mirror was a regular mirror behind the bar, and patrons would only see themselves in the glass. But a couple of times each evening, for a very brief interval, the house lights would dim and the lights behind the Magic Mirror would turn it into a window, revealing a velvet upholstered bench upon which reclined a beautiful nude woman. You couldn't see much — remember we're talking about the 1930s — because the lights behind the Magic Mirror were bluish so the set was dark. Plus, the naked girl placed her arms and legs in such a way that covered her private parts. In other words, no boobs or pubes. All very tame by today's standards, but titillating nevertheless, and pretty hot for those days.

At one point I got myself banned from the night club for imitating one of the acts I saw there. It was a so-called Hawaiian number, which is probably why I was allowed to see that particular show. The chorus girls did what they thought would pass as the hula and then, at the end, put their hands in front of their faces and did a sort of half-slide, half-skip sideways around the stage while wiggling their hips.

The dance-step intrigued me and, since I had a cellophane hula skirt more or less like the ones they wore, I decided to perform my version of the routine for my parents one afternoon. I got all dressed up in my costume, which I tried to make as much like the chorus girls' costumes as possible. They had flowers in their hair, I put flowers in my hair. They wore fake flower leis, I put on a fake flower lei. They wore cellophane skirts, I put on my cellophane skirt. My mistake was that, because I couldn't see their underpants and my child logic concluded they weren't wearing any, I didn't either.

I was probably four years old. My audience seated around our living room consisted of my parents, Uncle Ace and Aunt Skeeter. I entered from the bedroom hall and launched into my imitation of the floorshow number. I hadn't done more than a couple of bars of my exotic dance when my mother shrieked, "Betty Ann, where are your panties?" I answered matter-of-factly "Well, they didn't wear any," whereupon my mother quickly whisked me out of the living room, back to my bedroom.

I was only dimly aware of heads wagging and tongues clicking as I was ushered away to change back to my blue corduroy overalls as my mother scolded all the way. "You should know better. Wherever did you get the idea the dancers don't wear underclothes? Oh, my goodness!" Needless to say, I didn't risk much interpretative dancing after that — at least not without panties.

On other occasions when my brother and I were allowed to see a floor show, if we didn't get a front table, we watched from the crow's nest. It was a tiny wooden room — really more of a box than a room — hanging down from the ceiling from which my Uncle Earl operated the spotlights. You entered the crow's nest by climbing up a vertical wooden ladder and crawling through a square hole cut into the floor. Just getting into the place was an adventure for me — like accessing your big brother's secret clubhouse, but better because it was the window onto the world of grease paint, spangled costumes and spotlights. The furnishings were sparse — just spotlights and a couple of old chairs. Uncle Earl sat on one; my brother and I would share the other one, lean our elbows on the raw wood frame of one of the square glassless windows and watch what most kids our ages couldn't even imagine seeing.

Uncle Ace was a bit-part actor, mostly in Westerns, playing the part of the bad guy in the black hat. His big brawny build and bushy eyebrows made him look sinister, but in real life he was a pushover, at least for us kids. Childless himself, he was everyone's favorite uncle. Flashy, funny and extroverted, he was as popular with the under-six set as he was with the chorus girls. He could make the best faces, wiggle his ears, do funny things with his eyebrows and he didn't seem to mind our combing his hair endlessly, which, you know, is a favorite thing for little girls to do. And he made kissing him into a game: "Hey, how about a butterfly kiss? How about an Eskimo kiss?" But the best reaction was when I told him I was going to give him a Hawaiian kiss. We rubbed noses for both that and the Eskimo kiss. Actually, most of the kisses were the same, and *always* on the cheeks. He just made each of us kids think we were very creative and very special.

Uncle Ace sang catchy and easy songs and taught them all to us kids. They were not songs you would learn in school, but they had sing-song melodies and lyrics that were easy to memorize, so we made them our own and repeated them at home or on the playgrounds at school. Years later, when I was in the sixth grade and sang one of Uncle Ace's songs to my class, I found out they weren't socially acceptable in all circles. The song I sang to the class was about a "Gay Caballero coming from Rio de Janeiro." Another, more acceptable, Uncle Ace favorite was:

*No matter how young a prune may be*
*It's always full of wrinkles*
*And you may have them on your face*
*But a prune it has them every place.*
*How sad to be a prune.*

Uncle Ace would sing those songs to us at the top of his lungs and was either unaware or didn't care if they were in bad taste!

He was definitely a better uncle than he was a husband. Poor Aunt Skeeter. Uncle Ace just couldn't seem to keep the chorus girls out of his bed. He and Aunt Skeeter lived in an apartment they had built in the back of the nightclub. Probably Uncle Earl built it. It was unadorned functionality. At the end of the hall past the storage shelves and cleaning supplies, it was just a big room with a bed, a couple of chairs and a desk where Uncle Ace could count his money and keep his accounts. Aunt Skeeter didn't cook, so there was no kitchen. As far as I know, Henrietta cooked all their meals in the club, at the grill at the end of the bar.

Their dog Rowdy and their Persian cat Silver Fizz also lived in the big bedroom. Silver Fizz was quite a beautiful creature, Rowdy was a wire-haired mutt and they were both much loved. The affection Uncle Ace and Aunt Skeeter had lost for each other was lavished on their pets. My mother, who thought all animals belonged outside in the yard, disapproved of Rowdy and Silver Fizz sleeping in the same big bed with Uncle Ace and Aunt Skeeter, and shook her head about how foolish they both were to be so ga-ga over their pets.

Uncle Ace liked all the chorus girls, but his favorite was a strip-tease dancer who also played the trombone and called herself Jibouti. A small scandal unfolded one night when Uncle Ace and Jibouti were locked inside the apartment when Aunt Skeeter tried to get in, and Uncle Ace refused to open the door. Our family got mixed up in it because Aunt Skeeter came over to our house in the middle of the night, crying and asking for a place to sleep. I didn't understand all the implications of it at the time, since I was only about five years old, but I did realize Uncle Ace had done something mean and cruel.

Aunt Skeeter didn't bang on the door or create a scene. She didn't scream and holler. She just whimpered and came next door to our house. I remember other relatives talking about what happened but without any sympathy for Aunt Skeeter. There might even have been a touch of scorn in their voices because she didn't fight back. The next day, Jibouti stayed in the chorus girls' dressing room, the apartment door was no longer locked and life at Ace Cain's Cafe went through its normal paces. What would have been a huge event in most families was just a little glitch at Ace Cain's Cafe.

Jibouti was probably from some Small Town USA, but her stage name transformed her into an exotic woman from a foreign country. All the men who worked around the nightclub talked about her. My brother and I could hear a lot of gossip because our back yard was also the back yard of the nightclub. Every once in a while, we would hear one of the employees telling another, "Hey, did you hear Jibouti went out with so-and-so last night?" Even at the age of five, I could hear the difference in the way they said that and the way they said everything else. Jibouti passed over the other guys for Uncle Ace. And why not? He was definitely the boss of the nightclub. He was the Lord of the Manor.

Uncle Ace presided over his little domain with almost regal authority. His stature helped — he was 6 feet tall and had a hefty build. To ensure his king-pin status, he added a couple flourishes. He wore a huge diamond ring on the pinky of his right hand. That big gem flashed and sparkled every time he moved. He also carried a big wad of bills in his hip pocket. Maybe it was a reaction to the poverty of his youth and a salute to the affluence he had achieved. I have no idea how much money was in that wad, but it had to have been a lot and he wasn't shy about showing it. He often paid people in cash so he frequently had a reason to reach into his pocket, take out the wad and peel off a few bills. He was also very generous. Anybody who needed a little help getting to the next paycheck could come to Uncle Ace, tell him their story and get a few bills off the big wad. He was really The Man in the world he had built at Ace Cain's Cafe.

It was very different in the liquor store that my father ran. No relatives worked in the store. My dad's main clerk was an older man we called Mac. His daughter was a nurse who apparently took a dim view of the nightclub as a major part of my environment. I think she was afraid I would grow up uncultured — or worse — and took it upon herself to provide me with "advantages." On her days off she took me to the movies. We saw every Shirley Temple movie as soon as it came out. We also went to see all the Deanna Durbin films and other movies Miss Nancy considered worthwhile. I don't remember going to the movies with my mother, but she loved live theater and her favorite performer was ice skating superstar Sonja Henie. We saw the Sonja Henie show every year when it came to Los Angeles - even after we moved to the country when attending meant an overnight stay in the city. Movie-going for my brother and me meant the Saturday afternoon kiddie matinee at the Sunset Theater one block up Western Avenue.

Going to the movies with Miss Nancy, however, was a special event. Movies with her meant going downtown. Miss Nancy lived in an apartment building that seemed to be a world away from our little duplex next to the liquor store, and after the movie we'd go there for hot cocoa. I can still remember the thrill of walking down the hallway to her front door — so much more elegant than just walking in off the sidewalk to our front porch. Miss Nancy's kitchen seemed much more modern than ours, and her bathtub didn't sit on claw feet like ours but was squared off straight to the floor. The lid on her toilet had a fluffy cover. It was all so wonderful. I loved going there.

Miss Nancy had waist-length brown hair that she sometimes let me brush. That was really heaven! She would lie on her sofa, rest her head on the arm and let her long hair cascade over the end. It went almost to the floor. I would brush it and brush it. I would have brushed her hair forever if she had let me. But then, one day, there was an even bigger treat. She said her masseuse was coming and she wanted to take a bubble bath. I didn't know what a bubble bath was. I had to wait in the living room until she called me, and then I could go into the bathroom to talk to her. There she was in the tub, up to her chin in a sea of perfumed bubbles, and she used a soft sponge to wash her arms and neck. My eyes nearly popped out. I had never seen anything like that before. My baths were generally shared with my brother with as little water as possible and bar soap that only reluctantly gave up suds to our very plain washcloths.

When Miss Nancy's bath ended, she sent me back to the living room, and the next view I had of her was on the massage table where a man dressed in a white smock and white slacks was slathering cream all over her back with both his hands. I remember the long strokes he took, starting on her sides and coming up to the middle of her back, one hand following the other. I thought "That looks like the *lomi-lomi* (Hawaiian for massage) our mom gives our dad sometimes, but in our house it was performed on the living room floor and without aromatic creams.

We moved away from Hollywood just before my eighth birthday, and I never saw Miss Nancy again. But I will never forget her. She was the first in a list of very special women — my surrogate moms — in my growing-up years who came along to fill in empty spots in my life, and I loved them all. But Miss Nancy will remain the most enchanting, the most mystical, maybe just because she was the first and I was such a blank slate. She was part of the liquor store/nightclub scene but managed to lift my eyes to another level. She gave me alternatives. She gave me Shirley Temple, Deanna Durbin and the hope of bubble baths.

In the late '40s or early '50s, Uncle Ace sold the nightclub and bought a little bar called The Black Light a few blocks down Western near Santa Monica Boulevard. He took along many of the relatives who had stayed in the area although, after the nightclub closed, some moved away and started independent lives. Those who went with him lived in an apartment building behind the bar: his brother Uncle Earl with his family, and Auntie Hattie and her family. Grandma Cain had a little apartment there too. During her years in Hollywood, she had learned how to shut out the hedonistic sounds of the bars and the nightclubs. She turned up the volume of her radio evangelists and lived in her own world.

While I was in high school, I used to drop by Uncle Ace's compound whenever I was in Hollywood, but he wasn't the same funny character to teenage me that he had been to little-girl me. I gradually realized he saw women only as playthings or love things — creatures to tease or squeeze. Nevertheless, I will always cherish the memories of him as my favorite uncle. No amount of feminist conviction or reason will ever change that.

Uncle Ace spent the last few years of his life in the little desert town of Saugus on the northern edge of Los Angeles. He had a small, low-key resort there with a bar, cafe and swimming pool. No chorus girls. No floorshows, but Uncle Earl was still the fix-it man and his wife Henrietta still served up the burgers. Others in the family had moved on — either in this world or the next.

# CHAPTER 4

# AUNTIE BERDIE

A MOUNTAIN OF A WOMAN

E ver tried one of these?" Rosy asked as she thrust the bag of pickled olives in my direction. A pungent whiff invaded my nostrils.

"Auntie Berdie's house!" I shrieked, startling us both.

"Huh?" Rosy said, looking puzzled at the bag.

"Chinese pickled olives are the smell of my Auntie Berdie's house!" I repeated, thinking that explained everything. But of course it didn't mean a thing to Rosy, who had been my friend and co-worker for years. She had never heard a word about the elderly Hawaiian lady who lived in the other half of our duplex when I was a child.

The perfume from that bag blasted loose memories that had lain dormant more than 25 years. I buried my nose in the bag, took a deep breath and traveled on that spicy fragrance back in time to the 1930s and a little duplex on Western Avenue in Hollywood.

When I first met Auntie Berdie she was already a literal mountain of a woman. I was six or seven and have no idea how old she was, but I would guess 50-something, maybe 60. It was hard to tell. She had long, salt-and-pepper hair that she wore tied in a bun at the back of her head. Her brown eyes protruded slightly from their sockets, so there was an almost bovine aspect to her when she blinked.

Encumbered by fat, her every movement seemed difficult. Her

clothes were mostly tent-like muumuus sewn from a dozen yards of cotton print. The one exception was a black wool dress with long sleeves that hid her hammy upper arms. That was the only Western-style outfit I remember seeing her wear. On the rare occasions when she wore that black wool dress, she also put regular shoes on her feet, but most days she padded around in a pair of misshapen slippers — crushed by her weight with paper thin soles and a bulge on the inside edges to accommodate her bunions.

As a child, I was fascinated by her and studied her details; she was so different from everyone else I knew. Despite her enormous bulk, there was a loveliness about her. She exuded an aura of freshness and her skin was silky smooth. At her sink, water drops ran off her hands and arms like rain off a newly waxed car. And she was, for me, a real connection to the Hawaiian culture I felt connected to in name only. Auntie Berdie was the real McCoy Hawaiian, different from my mother's selective Hawaiian-ness, which I witnessed only occasionally when she visited her Hawaiian friends and spoke the language to them as she served raw-fish and poi. I never heard that language at home. Auntie Berdie on the other hand, always wore a muumuu, made Hawaiian leis and always had poi in the house. It seemed to me that all her friends were from the Islands, and maybe I hoped some of that would rub off on me. All I know is that I loved being around her.

Auntie Berdie was well known in Hollywood circles in the 1930s as the *lei lady*, in the films Hollywood loved to make about Hawaii. Her biggest role was the featured character Auntie Pinau in "Hawaii Calls," a 1938 RKO Radio Picture. One needed only to refer to the *lei lady* for anyone and everyone in Hollywood to know about whom you were talking. Both her physical and mental attributes made people remember her. Auntie Berdie had the kind of personal power that attracted attention and let everyone know she was a leader. She had a quick mind and could banter with the best of them, but her comebacks were always soft, never harsh and never unkind.

Off screen, Auntie Berdie was a real-life lei lady. She crafted garlands from crepe paper that she stacked at one side of the dining room table and sewed into leis by the hundreds. They hung in colorful bunches from every hook and knob and gave her home a festive atmosphere, as though a party was about to begin any moment. She sold the leis for $.50 to $1.50 each, depending on how thick, how fancy and whether they were one color or two.

To make them, first Auntie Berdie cut across packages of crepe paper to make strips; then with a sure needle and a strong thread she sewed a running-stitch rib straight down the middle of each strip of paper. She made multi-colored leis by holding two or three pieces of contrasting paper together and stitching them at the same time. The finishing step was twisting the paper round and round their thread spines, fluffing them out and, *voilá*: petals, points and other flower parts would suddenly appear in all colors and color combinations.

Auntie Berdie made some money from her leis but earned most of her income by catering Hawaiian luaus. In the 1930s, Californians were in love with the South Seas, and wealthy party hosts in Los Angeles could replicate the Islands with lavish evenings planned and catered by Auntie Berdie.

I remember one party at a posh Beverly Hills estate where white tents were set up on the front lawn to keep the evening chill off the sarong-clad guests. I was then in high school, but I stayed with Auntie Berdie that weekend to help out at the luau. She asked me to help sell her leis to the guests and also to dance a hula in the show. I was thrilled to oblige.

A brook babbled through the landscape and, for the evening, it was stocked with catchable-size trout. A stack of fishing rods stood ready for guests who wanted to try their luck at reeling in their own dinner. Inside the tents, guests entered a tropical paradise the way only Hollywood could do it — with fake palm trees, artificial waterfalls and tiki statues. The tent poles were surrounded by flower-bedecked cages housing live exotic songbirds. A carpet of fake grass covered the lawn and protected the guests as they sat *Island style* at the dinner tables which, for that evening, were long mats on the fake lawn. Wooden platters down the centers of the lauhala mats were piled high with fresh fruits and other Auntie-Berdie-luau specialties: whole pigs cooked over lava rocks, *lomi-lomi* salmon, *laulaus* and fresh Hawaiian poi.

Not many *haoles* ever liked the poi, but they had all heard about it, so it was a must on the menu and was introduced with the usual patter. "You all know about poi," the emcee would begin. "It's the Hawaiian staple food — what potatoes are to the Irish, or bread to the French. It's made from the root of the taro plant — first cooked, then mixed with water until it's the right consistency. The more water you add the thinner it gets and the farther it goes, so a person's generosity is judged by whether he serves you one, two or three-finger poi. If you're served four-finger poi, you don't ever want to go back there!"

And then came the inevitable deprecating line. "And if you don't like the poi, take it home and use it to hold up your wallpaper!" Whereupon everyone would laugh, and I would cringe from the pain of that humiliating joke.

Auntie Berdie sensed what her clients wanted, and she made it happen. I say she did all these things, but in fact she didn't do any of these things; she just made sure other people did. Auntie Berdie was a great executive. She not only knew every Hawaiian in Southern California, she also knew exactly what anybody might do for her and how much she had to pay them to do it. She made all arrangements for her luaus on her black rotary dial phone as she sewed leis right there at her dining room table. Her business dealings probably qualified her for a black leather swivel chair in a corner office, but Auntie Berdie chose a spindle-backed, maple kitchen chair in her dining room. Her dining table was not a place for eating, it was her executive desk — covered with business papers, long lists of phone numbers, price lists for luau supplies and, of course, piles and piles of lei-making ingredients. She negotiated, bantered, bartered and schmoozed on the phone — all the while pushing her lei needle through the ubiquitous strips of crepe paper. Not your normal corporate image, but nevertheless she was an effective multitasker before the phrase was invented.

Any CEO today would envy her executive skills. She had a way about her that made people feel special if she picked them to run an errand for her. I became a part of something really important when she asked me run to the back porch or to the kitchen to fetch something. I know others felt the same way when Auntie Berdie called them, and she always used the Hawaiian phrase of endearment as she gave them their next assignment. "*E i nei*," she would coo softly, slowly blinking her watery eyes. "*E i nei*, could you please bring Auntie … blah-blah-blah."

She always referred to herself as "Auntie." In this way she seemed to be someone outside herself, the voice on her phone was just the agent for a higher power. Everyone on her long phone list would gladly have run to the ends of the earth to serve her.

Auntie Berdie's catering business gave her control of the poi supply, which was the lifeline to the heart of Southern California's Hawaiian community. Every Hawaiian who came to California soon learned the only way to get poi was from Auntie Berdie. After World War II, a few Chinatown stores carried poi, but in the '30s and early '40s, Auntie Berdie had a monopoly and she used it to build her business empire. In exchange for a bowl of poi and a bit of meat or a piece of dried fish, a recent arrival from the Islands would bring her the latest local news.

Hawaiians have always been very interested in news about other Hawaiians, perhaps because of the Polynesian tradition of oral histories that continues to the present day. Put two Hawaiians together and within half an hour of sharing family histories and reviewing whose kids are married to whom, those two Hawaiians will have found connections to each other. The latest family news from the Islands was social tender for Auntie Berdie, and she traded it to other people. In return she got gratitude, loyalty and new phone numbers to use when she would need to get a job done or an errand run.

Poi from Honolulu arrived frozen in 20-pound cotton sacks. Auntie Berdie kept track of ship arrivals, knew where they docked and, by working her phone lists, always found someone to go down and pick it up for her. Cooking the poi was the only part of food preparation Auntie Berdie always did herself. Poi is very special to Hawaiians. Preparing it is a task reserved for the most experienced people and, when done right, the task becomes a ceremony. Watching Auntie Berdie make poi was watching a master craftsman at work.

I remember piles of poi bags thawing in Auntie Berdie's tiny kitchen. As the frozen poi softened, she broke off chunks and stirred them into boiling water, covering the bottom of a huge cauldron on her four-legged gas stove. This was the only task for which she stood for any length of time. It must have been very difficult for her to stir bubbling poi until all lumps disappeared, but she did it because she was the poi lady. It wasn't a job to delegate to anyone else. After the poi cooled enough to handle, Auntie Berdie would strain it to perfect smoothness.

She would line a huge bowl with cheesecloth, fill the bowl with poi, then gather up the corners of the cheesecloth to make a bag.

By rotating the bag around and around, she would force the poi through the mesh. When I was a child, this was my favorite part of the process. At the first twist, the poi came through the cheesecloth like a million vermicelli, then a second later it would melt into a viscous mass and cascade into the bowl. Understand, this was before lava lamps, screen savers and movie special effects gave us endless morphing colors and shapes. I was fascinated by the oozing of the poi; I loved watching its transformation. Auntie Berdie would keep twisting the cheesecloth, round and round, her fat hands drenched in the sticky poi, and she wouldn't stop until all the poi had gone through the cheesecloth and into the bowl. The bit of gritty poi residue remaining in the cheesecloth got thrown out and the bowl full of poi was ready to cool and serve.

Dishing it up also required skill, and Auntie Berdie, like all master poi handlers, used deft and forceful hands. She would hold an individual serving bowl in her left hand while her right hand would dive into the big bowl, swirl around just so, pick up exactly enough and then take aim and lob the poi right into the target. Plop. Direct hit. Every time. I didn't dare try it — too messy if I missed!

Auntie Berdie was a gambler. She had a circle of friends who loved to play the horses and they were all in daily contact. She placed her bets the same way she conducted the rest of her business — from the black dial phone at her dining room table. She loved the risk and the adventure of the horses. I knew her bookie spoke Hawaiian, too, because whenever she was telling him something she didn't want me to know about, she reverted to Hawaiian, which I didn't understand. If things had gone well at the track that day, however, she would give me a wink or a little chuckle as she hung up the phone.

The horses weren't her only gambling sport. She also loved Rummy 500. Auntie Berdie and her rummy buddies used to play for 10 cents a point, BIG stakes in the '30s and '40s. A zero-point game could cost a loser $50 — a month's pay for some people in those days. I played cards with her too, but since I wasn't old enough to gamble money, she and I played gin rummy for match sticks.

When I was eight, and my family moved to the country 100 miles away from Hollywood, I only saw Auntie Berdie occasionally. My visits became limited to times when my mother was willing to make the pre-freeway-three-and-a-half-hour drive. After I turned 10, my parents would let me take the bus to Los Angeles to visit Auntie Berdie for days at a time, which I did as often as they would say yes and give me bus fare. My cousin Peggy Jo and her family were living in our former half of the duplex, so my trips to Hollywood were doubly pleasant affairs. She and I were the same age; both her parents worked at Uncle Ace's nightclub, so Peggy Jo had a wondrous trunk filled with discarded costumes from the floorshows. She and I spent many happy hours digging through that trunk for glamorous combinations of satins and sequins. Auntie Berdie always seemed very appreciative of our creations, but they must have been pretty outrageous, considering the source of their component parts. Of course, Peggy Jo and I thought we were the picture of sophistication, and Auntie Berdie never disillusioned us directly; she just made sure we didn't embarrass ourselves again in public.

One day, after we had draped ourselves in finery from the trunk, we decided to show off our outfits to Auntie Berdie, but the inside door between the two apartments was locked on Auntie Berdie's side. We weren't going to let that stop us from sharing our splendor with her, so we clomped out Peggy Jo's front door, up the sidewalk on Western Avenue — a very busy thoroughfare — and turned left to Auntie Berdie's front door. It was a short but difficult journey. The cast-off, high-heeled dancing shoes we wore didn't come close to fitting our little-girl feet, but both Peggy Jo and I were convinced they topped off the glamour of our ensembles. So, with ankles bending and twisting, we shuffled our glitzy way up the street to Auntie Berdie's door. We only took the street route once. After that, Auntie Berdie made sure the inside double doors between the two apartments were unlocked and open when Peggy Jo and I played dress-up, and we believed it when she told us she did it so she wouldn't have to wait so long to see our fashion show.

Now the semi-secret in this story is that Auntie Berdie wasn't really my aunt at all — nor anybody else's for all I knew. She didn't have any real nieces or nephews — at least not real by Western standards — but she was everybody's Auntie Berdie. It was, and still is, Hawaiian custom to address anyone older than you by a family title followed by the person's first name. Hawaiian children never address adults by their first names alone. Adults are either Auntie or Uncle So-and-So, or, if the adult is beyond middle age, the title is Tutu, meaning grandma or grandpa.

People could have called Auntie Berdie "Mrs. DeBoalt," which would have been acceptable but not at all Hawaiian. The formality of Mr. or Mrs. is too stiff for the Hawaiian culture so, although I called her Auntie Berdie, she wasn't my aunt and I didn't know anything about her actual family. I didn't even know whether she had ever had any children of her own. I thought she might have had a daughter because there was a portrait of a beautiful young woman on her bureau. The young woman was very chic — a slim, longhaired beauty, with languorous dark eyes looking out from under the wide brim of a stylish hat. I used to stare at the picture, trying to figure out who the young woman was. Daughter or self? I couldn't decide. I tried to reconcile the young woman's features with Auntie Berdie's, but any resemblance had long since vanished.

But I did learn that before Auntie Berdie came to Los Angeles, she had lived in Honolulu and was the wife of a prominent judge. He died suddenly in an auto accident, and she literally buried herself in grief and hid in the mountain she made of her own body. Finally, I got up enough courage to put the question to her directly. "Is this you, Auntie Berdie?" I asked one day when she caught me staring at the picture of the beautiful young woman.

"Yes, that's me."

"When, Auntie Berdie, when?"

After a long pause, she murmured, "A very long time ago." Her eyes misted and focused on something way behind the beautiful woman in the picture.

The last time I saw Auntie Berdie, I had just graduated from college. I was 21 years old and on my way to a job on the East Coast. I went to Hollywood to say goodbye to her and the few other relatives who still lived in the old neighborhood. Peggy Jo had married and moved away, and most of the people I had known there were gone. Although Auntie Berdie still occupied her half of the duplex, she and her life were much changed. She wasn't in movies anymore; she hadn't catered a luau in years or sewn a crepe paper lei, and she bought little 3- pound bags of poi from markets in Chinatown just like everyone else did. But I know those Chinatown grocers didn't prepare it the same way she had. I know they didn't squeeze the poi through cheesecloth to make it smooth. I know they didn't trade it for tidbits of news about folks in the Islands. They just stuck a price tag on it and sold it as though it were a sack of rice.

Auntie Berdie's hair was dyed an awful blue-black color and didn't look good at all around her aging face. And, she wasn't fat anymore. She said her doctor had told her that her heart was bad and she needed to lose weight. She had — more than a hundred pounds. But in the process, she had lost something else. She had lost her persona and her empire, maybe even her confidence. Or, if it wasn't just the weight loss, maybe time had just passed her by. On my last visit to her, Auntie Berdie was a mere hint of what she had been. She was living with the ghosts in her memory. A few old-timers (and I include myself despite my youth) still came to pay their respects to her, but she was on the periphery of the action now, and getting closer to the edge. She would slip off soon and join her husband, but she had made her mark in Hollywood, way beyond being Mrs. Wife of Judge DeBoalt. She had made her mark being Auntie Berdie — the one and only lei lady, the luau lady, the poi lady, whose essence still lives in the exotic perfume of a pickled olive.

# IN THE COUNTRY

# CHAPTER 5

# ON AND OFF THE HORSE

"The air here in LA is not safe for you to breathe. Get out of town. Move to the desert where the air is decent." My dad's doctor spoke those words to him in the spring of 1939, before the word *smog* was invented. He didn't need the word to know the polluted air of the Los Angeles basin was detrimental to his patient's health. The implications for my dad were so serious that, as soon as school was out for summer vacation, he and Mom piled my brother and me into the back seat of our tan Chevy and off we went to search for a new hometown with clean air.

First we visited Palm Springs. Movie stars wintered there, so my parents thought of that desert community as a Hollywood annex, and certainly the dry air was clean. But they eliminated that oasis on the first visit because the temperature was 112 degrees and summer had just begun. They didn't need to see what temperatures July and August would bring.

A few miles west, on the other side of Mt. San Jacinto, however, was a picture-perfect, agricultural valley, and Daddy liked the idea of settling his family on a small farm. He had grown up on a farm in the Texas panhandle, and raising a few chickens and milking a cow appealed to a yearning deep inside him.

After we said "no thanks" to a turkey farm on a parched, rocky hillside, miles from anywhere, the realtor showed us a pretty little farm just outside the small town of San Jacinto. The property fit the image of idyllic-farm America. Ten acres were broadly divided into two agricultural areas: an apricot orchard to the side of the farmhouse and a pasture across the back of the property. The apricot trees were loaded with green fruit promising a bumper crop in July, and a dozen different kinds of fruit trees hung heavy with several varieties of pears, plums, peaches and figs. A tire swing dangled invitingly from a towering cottonwood tree between the house and the barn. Oh, the barn! What a treat to our city senses. Inside, the air smelled sweet from alfalfa hay and feed for the horses, cows and chickens.

My mother delighted at the roses bordering the front lawn and squealed when she saw the lilacs, petunias and geraniums. A grape arbor shaded the west side of the house, and on the east, an English walnut tree filtered the morning sun. Tamarisk trees bordered the driveway, blocking the east winds and separating our farm from the neighbor's field on the other side.

It was love at first sight. Every dream either of my parents might have had about life on a farm seemed likely to come true here. The owners weren't home that day, so my parents couldn't go inside the farmhouse, but they didn't need to. To them the house was not an important part of the property. They could see what was important to them, and they liked what they saw. They bought it for "cash-on-the-barrelhead," as my father used to say, and we went back to Hollywood that night with happy fantasies about how life on the farm would be for all of us.

Dad: "Maybe they'll sell us that workhorse I saw in the corral. And there are enough harnesses and plows on the property to do whatever is needed."

Mom: "Those roses are gorgeous mature bushes and will make lovely cut flowers for the house. And I think I'll turn that little patch out by the water pump into a vegetable garden. And water from our own well! Imagine how sweet that will be."

Dad: "We can get some pickers in to take care of the apricots, and I could get a milk cow too, and maybe even a pig for home-cured bacon and ham. We used to cure our own in Texas, and — you'd better believe it — there is *nothing* tastier than that! Mmm mmm."

Mom: "The fruit trees will produce all the jams and jellies we would ever want, and it'll be nice to have a few chickens and gather our own fresh eggs."

My dream had only one thing in it — my very own horse. I saw myself riding all over the farm, up into the foothills, down the dirt road to who knows where. My own horse! I couldn't remember when I did not dream about having a horse. And I mean that quite literally. Sometimes when I woke up from a wonderful horse dream, I would keep my eyes closed tight to hang onto the images in the dream for just a few more seconds. The fact was, the closest I had gotten to a horse was at the ten-cent pony rides my parents let me take every once in a while. There were concessions here and there throughout the Los Angeles area where, for a dime, you could get strapped into a saddle and ride around a ring a couple of times. I always found each ride disappointing because it always ended too soon, but whenever I saw a pony ride, I nagged, begged and pleaded to do it again. Perhaps the biggest horse thrill of my life was in the show at Uncle Ace's nightclub when I was 4 or 5 years old. The first time it happened, I was sitting in the front row watching the 8:30 floorshow when the trainer asked the horse if he wanted to give someone a ride. To my amazement and delight, the beautiful white horse came right over to me and put his muzzle in my lap. I felt like someone was offering me a golden crown. And when the trainer put me up on the horse's back and I rode that mighty steed all around the stage, I was a princess.

The prospect of living on a farm set my horse dreams on fire. I imagined myself galloping over the rolling hills of San Jacinto

Valley, hair flowing wildly behind me, and my horse — my best friend — would bear me safely and speedily to the crest of the hills where we would both pose majestically and survey the world below.

The farm was never intended to be the family's source of income. It simply replaced our half of the duplex on Western Avenue. Soon Daddy would sell the store in Hollywood and transfer his liquor license to two small stores in the Valley, one in each town, both on Main Street. It was a great life decision — better health for him with the clean air, good business move because he had the only liquor stores for miles around, plus the farm offered a much better environment for the family, compared to the nightclub. But the road forward was not without a few bumps.

The car ride from Hollywood to our new lives in San Jacinto was a very long one. By the time everything in our old house and store were taken care of, it was already late in the day, and in those pre-freeway years the 100-mile drive took three-and-a-half hours. We arrived at the farm after dark.

None of us will ever forget that night. Remember, Mom and Dad had not gone inside the house the day they bought the farm because no one was home and the house was locked. When my parents opened the door that night — now as the new owners — they did not expect fancy, but they did expect the basics. After all, it was 1939. My parents were not prepared for what they found.

After the long drive, the first room all of us wanted to use was the bathroom — but after opening every inside door in the place, we couldn't find it. We did find a bathtub in what should have been the pantry off the kitchen. Later however, we found the tub wasn't connected to any plumbing. You filled it by hauling buckets of water, and when you finished bathing and pulled the plug, the water drained into the grape arbor on the other side of the wall.

The only running water in the house was one cold-water tap at the kitchen sink. A cotton sack was tied over the faucet to filter out impurities like sand, sticks, leaves and insects. The only toilet on the whole ten acres was outside — a two-holer outhouse near the barn and chicken coop. Mom and Daddy had of course seen it when they initially toured the farm, but they thought it was just a useful relic and never dreamed there was not a fully-plumbed bathroom inside the house.

Needless to say, the first improvements to the house were plumbing in nature, but that didn't happen overnight, so for a few weeks the outhouse was it. My brother and I took late-afternoon baths in a galvanized tin tub that Mom filled in the morning so the sun could have all day to warm the water — simple, direct solar power.

My brother and I were young, and the closest neighbors were a hundred yards away, but I still wasn't comfortable stripping down in the back yard for my daily bath. Modesty had been thoroughly preached to me, and my nude scene in the movie *Hurricane* had been such a traumatic experience, I did not enjoy bathing in a space without walls. I have no idea when my parents bathed.

My extreme body shyness made the cesspool incident all the more embarrassing. The city sewer lines did not extend to our rural neighborhood, so every farm had its own system. Our choices were: (1) staying with the good old-fashioned outhouse, (2) installing a septic tank system or (3) digging a cesspool. My father opted for the cesspool — to be located at the end of the grape arbor, about 15 feet from the back corner of the house. One afternoon while some men were working on it, I needed to pee but didn't want to go all the way to the outhouse, so I squatted in the bathtub which, if you remember, drained to the grape arbor. When I finished and went back outside, I saw all the men looking at me and then at the little yellow puddle at the end of the drainpipe. They obviously thought it was very funny and were enjoying a big laugh, but for me farm humor was going to take some getting used to, especially when I was the butt of it, so to speak.

The first morning at the farm we all woke up early, anxious to go exploring. Everyone in the family was excited about the property and hoped the lovely outside would boost our spirits, which were sagging because of the depressing inside. The morning dew still glistened on the leaves, everything looked fresh. The pens and corrals were empty, but our imaginations filled them up with friendly cows and horses. As soon as my brother and I saw the umbrella tree growing in the middle of the back pasture, we immediately visualized a clubhouse nestled in its branches. That didn't happen, but it didn't matter because the farm was full of great places to have secret meetings, or to be alone and daydream. We didn't need to build anything. There were places in the sheds, in the hayloft, in the feathery branches of the tamarisk trees, up in the cottonwood, in the tank house, endless places. All you needed were friends to make up your circle of secret cohorts.

The first friends we found were at the next farm over. On our first afternoon, Everett and I crossed the orchard by ourselves and arrived at the barbed wire fence separating the two properties. Three children about our ages suddenly appeared on the other side. I don't remember anybody saying anything much; I think we stood there and stared at each other until an adult came up behind them. After finding out we had just moved in, he invited us to come back that afternoon and swim in their reservoir. My reaction was immediate — I turned and ran.

My mother had taught me to always assume the worst about strangers, which was a good survival tactic if you were growing up in Hollywood next door to a night club. In rural San Jacinto though, it was a bit much and I kind of knew it, but I kept on running anyway. As I pounded through our orchard, the scenario running through my head was that the man who had invited us to swim had kidnapped those children and had lured them inside his barbed wire fence with promises of candy and a cool swim. Now they were trapped and couldn't go home again. Well, that wasn't going to happen to me. If Everett wanted to get himself held hostage, he could, but I wasn't! I ran home and stayed there.

My brother, who wasn't burdened with my little girl's fear-based survival kit, came home, changed into his suit and went to the neighbors by himself. When my mother asked me why I wasn't going too, I made up some lame excuse. I was too embarrassed to expose my fears to her. There was a tinge of guilt and suspicion I might never see my brother again, so when he came home later that day, refreshed from a delightful afternoon in the reservoir, I hid my envy by pretending I had done something really fun too, although I don't remember what it was.

I later learned the "kidnapper" was named Tony, and in real life was the older half-brother of the three younger kids who were the same ages as my brother and me. Joe and Josephine Yorba were twins, and Eddie was a couple of years younger. After that first day, my fears evaporated and I was able to enjoy spending time at the Yorba's turkey farm. They had hundreds of the birds in large pens, and we had a game to make them gobble. It was very easy. All you had to do was make a loud noise and all the turkeys would answer, "Gobble, gobble, gobble." *All* the turkeys. It was so much fun. We couldn't do it for very long, though, because an adult would always hear the turkeys and come out of the house and make us stop. Once in a while, Mr. Yorba would let us help pick the feathers off a turkey he had just butchered. He would tie the turkey's legs up to a post near the chopping block, and we'd all stand around and pull the feathers out. At the time it seemed a perfectly natural childhood activity, although now, after decades in the city, I look back at those days as rare and cherished memories.

We didn't have turkeys on our farm, but we did have chickens and a few ducks. We bought baby chicks 100 at a time. They arrived in perforated cardboard boxes so the three-day-old chicks wouldn't suffocate in shipment. As soon as they came, we transferred them as quickly as we could to incubators where they lived until they grew enough feathers to leave the artificial mother hen. The incubators were about four feet in diameter, looked like low tents of galvanized tin and had a couple of light bulbs inside to keep the chicks warm.

We also got new chicks by letting a few of our hens hatch eggs the old fashioned way. "Settin" hens had status and got their own little A-frame houses where they could sit on their nests in relative peace, away from the hurly burly of the crowd. As soon as a hen began "settin," we would place as many eggs in the nest under her as she could cover. Then we'd mark the calendar for 21 days, and wait. It was fun seeing new chicks hatch — watching those first holes in the shell, then seeing the little beaks pecking larger and larger holes until finally the chicks would emerge all fluffy and soft, and you'd hear the peep-peeps of the new generation.

Birthing days were always cause for celebrations on the farm, whether the newborns were chicks, calves, colts or rabbits. We marveled at them all. Sometimes a newborn had to be bottle-fed and quart wine bottles became nursing bottles. We filled them with warm cow's milk and vitamin supplements, capped them with rubber nipples and struggled to hold them steady while a baby calf, kid or lamb punched and sucked like he was at his mother's teats.

We brought one animal with us from Hollywood — our dog Poochie, a Heinz-57-variety puppy from the pound. He was the first of a long string of four-legged playmates (not all dogs) I would have during those years on the farm. Poochie's distinguishing feature was his devotion to fetching. He not only lived for it, he was obsessed with it. The instant anyone stepped outside the door of the house, Poochie would immediately run to find a stick, then lay it at the person's feet and look pleadingly at him until he threw it.

There was no rest from this game for him, but after a dozen stick tosses, that game got pretty boring for me. So I developed a twist to make the game as interesting for me as it was for him. It was a version of hide and seek, with Poochie being IT all the time. Since he couldn't count to 100 while I hid myself, I had to come up with something to keep him busy for a minute or two while I ran to find a hiding place. I discovered that if I put the stick on a high rung of a ladder, I could slow him down long enough to give me time to duck into a good place. Most dogs do not like to climb ladders, but Poochie was so determined to retrieve the stick, he learned to climb a six-foot fruit-picking ladder. He'd hunker down close to the rungs and sort of crawl up the ladder until he reached the stick, but once he got the stick in his mouth, he would leap off triumphantly and race to find me.

He always found me, no matter how cleverly I hid, and when he did, he would pounce excitedly on me and drop the stick in front of me as though to say, "Hah! I did it! Now it's your turn again." With tail wagging, he'd sit back on his haunches and wait for the next round.

Looking back on those days, I think I was really lucky to have such a plucky, eager, canine companion, because human playmates were simply not readily available. Their farms were too far away and after school we all had our own chores to do.

The corrals and pens around the barn gradually filled with four cows, one grouchy milk goat named Maggie who loved only my dad, and a workhorse we called Brownie. He was good at pulling the plow, which pleased my father, but my only interest was in riding him.

"The Yorba kids ride their Brownie," I reasoned, pleading with my dad "So why can't I get on him? "

"He hasn't been broken for riding, Betty Ann," cautioned Daddy, "and he might not like anybody on his back."

"Oh, puh-lease. I know how to ride," I insisted, sure my brief experience on horseback at Ace Cain's Cafe was sufficient experience. Besides, I trusted Brownie would understand I loved horses and wanted to ride so much he would love to have me on his back. I just knew I would have the same love connection with Brownie as the heroines in all the horsey books I had read had with their gallant steeds. I finally convinced my father to put a bridle on old Brownie and give me the reins. We didn't have a saddle, so I rode bare-back, the same way the Yorba kids did. Brownie let me ride for quite a while that first time before he dumped me off with a little buck.

After that, each time I rode him the riding interval got shorter before he bucked me off. I think he learned the connection between dumping me and getting to go back to the corral where he could eat and hang out. Over time, my pleasure in riding decreased as surely as his bucking increased.

The last time Brownie bucked me off, everybody was watching — Daddy, my brother, and all three Yorba kids. I was hurting from the fall, and the trauma of it activated my bladder. My father was giving me some tips about how to hang on longer and "teach Brownie a lesson," but all I could think of was I had to pee. Well, horror of horrors, I stood there and lost control — in front of all those other kids. I started to cry, but when all the other kids started to laugh, I tried to laugh too. My father just said, "My goodness, Betty Ann, why didn't you say anything?" So why didn't I say anything? I didn't know. I just couldn't. I was just a kid, eight years old, with bruises on my arms, legs and pride.

That Christmas I got a saddle, a lovely English style saddle. In a smaller box was a ceramic horse with "Here's your saddle horse" written all over it in laundry marker ink. My parents thought it was a pretty good joke. "Oh, that's pretty funny," I said, blinking hard to keep tears from falling. I didn't think I would ever catch on to adults' sense of humor.

Daddy didn't say anything more, but the next time he went to the stock auction in Ontario, he came back with a beautiful riding horse, a small mare, brown with a black mane and tail, a white star on her forehead and four white socks. She was in the corral when I got home from school that afternoon. I could hardly believe my eyes. "Wahoo!" I yelled. "Wa-hoo! Is she mine?"

"Yes, she's yours," my mother answered. "And let's call her that!! Wahoo is a great name for a horse!!"

"Let's put your saddle right on her and see how she goes," added my dad, as he brought the tack out from the barn.

I was still in the third grade and caught the early school bus home; my brother, in the fourth grade, came home about an hour later. By the time I had changed into my play clothes and Wahoo was saddled up, that hour had passed, and I turned out onto the street just as Everett's bus stopped to let him off.

"Hey, where'd you get that horse?" he hollered.

"She's mine!" I yelled back. "Daddy just brought her home from the auction. She's my riding horse!"

"Well, I get a turn!! Lemme on her!"

"No! I just got on her. This is my first turn!"

"No, it isn't! You've been home a whole hour. It's my turn now. Get off!"

"No, honest, I just got on her. I haven't had my turn yet."

"Like heck," he said, and he picked up a handful of rocks and began lobbing them in my direction. Some of them found their mark on Wahoo's flank, and she took off like a shot down the street.

I had never even been on a trotting horse before, and there I was, suddenly at full gallop, trying to just stay in the saddle. I let go of the reins and grabbed for the saddle horn, but there wasn't any because this was an English-style saddle — no horn to hang on to. I dug my hands under the edge of the front of the saddle and hung on tight. I did not want to be in that saddle anymore, but I knew if I fell off I would die. That was not the way horseback riding was supposed to be. Horseback riding was supposed to be fun. This was not fun. Wahoo galloped on for what seemed like forever. It was probably a quarter of a mile.

Just chalk it up to fate. I wasn't meant to be an equestrian. All of Brownie's bucking, and now the runaway incident with Wahoo cooled my ardor for being on the back of any horse. I rode Wahoo a few more times, but I was never able to control her well and she seemed to know it. Right after we left the driveway and turned onto the street, she would head over to the side of the road and proceed to graze. She was always reluctant to go away from the farm, but when I'd turn her around and head home, she always galloped until she got to the barn.

My dream of a beautiful relationship with my horse, and the long, graceful rides over the hills didn't come true, and in time even those dreams faded away. Getting my riding horse cured my yearning for a riding horse, but not in the way I thought it would.

Fortunately, other animals on the farm were more amenable to playing games with a little girl. Besides my buddy Poochie, there was my pet lamb Lammie, my pig Tiny, and my baby goat, who was one of twin kids born to Daddy's grouchy milk goat Maggie. When the twin kids were a couple of weeks old, Daddy gave them to my brother and me to raise and to bottle-feed with cow's milk. My brother took responsibility for Billy, the boy, and I took over the little female, whom I named *Nani*, which means "Pretty one" in Hawaiian. The twins were so much fun, playing constantly, jumping, running and chasing. We kept them away from Maggie because Daddy didn't want them nursing. Maggie stayed in her pen, but the kids had the run of the farm. They were as free as Poochie, and he enjoyed playing with them too. To him, they were just a couple more critters to play run-around with. My mother thought it was cute when they wanted to get in the car, so she let them ride along whenever we ran errands. When I had my tonsils out and stayed overnight at what was called a rest home (because there was no hospital in the Valley), Mom, my brother, and the two kids all came down to pick me up. I was as glad to see Billy and *Nani* as I was to see the rest of my family.

One day, however, tragedy struck. One of the hired hands backed his car over the little billy goat and crushed him. Remember, this was a farm, and farm animals are not raised solely to be pets. Also, nothing goes to waste and goat meat was highly prized, so my father dressed the meat and put it in the freezer locker downtown.

A short time later, Uncle Ace and some other relatives from Hollywood came out to the farm to visit. They loved to come drink the fresh milk, eat fruit right off the trees and breathe the fresh clean air. They also raved about the sweet well water we had on the farm — still filtered through the cotton sack but so much better tasting than the stuff that came out of the pipes in Los Angeles.

My mother prepared a special farm dinner, with heaping platters stretching the full length of the long table: fresh corn on the cob; green beans and beets from the garden by the water pump; assorted homemade pickled peaches; three kinds of pickles from watermelon rinds and cucumbers; butter we had churned ourselves; fried chicken from our own coops and to top it all off, barbecued goat's meat. Everyone was raving about what a special treat it all was, and the chatter around the table was happy and centered on the good food, especially the barbecued goat's meat. I winced at the fact those little chops had been one of our pets, but I kept telling myself I was a farmer and had to accept the fact that part of life on a farm was butchering and eating what you raised. I suppressed all sentimental thoughts and tried to be grown up. In hindsight, I may have gone a little too far.

I polished off my plate and looked around for seconds. The barbecued goat's meat was really very tender and flavorful, so that's what I chose. Pulling myself up so I would look like a big, tough farm girl, I asked in my loudest and strongest voice, "Please, may I have another piece of Billy's leg?"

My request rose over the table like a mushroom cloud. The happy chatter ceased. Eating ceased. Hands came up from laps and quietly pushed plates just a bit toward the center of the table. No one said a word. No one passed the plate of barbecue either. In truth, I didn't really want any more. I was just trying to be more grown up, just trying to do what I thought was expected of me. So, okay I went a step further than I needed to. I just didn't realize some things are better left unsaid.

CHAPTER 6

# A TINY PIG

About two years after we moved to the farm, the 20-acre place across the street was put up for sale, and my dad bought part of it — the alfalfa field directly facing our house and orchard. The other part of it, with the big house, the barn and some pens, was bought by the Matsons. The really great thing about all this was that the Matsons had a daughter who was the same age as I was. In farm country, having neighbors nearby was rare enough; neighbors with kids your same age was even rarer. But there we were, with playmates on both sides. It was almost like a real neighborhood.

After the Matsons got settled they began filling the pens with pigs — hundreds of them. Fortunately for us, the pigpens were at the end of their farm, farthest away from our house, so we didn't suffer too much from the downwind drift. All the kids in the neighborhood thought the pigs were more interesting than the Yorbas' turkeys, so we began to hang around in the Matsons' yard after school, watching the pigs grunt, squeal and push each other around over slop and garbage. The only times the pigs weren't jousting over food was on very hot afternoons when they lay in mud puddles the Matsons created for them. Then the pigs would crowd around, all trying to fit in the water at once and grunt and snort the time away.

Our favorite pigs to watch were the new mothers nursing their babies. Pigs have big litters, eight to 12 piglets at a time, and the babies line up to suckle at the sow's double row of teats. That's when the pecking order gets established, at their mom's bosom, so to speak. Some teats are better than others because they produce more milk, so the largest piglets in each litter scramble to nurse at those teats, which makes them grow even faster than the smaller piglets that have to nurse at less abundant spigots.

One day, Mrs. Matson offered me a baby pig. "She's only two days old," she explained, "the runt of the litter and, because it's such a big litter, I'm afraid this little one won't make it if she has to compete with the others. They're all larger and will push her out of the way so she won't get in to nurse. She'll starve unless someone bottle-feeds her, and we just don't have the time. If you'd like to take her home and take care of her, she's yours."

I put out my arms and carefully cradled the tiny baby close to my chest so she wouldn't be scared. Runt of the litter, she looked so helpless with her sweet face and snout. I walked home with her immediately, cooing to her all the way. She was reddish-brown with a white band over her shoulders. Her little legs and hooves weren't any bigger than my own fingers. She was so tiny, that's what we named her.

At home, Tiny joined the retinue of our bottle-fed babies. Every day after school I raced to her pen and took her out to play. Soon she recognized me and ran to greet me as soon as she saw me coming. She had a little bed in the barn for a while, but Daddy built a pen for her next to Maggie the grumpy milk goat's enclosure so she could have her own mud puddle to lounge in. When I was home, however, Tiny didn't have to stay in the pen, she was free to roam the farm and was never more than a few feet away from Poochie, *Nani* or me.

Tiny thrived on the fortified cow's milk we fed her from the bottle and, as she grew older, we added other foods to her diet — clabbered milk and some vegetable scraps. She also got a mixture of grains that, true to her species, she consumed enthusiastically. In fact, without competition at the bottle or the trough, she ate so much every day she outgrew her siblings and by her first birthday was a very large adult pig.

Then one day, my dad announced he was going to take Tiny back to Matsons' for a one-day visit. He wouldn't tell me *why* he was taking her there, so naturally I feared the worst. "Is she going to come back tonight? I mean, they're not going to do anything to her, are they?" (Read that — make bacon out of her.)

"No, she's just going to visit some of the other pigs. She'll be back and she'll be fine," assured my dad as he loaded her into the panel truck.

"Can I come?"

"No, you have to go to school. She'll be here when you get back tonight. Don't worry!"

Four months later, Tiny had ten little piglets — the cutest little things, with curly-Q tails and high voices — all clamoring for attention and teats. Tiny had enough for them all and, as mother pigs go, seemed to be quite a good one. She now had to spend all her time in the pen, however, because the piglets couldn't follow us all over the farm. But I used to spend a lot of time playing with them, and named each one: there was Flopsy, Mopsy, Cottontail, Peter, Nutkin, and so on down the line.

I was nine or 10 years old when Tiny had her babies. Mom and Dad took turns tending the liquor stores and weren't always home when my brother and I got off the school bus. In those days, there was always a hired hand who lived in a small house Daddy had added near the barn complex. The hired hand took care of the livestock so my parents didn't have to do the day-to-day chores around the farm. My brother and I both had our own chores. We fed the rabbits, the dog, the cats and the chickens, and gathered the eggs. The hired hand pitched hay for the cows, horses and goat, distributed oats and did the milking.

One day when both Mom and Daddy were at the store, I was playing with my piglets and decided we all needed a nap. I tucked Flopsy and Mopsy, my two favorites, under my arms and took them inside. You'd have to know my mother to realize what a big risk this was. "Animals stay outside! No animals in the house. The house is where we live, and I don't want any hair or any other kind of animal mess to clean up. I have enough to do ... blah blah blah." Well, you get the idea. Mom did not even allow the dog or the cats in the house.

We all knew better than to break those rules. Consequences for doing so tended to be severe. Even in the worst weather, the dog never got beyond the screened-in porch, and the cats had to seek shelter from storms in the barn or under the house. But at that moment I was too much into my two little pigs to appreciate the serious nature of what I was doing. Mom was at the store — out of sight. My two little-doll piggies were right here in my arms and were the only things that mattered. The best place, by far, for napping was the living room sofa, so that's where we headed. I arranged the three of us very nicely with pillows and a light blanket, and we all dropped off to dreamland.

When I woke up, I quickly hustled the two piglets back out to the pen. Daddy's car was in the driveway, so I knew he had come home, but he was out in the barn, so I just put the babies back in their pen and went on with my chores.

Mom didn't come home until much later, but she had no more than stepped foot in the house than she wrinkled up her nose and sniffed. Peeuu! There's manure in the house! Everybody! Check your shoes!! Oooph! *Pilau!! Pilo, pilo!*" The last two words are Hawaiian epithets for bad smells, and when my mother resorted to

Hawaiian it upped the level of drama. You didn't have to understand the words to know she was not pleased. Someone was going to be in big trouble!

I dutifully checked my shoes and held up the soles for her inspection. They were clean. We all walked around the house bent over, studying the floor, looking for spots, piles or smudges of offending animal scat. Nothing. My mother finally simmered down and gave up the hunt for evidence of sloppy shoe-scraping. Life went on.

This is the way my mother tells the story: A week after the *pilo pilo* incident, my dad raised the subject with my mother again. "Remember, Hon, last week when you came home late and you were sure someone had tracked in some manure? Well, if you promise not to get mad, I'll tell you what happened."

"Okay, I promise," she said eagerly. "What happened?"

"You were right on the money when you came in and said the house smelled like a pig pen. I didn't want to tell you at the time because I didn't want Betty Ann to get into trouble, but when I came home in the afternoon and walked into the living room, there she was, sound asleep on the sofa with a piglet on each arm. All three were asleep. It was the cutest picture you ever saw. I didn't wake them up but went right on outside without making any noise. She came out a few minutes later and put the piglets back into the pen. I really don't think she even thought about having the pigs in the house when you were asking everybody to check their shoes. You have a nose like a bloodhound you know, and I am sure she didn't notice the little pigs do have a scent. They didn't make any mess; they just took a nap on the sofa. She really didn't mean to do anything wrong."

Since a week had passed, and because she had promised not to get mad if my dad told her the truth, she didn't. In fact, as the years went by, this story became one of her favorites when she talked about life on the farm.

Every summer, hundreds of Oakies (as we all called them at the time) came to the Valley to work in the harvest. They would set up a camp town on a 20-acre field between Hemet and San Jacinto, and overnight what had been a wheat field became a tent city, with water faucets, community showers and outhouses.

All of us kids loved to go to the Oakie Camp on Sunday afternoons. It was the day off, and Oakie Camp buzzed with fun activity. As I look back at it now, I can see the camp leaders were trying to keep the camp residents from making any trouble in the town by entertaining the folks in their own area. We local kids felt Oakie kids had a lot more fun than we did because their parents planned all kinds of neat things for their amusement, while ours pretty much left our entertainment up to us.

Sunday mornings, Oakie Camp had its own preachers doing services in the community tent, but the afternoons were solid theater. There were games, contests and entertainments. I was always too shy to join in any of the activities, but I loved watching my brother and his friends jump right in.

"Who of you kids can whistle?" asked the emcee at one of the afternoon shows. Nearly every young hand in the audience shot up in the air.

"Well, we're gonna have a contest to see who's the best whistler here. Who wants to come up on stage and try?" My brother and a dozen other little boys climbed up on the platform. "Okay, let's hear y'all whistle," coaxed the announcer. He'd no sooner finished the word 'whistle' when he was besieged by a gaggle of little guys all whistling in his ears.

"Okay, okay! I hear ya," he cried, cringing as if asking for mercy. "But here's the deal on the contest. Anybody can just plain whistle, but what we want to find out is who will be the first person to eat four soda crackers and then whistle." He held up a box of crackers and passed them out, warning the contestants not to start eating them until he gave the signal. When he said, "Go!" all the soda crackers disappeared inside open mouths and then, almost immediately, started coming out again. Showers of cracker crumbs rained all over the stage as the emcee jumped around ducking the projectiles. The audience cracked up with laughter at the boys rushing up to the emcee, trying to whistle but succeeding only in blowing wet cracker crumbs all over him.

Those Oakie families sure knew how to have fun. Every Saturday night they had a dance right there in Oakie Camp. We local kids were sure the Oakie kids had a good life traveling around, getting to live in a tent and having all that fun all the time. The hard work those migrant worker parents did in our valley, from sunup Monday morning until sundown Saturday evening, didn't enter our thoughts. We didn't bother thinking about their long hot days in the fields and orchards. Even the few women who stayed behind in that tent city to tend the babies couldn't have had much fun with summer temperatures hovering over 100 degrees throughout July and August.

One summer, my parents hired some workers from the camp to help harvest our apricots. The men picked the fruit, and the women — along with children over five — worked in the cutting shed. I say "shed," but actually our cutters worked under tarps strung between trees in a corner of the orchard. The women would cut and pit the fruit, dropping the halves into a pan. The children took the full pans and spread the halves out on the drying trays, cut side up. When they filled one tray, another empty one would be placed right on top of it, and when the stack of trays got so high the children couldn't reach the top, someone would haul the stack away and place another tray down to start another stack.

A fast cutter, with a crew of hard-working kids, could cut a dozen, maybe 15 field boxes of 'cots in a day. At 45 cents a box, you can figure out how much they took back to camp in the evening. Their husbands, if they were good pickers, could pick up to 45 boxes in a day, at 25 cents a box; so the men could make up to $10 a day. That wasn't bad money in those days, but it took the whole family and the season was short. After the 'cot season ended, the Oakies would move on to another valley with another crop to harvest. Oakie Camp in San Jacinto would be gone by mid-August, and the big field would get plowed and planted in wheat or field corn again.

The Oakies only worked one season in our cutting shed. After that, we kids and our friends did all the work. My mother and my brother oversaw the operation. I was relegated to the cutting crew. My brother got a percentage of the profits after the dried cots were sold, but I only did piecework. Since I had to do everything myself — cut, pit, and lay the cut 'cots on the tray — I couldn't even aspire to 12 boxes a day like the Oakie family teams did. My best was 7 boxes in one day and, at the end of the two-week season, I might be able to put a very hard-earned $14 in my piggy bank.

Those years of life on the farm were very special, and I feel so lucky to have had them. They were difficult sometimes, and at other times they were lonely. Some things about farm life are harsh, but the lessons from the animals, the people, the chores and the games are unique to that life, and I am thankful to have had five years on that funky little 10-acre plot of land. I was 13 when we moved to the *city* — that is to Hemet, the larger of the two towns in the valley. It was only three miles away but, compared to life on the farm, it was another world in lifestyle and experience.

The population of San Jacinto in those days was 1,800. Hemet had almost twice that — 3,400 residents *and* a traffic light. Valley kids considered Hemet a metropolis. For me, moving day was a day of high excitement and anticipation. Not only were we moving to a city almost twice as big as where we had been living, but the Craftsman-style house we were moving to had two floors and was twice the size of our little farmhouse. Plus, there were two bathrooms — one downstairs for my parents and one upstairs for my brother and me. Everett and I each had a large bedroom, and we also had our own living room upstairs. Such space! Such luxury! The biggest difference, though, was we had neighbors. All around us. Across the street. Right next door. You could walk downtown in 10 minutes. School was five minutes away on your bike, and it took a while to get used to seeing people walking past our house on their way home.

Several years later, during a college vacation, my mother and I went back to that little farm to see if the years had changed it. We were astonished. Eighth Street, which had been a washboard dirt road barely wide enough for two cars to pass each other, was now smooth, black asphalt with a white line down the middle.

Our 10-acre farm was gone, replaced by a subdivision. The house at our old address didn't look at all like the one we had lived in, but the woman who lived there welcomed us and invited us inside. She showed us how they had remodeled everything — modernized and improved. No flour sack on the kitchen faucet anymore. That was all fine. The sad part was, none of the landscape was there; not the tamarisk trees, not the cottonwood tree, not any of the fruit trees, not the tank house, not the barn or the corral.

The more we saw, the sadder we got, and then our hostess raised her hand and exclaimed, "There is one thing we couldn't do away with. We just had to keep it. It's right over here — the other side of the garage. Look, there!" As she pointed, we looked and burst into laughter. A minute passed. The three of us stood there giggling, hands over our mouths, shaking our heads at each other — instantly and joyfully bonded by the little old two-hole outhouse with the new moon carved into its door.

# CHAPTER 7

# TRYING TO BE CATHOLIC

For almost 15 years, I was a Catholic and, for 10 of those years, an ardent one.

I went to my first Catholic mass shortly after I turned eight. Our family had just moved to the farm in San Jacinto and one of my mother's cousins stayed with us for a while. Cousin Henry was returning to Honolulu after dropping out of seminary in Belgium, where he had tried to become a priest. But even though Henry was no longer going to be a priest, he was still a very devout Catholic and, when his first Sunday with us rolled around, he announced he planned to attend Mass and invited the family to go with him. Our family didn't go to church, but I thought it sounded interesting, so I accepted his invitation.

I didn't have a dressy dress to wear, so my mother suggested one of the dancing costumes I had worn in the last Bud Murray Studios Revue when we lived in Hollywood. I loved having an excuse to put those costumes on again. One was light blue taffeta with dark blue ruffles on the sleeves and short skirt. Another was white satin, with a wide, red-sequined belt. I wince now looking back on going to church in those glittery getups, but at the time I enjoyed the glamour of wearing fancy outfits.

I thought they matched the glamour of the Catholic Mass itself. And I loved it all, especially the Gregorian chants with responses back and forth between priest and congregation. I liked the choreography of the Mass, kneeling on cue, rising in unison with everyone else to say something in Latin or to sing a hymn. I loved the rule of genuflecting every time you crossed the center aisle of the church. There was so much to do and see at St. Anthony's Catholic Church. It was a lot more fun than Sunday School at the First Methodist, where I'd gone a couple of times with our neighbors, the Cochrans.

The first time I went to Mass with Henry, I was so dazzled by the pageantry I told the whole family I couldn't wait until I could go back the next Sunday. Henry said I needed a hat if I was going to be a regular at Mass, so my mother took me to J.C. Penney's and bought me the prettiest hat in the store — a heart-shaped white straw bonnet with white flowers nestled inside the brim. A navy-blue net sash went around the crown and tied in a bow under my chin. Going to church was so special.

In those days, all females had to cover their heads in the church. Later, in catechism class, I learned the reason women had to wear hats was because *our* prayers couldn't go straight up to God — only *men's* prayers could do that. I imagined women's prayers, like word balloons in the funny papers, deflecting off the crowns of their hats and bouncing over to their husbands' heads, or their fathers', or the nearest male relay station, and then floating up to heaven. It was all part of the Catholic conditioning that girls weren't worthy of anything except secondary service. Only boys got to serve the priest at Mass and carry the incense burner for him. Only boys got to take the long brass-handled wick and light the candles on the altar. Only boys got to wear the long, red robes with white, lace-trimmed smocks over them. Only boys got to ring the bells when the priest said certain important words.

What little girls got to do, once a year, was put a crown of flowers on the statue of the Virgin Mary. It was the only time we were permitted inside the railing that separated the altar from the general admission section of the church. For that day, one little girl was chosen to wear the light blue silk cape the nuns would bring from their convent. Two other girls got to walk behind her and carry the train of the cape, and two would walk in front scattering flower petals on the aisle. Then the one in the cape got to climb a stepladder and place a wreath of flowers on the Blessed Mary's head. I always wanted to do that so I could wear the blue silk cape, but the closest I got was carrying one tip of its train. Even as a child, I understood I wasn't quite as good a member of the congregation as I would have been if my parents had also been members.

As long as I got to wear my hat and my taffeta dresses, however, I didn't begrudge other boys and girls their privileges. I loved just being any part of the action. I could smell the incense, dip my middle finger in the holy water basin at the front door and make a cool wet sign of the cross as I entered God's house. I loved hearing the priest read the Mass in Latin with his hands raised, palms open. I especially loved it when Bishop Buddy came to San Jacinto and sang a High Mass with other priests — not just altar boys — in attendance.

From age eight to 18 I totally believed everything the Catholic Church taught. I believed in the miracles, in the reward of heaven and the punishment of hell. I wanted to be as good as the saints I read about in my catechism books. I earned points in the celestial ledger by saying all the recommended prayers, and when the Church asked for support I conscientiously made donations — sometimes to the point of sacrifice (not to the point of martyrdom, but I did want to feel a pinch).

When Lent came around, I would take home the little tuna can-sized donation container and check off each day after I dropped a coin inside. Filling the tuna can with money wasn't easy on my 50-cents a week allowance, but I set a goal for myself — a nickel a day — which left me 15 cents a week spending money. That was a real sacrifice and gave Lent true meaning. It made me feel closer to Jesus, who gave up meals and sleep when he spent 40 days and nights of the first Lent in the Garden of Gethsemane, praying and wrestling with the Devil.

One of my favorite people at the church was Miss Irene Hickey, Father Mackey's housekeeper. After Mass or Sodality club meetings, she would open her kitchen door to my best friend Pat and me, serve up large slices of chocolate cake with green mint frosting, and listen sympathetically to our adolescent concerns.

Miss Hickey had just moved to San Jacinto from New York City, and to us seemed so sophisticated and urbane. She loved to laugh and was extremely kind. Anytime Pat and I were at St. Anthony's Church, we'd knock on the back door of the rectory, hoping Miss Hickey would invite us in for a visit. She always did and she always had time for a chat. "Hi, Girls," she'd say with a big smile as she unlatched the back screen door. "Come on in. Sit down for a bit, won't you? I just finished baking a cake. Will you try a little piece with a glass of milk?"

As Father Mackey's cook, she probably baked a cake every day so he would have something to offer parishioners who stopped in to see him for advice, consolation or to arrange a special service. As her guests, we were the lucky beneficiaries of that hospitality. After we settled ourselves at her kitchen table, Miss Hickey would ask how things were going at school, what was new, what was going on in our lives, and we would pour out our pre-teen hearts to her. Within a short time, she knew all our thoughts and dreams, many of which, in those days, involved the church, because every once in a while Pat and I would wonder out loud what it would be like to become a nun. Miss Hickey knew what our hobbies were and how we spent our free time. Our visits with her were happy; she was a positive influence, a good role model and a devout Catholic.

In temperament and physicality, Father Mackey was almost the exact opposite — young, nervous, and extremely energetic. St. Anthony's got a new church building and a small-but-promising Catholic school shortly after Father Mackey took over. Maybe all that activity was contagious, too, because before long, members of the parish in nearby Hemet announced they had decided to build their own church to have their own parish in their own town. I didn't think that would affect my life at all, because I lived in San Jacinto, but in time it had major repercussions.

San Jacinto was the smaller of the two towns in the Hemet-San Jacinto Valley, so when the Hemet Catholics finished building their own church, the effect in San Jacinto was immediate and traumatic. For starters, the church organist lived in Hemet, and when she left St. Anthony's there was no one to play music at Sunday Mass in San Jacinto. From the pulpit, Father Mackey asked desperately for someone who could play a keyboard to come forward, but no one did. It was a shame, too, because our new pink stucco church had a choir loft in back of the Sanctuary with a brand new Everett Orgatron. Made of gorgeous blond wood, it had two keyboards with a whole row of foot pedals, and was so much better than the dingy old pump organ in the old church. But what good was a fancy new organ if nobody could play it?

Miss Hickey must have told Father Mackey that I played the piano and could probably learn to play the organ. After a Sunday or two with no music, Father Mackey told me he would arrange for one of the nuns from the convent in San Bernardino to give me organ lessons if I would agree to play for Mass. I went directly to Miss Hickey's kitchen to seek her advice, which, of course, was predictable. "That's wonderful!" she exclaimed, "Grab it! It'll be a challenge, but it's a great opportunity."

So, at the age of 12 and-a-half, I became the organist for St.

Anthony's Catholic Church in San Jacinto. A grouchy nun came out from the convent every Saturday morning to give me lessons on how to use the stops, the two keyboards and the foot pedals. The organ was difficult for me because I was pretty short and, even when I perched on the edge of the bench, the tips of my toes could barely reach the center pedals. Until I grew taller, I didn't have a chance of reaching the foot pedals on the outside edges, but I loved playing the organ and stopped by church every day after school to practice.

A couple of weeks after my debut as St. Anthony's organist at Sunday Mass, Miss Hickey suggested I come to the 7 o'clock morning Mass on weekdays before school, so I could practice with the service. Timing of the music during Mass was important because there were certain times when music was appropriate, but other times — like when the priest said particular phrases in Latin — when the organ had to be silent.

Attending daily Mass held an added plus for me. My dad was always up by 5:30 or 6 to milk his goat Maggie and take care of other chores before he went downtown to open his liquor store. My mother liked to sleep in until 9, so early morning became my dad's and my time together. He made breakfast every day: bacon, eggs and toast, plus fresh-squeezed orange juice served in little flowered Velveeta Cheese glasses. It was very special because, while the rest of the house was asleep, I got an edge on the day with my dad.

On any given weekday, about three people attended early Mass at St. Anthony's. Miss Hickey sat in the first pew on the right hand side of the church. The lady who had donated the land on which the church stood, and who lived next door in what would eventually become the rectory, sat in the first pew on the left. An old man, who had appointed himself groundskeeper, sat in one of the back pews under the choir loft. I couldn't see him, but I knew he was there. Sometimes one of the altar boys would show up on weekdays to serve, but most days Father Mackey said Mass unattended. I would begin playing about 6:45, to give the congregation some pleasant music as they came in and took their seats. Two minutes of music would have been sufficient for that weekday crowd but — what the heck — I needed the practice.

I had a book of classical songs to play from, and the nun who gave me organ lessons gave me a book of sacred music. She sometimes came to Sunday Mass, but on weekdays I was on my own and, gradually, I found myself playing more of the classical songs from my own book throughout the Mass because, frankly, I found many of the so-called sacred songs boring. Mostly, they were just sequences of chords and didn't have much in the way of melody. The good sister had not, however, made it clear that the Church distinguished between liturgical music and worldly (also called "profane") music. I thought anything with long, arching melodies full of rich chords and arpeggios sounded like religious music, so I played classics. Some of my favorites were *Thou Sublime Evening Star, Le Cygne*, some Rachmaninov, and, of course, Gounod's *Ave Maria*. All in all, it was a pretty good gig for a young girl. As time went on, in addition to playing at Mass 7 days a week, I also played at funerals and weddings, for which I sometimes got paid $5, and to me that was big money. Then one day, I was suddenly, abruptly and loudly fired.

The weekday Mass had just ended, and I was playing exit music so the three attendees could have music while they strolled toward the doors. My habit was to keep one eye on the parishioners as they made their way down the aisle and out of the building to make sure I played until everybody was out. What I saw when I glanced down that morning was startling. Miss Hickey and the neighbor were coming up the aisle side-by-side chatting as they walked. Father Mackey, apparently in a big hurry to get out, couldn't get by them in the aisle so he jumped up onto a pew, pounced to the top edge and was springing from the back of one pew to the next, rushing toward the front door. His jaw was clenched. He didn't look happy. I kept playing and for a second wondered what could have happened to make Father Mackey pound out of church in such a lather.

My wondering couldn't have lasted longer than a second, because that's how long it took for Father Mackey to get to the back of the sanctuary, fly up the stairs to the choir loft and materialize in all his fury at the side of the organ. I glanced up at him and then gasped because, obviously, I had something to do with whatever was so terribly wrong. He was fuming. I could almost see puffs of smoke coming out of his ears. I removed my hands from the keys as though I had just touched hot lava.

"What do you think you are doing?" he yelled. "Don't ever play that music in here again. In fact, don't ever play in here again. Get away from the organ. Get away! Get away!" He was so angry, and there was no fury like Father Mackey's. I realized I must have done something awful, but I had no idea what it was. He went on sputtering about something, but I just didn't get it. The bottom line, however, was clear: I was fired — terminated — kaput!

My ears were ringing, and my face flushed hot. Blinded by the tears that sprang to my eyes, and moving like an automaton, I closed the music books, stacked them and put them in the bench. I couldn't think. I couldn't see. I felt as though I had been whipped. I kept asking myself what was wrong? What had I done? But I couldn't come up with an answer. I had just played for the mass. I didn't understand.

I have no idea how many minutes passed before I was able to gather my schoolbooks and make my way down the stairs to the front door. Miss Hickey was standing there just outside. "You look like you could use a nice cup of hot cocoa and a rye bread and honey treat," she said to me. "Come on, let's go. We can talk in the kitchen."

Blindly, I stumbled along after her because I couldn't think of any other choices I had at that moment. My only thought was, what had I done to make Father Mackey so angry? As we settled down at the familiar green table in the corner of the rectory's kitchen, Miss Hickey set out a plate of hot rye toast, the honey-jar, and a cup of steaming Dutch chocolate with a marshmallow melting on top.

I couldn't say anything, and just looked up at her through my tears. She was looking down at me, and she was smiling. That puzzled me. I didn't see anything in my situation to smile about. "Don't worry, Betty Ann," she said. "Father Mackey just has a temper. In a day or two, he'll realize he has put himself in a corner because, now he has no organist for Sunday. Just wait. He will apologize and then ask you to come back. It's really nothing serious anyway. You can ride it out."

"But what did I do?" I wailed.

She burst out laughing. "You really don't know, do you?" When she stopped laughing, she explained with a grin that my transgression was playing *The Indian Love Call* during the holy Mass. That, she said, wasn't considered appropriate music for a holy Catholic service.

"But it's a pretty song, Miss Hickey!" I insisted lamely, still not seeing the humor in the situation.

"Yes, it is pretty, Betty Ann, but it's really not what you ought to be playing when he is saying Mass. It's just the difference between liturgical or religious music and popular music. And *Indian Love Call* is very popular these days, thanks to Nelson Eddy and Jeanette MacDonald. Everybody in the country recognizes that melody because of them. I tell you, it'll blow over. Just give it a couple of days. He'll be fine. He's just blustery when he gets upset. He doesn't mean anything by it."

She might have known that, but I didn't. After her comforting words, the hot chocolate and the honeyed rye toast, however, I managed to pull myself together enough to go on to school. Fortunately, none of my friends there would hear about my humiliation, so at least it was confined to the small group who were at Mass that morning.

The day at school was busy, and I didn't have time to feel bad again until after I got home. I kept the morning's debacle to myself because I assumed my parents, like Miss Hickey, would be surprised too and feel I should have known better than to play *The Indian Love Call* during the Mass. I clung to what Miss Hickey said about Father Mackey's temper being short-lived, and as each day passed I prayed that would be the day he realized he wouldn't have an organist for Sunday Mass, tell me all was forgiven and beg me to come back. Until then, however, I couldn't practice the organ after school like I usually did, because Father Mackey had told me to stay away. One long day after another long day passed that week, and there was no call and no forgiveness — until Saturday.

That morning, Father Mackey's car steamed into our driveway and screeched to a halt amidst a huge cloud of dust. "I want you to come back to play, but you can't play that *Indian Love* thing again," he sternly announced. "Get some more songs from the Sister, and only play what she gives you. Nothing else! Understand? And here, here's something for your wall." He handed me a flat box about 3 feet long and 2 feet wide. "Give my regards to your parents." And with that, he disappeared down the driveway in another cloud of dust and was gone.

"Thank you, Father," I murmured to the cloud of dust. I went inside the house, opened the box and pulled out a 2-foot x 3-foot oil replica of Jesus in his crown of thorns. It was a major item — an extravagant gift. Father Mackey hadn't said he was sorry he lost his temper, but that was okay with me. I still felt exonerated — and very honored. I hung the painting on the wall above my bed.

Later, I realized it was going be a little hard to live with. It was one of those portraits with the eyes that follow you wherever you are. Whether you are directly in front of it or off to one side, the eyes are looking at you. There are a lot of pictures like that of stern ancestors in old English castles. Mine wasn't an ancestor, but the all-seeing portrait of the Son of God was an intimidating presence in my bedroom. The portrait was especially oppressive because of the period in my life when it took up residency on my wall: I was 13 years old and just beginning to experience the physical changes of adolescence. But, whenever I was tempted to explore those changes, there'd be the eyes of the Son of God glaring right at me from two feet away. I found myself wishing they would go away, but I couldn't bring myself to get rid of the painting. I just accepted that another layer of guilt was one more burden to bear.

It was all because the song, *Indian Love Call,* had a title that disqualified it as church music. I thought being beautiful music was qualification enough, but I was just a kid so what did I know? Lesson accepted. I never played *Indian Love Call* again in church, but many years later I learned something about one of the other songs I played regularly that, if Father Mackey had known, he would have fired me all over again — out of a canon. That song, *O Thou Sublime Evening Star,* also beautiful and gloriously melodic, is about yearning — not for love but for sex. It's from Richard Wagner's opera, *Tannhauser,* in which the hero has just returned from a yearlong orgy with Venus, the Goddess of Love. He confesses to the Pope but is denied absolution, so he decides to return to the bacchanal. His song doesn't have anything to do with the evening star the rest of us see in the sky. Oh, the power of a name — if you don't know the meaning behind it.

Just before my fourteenth birthday, we moved three miles away, from San Jacinto to Hemet, but I was able to continue going to St. Anthony's every day because I got a ride from another parishioner who also lived in Hemet and attended the early Mass in San Jacinto. I was so happy, because I didn't have to miss a beat in my job as the organist. St. Anthony's was such a big part of my life I didn't even think about changing parishes. But Hemet's new priest saw it differently. He thought, if you lived in Hemet you were automatically a member of his parish. Shortly after we moved, Father Hyland called in person to welcome me to his congregation. "Thank you very much, Father, but as you might know, I play the organ at St. Anthony's, and if I leave there I don't think they have anybody who can take my place."

That argument didn't impress the good Father Hyland. With a stern note in his voice, he told me I would be committing a mortal sin every Sunday that I did not attend Mass in the parish where I lived. Now I believed that not going to church at all on Sunday was a mortal sin, but Father Hyland's interpretation of the laws didn't seem fair or logical. "This is the second time a priest has threatened me," I told myself. "First I had to bear the wrath of Father Mackey's temper, and now this pressure. It doesn't feel right to me. These people are supposed to get their instructions directly from God, but what difference does it make to God which church I go to, as long as I go. What Father Hyland says doesn't make sense."

My mother, who never had much patience when it came to religious issues anyway, agreed completely. "That's just like these church-goers," she said shaking her head. "He isn't thinking about your soul; he's only thinking of himself. If you want to continue to play the organ at St. Anthony's, go right ahead. I'm sure God will understand." So I did. St. Anthony's was the church I had grown up in and I felt I belonged there. For the next three years, I continued to attend Mass at the little church in San Jacinto, but when I left for college St. Anthony's had to — and did — find another organist.

When I got to Stanford University, attending Mass in Palo Alto was difficult, both logistically and philosophically. Eventually I found myself missing more and more Sunday Masses, making the excuse I had too much studying to do. In reality, the more I learned about the history of the Catholic Church, the cruelty of the Inquisition, the contradiction between the Church's gold and the poverty of its members, the more I found myself withdrawing from the institution. During my sophomore year, despite several counseling sessions with the priest at the Newman Center in Palo Alto, I stopped going to Mass altogether and joined my agnostic classmates to dabble with other religious philosophies. When I attended a house of worship, which I did from time to time, I went to the Unitarian church.

Later in Oakland, I settled into the Montclair Presbyterian Church. At that time — the 1970s — MPC was known as the rad-lib church of the East Bay because it had offered sanctuary to young men of draft age who didn't want to go to Vietnam, and it also took in refugees fleeing terrorism in Guatemala and El Salvador. Rev. Duke Robinson preached morality, ethics and community spirit. He was just as apt to quote from the Koran or the Bhagavad Gita as from the Bible, and often began his *lectures* (nobody in the congregation called them *sermons*) with a news clip from the *San Francisco Chronicle* or *The New York Times*.

The first time I heard him speak, I thought he was clairvoyant because he seemed to know exactly what was going on in my life, with work, family and community. At MPC, no statues were crowned, and nobody wore robes or burned incense. There was ceremony, but it involved holding hands to form human chains of support in times of crisis. We burned candles while the choir sang beautiful music. There was much celebration, but of the beauty of the human spirit rather than the sins of the damned. As an adult, I found it a positive experience. But we can't go to that church anymore because we no longer live in the East Bay.

I don't go to any church at all now, but every once in a while I think I would like to find one that would nurture my soul. When Sunday mornings roll around, however, I usually go for a walk, pick at a few weeds in the garden, play with the cats, or have coffee and a croissant while I dawdle over the Arts section of the Sunday paper. The nice thing is, I can do all that without feeling I'm condemning myself to hell. I've put distance between the Catholic Church and me, and no longer feel the Church is going to come after me. It seems to have its hands full, not so much with its congregants but, as the world now knows, with its own priests and bishops.

# CHAPTER 8

# COUSIN HENRY HAD A SECRET

At 20-something, Cousin Henry was a husky, well-educated young man, much more refined than most of my Texas cousins who prided themselves on being tough, streetwise and unsullied by books and schooling. I liked my new cousin a lot because he seemed so worldly and talked about interesting things. He had traveled all over Europe and knew a lot about New York City too. Henry was the first person I was aware of who'd been anywhere except Hawai`i, Texas or California. I was impressed when I first started going to Mass with him at St. Anthony's church in San Jacinto, and thrilled when Henry told me he would take me to the catechism classes at 10 on Saturday mornings.

My age group was taught by Sister Bernadine, who drove 35 miles from the convent in San Bernardino to bring us the teachings of the church. Sr. Bernadine's pleated skirt of black gabardine covered her to her booted feet. A cardboard-stiff white cowl framed her sweet but plain, bespectacled face. A long necklace of black wooden beads held a large silver cross at her waist. Her habit set her apart from our teachers in grammar school downtown, and gave her an authority their mere civilian clothes couldn't match. I never questioned anything she taught us, even when some of the details about saints, martyrs and angels seemed pretty far-fetched. I liked the challenge of memorizing the lists. I especially loved reciting the Ten Commandments, the seven deadly sins and all the different prayers we learned.

There were many rules and punishments, but also many rewards. The rule was, a certain number of Our Fathers and Hail Marys got you X-number of days off your sentence to purgatory before you could go to heaven. Everything was laid out in the Church's books. The organization and specificity of the rules of the Catholic Church, as taught by Sr. Bernadine, were very attractive to me, and I welcomed them into my life.

Henry, who had appointed himself my Catholic mentor, saw to it I was baptized so, if I were to die unexpectedly, my soul could go to heaven and not have to stay in limbo for all eternity. Henry helped me get ready for my First Communion. For him, that meant drilling me on all the lists and church teachings we had to memorize. Henry spent hours with me, patiently reading the questions from the catechism book, and coaching me with the word-perfect answers. By the time Bishop Buddy came out from Riverside to test our catechism class, I knew all the answers, and was thrilled when Bishop Buddy extended his left hand toward me and gave me permission to kiss his ring. My reward from Henry was a miniature rosary, so tiny it fit into a little coral-colored plastic box shaped like a bell. As though that weren't special enough, Henry told me the Pope himself had blessed that little rosary. As soon as I learned which prayer each bead and link in the chain stood for, I used that rosary every day and felt sure I was directly connected to heaven.

My parents were neutral about the church. They didn't encourage it, but they didn't make fun of it either, or begrudge the time I spent memorizing prayers and lists of saints and commandments. When my First Communion Sunday rolled around, Mom sewed a very pretty white eyelet dress for me, and even made a little veil for me to wear on my big day. I also got a pair of new white shoes and socks, and Mom curled my hair. I was as spiffed up as I could get when I walked up to that railing and stuck out my tongue to receive my first little white wafer.

I loved being a Catholic, and I loved my cousin Henry — until I learned catechism wasn't all he wanted to teach me. I spent a lot of time with Henry. Our farm was a mile and a half from town, so when we got home from school in the afternoons, we were pretty much stuck there until we left for school the next morning. Afternoons were spent playing with the animals or doing little chores around the farm. One afternoon, my mother sent me out to pick some blackberries for dinner. Henry grabbed the colander and offered to help. As we walked to the back end of the farm, past the barn to the berry patch on the far edge of the orchard, Henry and I chatted about St. Anthony's and what lay ahead for me in the church. He told me that, when I got to be 12 years old, I could have my Confirmation. As he talked, I imagined myself marching down the aisle of St. Anthony's with my classmates, all of the girls in white dresses and pretty veils. It would take a while to get ready for it; I had a lot of studying to do, but then I had my cousin Henry to help me.

I chattered away happily as I scanned the berry bushes, looking for the sweetest, ripest fruit. We quickly filled the colander, but when I picked my last few berries to top off our harvest and turned to find Henry, what I saw made my stomach turn to ice. He was standing a few feet away with his fly unbuttoned and his penis, fully erect, sticking straight out at me. He was holding it with one hand. "Here, come here, I want to show you something. I want you to touch me," he said.

I had never seen an adult penis before, and it didn't look anything like what I remembered my brother had between his legs when we were younger and used to take baths together. "No, that's okay," I answered in a shaken voice. My face felt hot, my cheeks, flushed. I wanted to run, but at that moment I didn't know how to.

"I would like to take a bath with you and rub you all over. Wouldn't you like that?" he asked. "Here, come and see what it does when I rub it." His hands worked in and out, faster and faster. I watched in horror — not wanting to see but unable to close my eyes — wanting to run, but unable to move. I just knelt there by the blackberry bushes until he squirted something into his hanky and put his thing back in his pants.

We walked in silence back to the house. I don't remember dinner that evening. I felt dirty and ashamed. I had done something wrong and was carrying a heavy weight. I wanted my mother to notice something was amiss and ask me what had happened. Then I could tell her. But she didn't say anything. She didn't ask me anything. I guess she didn't notice. Everybody else in the family acted as though nothing had happened. How could they do otherwise? They didn't know what Henry had done in the garden.

The next day Henry gave me a book titled, "Little Lives of the Saints for Children." Although I was already an avid reader, I didn't have many books of my own. It was a nice gift. A few days later, Henry gave me the "Official Guidebook to the New York Zoological Gardens," a wonderful volume full of photographs of all the animals at the zoo, with a descriptive paragraph under each picture.

But whenever he could be alone with me — in the barn, in the back field, out of sight — he would repeat the masturbation scene and implore me to touch him. I wouldn't do what he asked but I wasn't able to tell my mother about it either. The more times he exposed himself to me, the guiltier I felt. My guilt also assured my silence. It was a miserable time for me. In between those sexual episodes, however, Henry took me to church on Sundays and to catechism on Saturdays. Henry sang in the choir and sometimes served as an altar boy. Other people at St. Anthony's thought he was so wonderful, having been to seminary and knowing the verses to all the hymns. Only I knew his other song.

It's difficult to remember how long Henry's exploitation of me lasted. I want to say maybe a couple of months and half a dozen episodes. It finally ended the day he tried to push things farther. That afternoon, Henry and I were the only ones at home. My brother was at band practice, and both Mom and Daddy were working in the liquor store. Henry asked me if I wanted to play a game of checkers.

"Okay," I answered, "soon as I finish my spelling homework."

"Good, I'll set the board up," he called from the room he shared with my brother.

I finished my list of words and went in to play checkers. Henry had set the board up on his cot and was waiting for me. He was naked with the board sitting between his legs. I didn't know what to do. Up to this point, he had done the masturbating thing in the field. I had been able to keep a safe distance from him. But a checkerboard isn't very wide, and his hard-on stuck out over it like a flagpole. I froze — wishing at the moment I could make myself invisible, or vanish from the spot, so what was happening really wasn't happening. But I didn't do anything. I just sat there convinced I didn't have a choice. After all, Henry was an adult. He had authority. He was also a guest in our house. He was the person who took me to church and knew all about God. I was just a frightened little girl who didn't know what to do.

I don't remember anything about that game of checkers except it didn't last long because someone came home. I don't even remember now who it was that came home. I just remember I felt relieved when I heard my dog barking, a sign someone had entered our driveway and I wasn't alone with Henry anymore. Henry muttered something under his breath and grabbed his clothes. I ran outside.

That night after dinner, even though I was very uncomfortable and frightened, I told my mother what Henry had been doing. I was afraid she would be angry with me and punish me for being bad but, without hesitation, she went to his room and told him she had something private to discuss.

The next morning Henry moved out. He took up residency at the local firehouse for a while. He never made a move on me again and, as far as I know, he never mentioned to anyone what he had done to me. I didn't mention it again either. Neither did my mother.

For the next year or so, I continued to see Henry at church until he joined the army and went off to fight the Nazis. After he left San Jacinto he wrote letters, not to my parents but to me. Long letters, about his experiences in the army and the places he was seeing. His letters did not contain anything inappropriate; he was just my great cousin Henry again. He continued to send me presents: a little bookmark from Holland, another rosary from Rome. I always answered his letters, not because I liked him, but I felt it was my duty. After all, he was a soldier and all civilians — even we children — knew we had to do our best during that Big War to help boost the morale of our troops.

The next time I saw Henry was in the mid 1960s. I was married, had two small children and was living in Oakland. Henry called to say he was on his way to the Trappist Monastery in Utah. "I have a couple of hours before I have to leave; can you come downtown to pick me up for a visit?"

Sure, I thought. Why not? Besides, I was curious. Could we have an honest conversation, or would we continue the charade that he had not exploited me? On the way to pick him up at his hotel, I pondered whether I could bring up what he had done when I was a child. I hadn't mentioned the incidents to anyone — not to my mother since my childhood, nor to my husband nor to any of my friends. It was something buried in the past, and I thought the past was better left buried.

We sat in my kitchen for a couple of hours over cups of tea while he told me he had divested himself of all his earthly goods so he could join the Trappist monks. He was 50-something then, and said he was looking forward to spending the rest of his life in meditation and menial labor in that cloistered community.

Three months later he called again to say he was on his way back to Honolulu. "I couldn't do the hard work," he said. "It's back-breaking labor. The Trappists are up at 4 in the morning and, after prayers and breakfast, they go out to the fields and pitch hay all day. I couldn't do it. I had to quit. I'm going back home." Again, there was no mention of our dark secret from all those years earlier.

The last time I saw him was in 1980, at my stepfather's funeral. Noah Kalama was much beloved in the Hawaiian community. He had brought the sport of outrigger canoe paddling to California some 25 years earlier and had seen more than a dozen clubs get organized and flourish before he collapsed and died suddenly one morning. He was the founder and coach of many of those clubs, and all the paddlers looked to him as their spiritual and cultural leader. They crowded into the home Noah and my mother had shared for 15 years. I think every Hawaiian in Southern California must have been there, plus several from the Islands.

I hadn't seen Henry for years, but he was there too, and brought his wife, an ex-nun. No one seemed to know he had even married, but it seemed fitting he would marry an ex-nun. When we saw her, however, we were shocked. She did not look like any of the nuns I remembered from my Catholic days, certainly not my lovely Sister Bernadine from catechism class. Her face and tone of voice told everyone she was a heavy drinker and smoker. Her language was edgy and a bit hostile. I gave her a wide berth. At one point, I noticed her talking to my sons in the kitchen. Dan and Mike were pressed backwards against the counter, and she was leaning toward them, talking intently. They looked like they wanted to escape but didn't want to be rude. They were both in high school and old enough to take care of themselves, so I decided to let them escape from her as best they could.

When they managed to break free, they made faces and rolled their eyes to each other. "Whoa, Mom!" they exclaimed. "She is really weird. You know what she was talking about? She was telling us how, on warm days, she and Uncle Henry like to walk around their house without any clothes on, and about how the neighbor kids come over and watch them on their screen porch! Crazy, huh?"

"Yeah, well someday I'll tell you about what Uncle Henry used to do to me when he was living with us on the farm. In the meantime, however, let's just all stay away from those two people!"

"You're not kidding!" they chortled, before disappearing into the crowd of cousins who had gathered around a guitar and an ukulele.

Later, my husband Craig told me Henry's wife had also cornered him in the kitchen. He had just checked out the supply of soft drinks and beer in the fridge, and she heard him offer to run to the store and get more. "She came up to me and asked if I wanted some company, saying there was something at her motel room she wanted me to see. Just the way she talked and looked at me, I decided the better part of valor was to get out of that detour. She is somethin' else, I'll tell ya."

I told him what the boys had said, and we agreed she and Henry really deserved each other — two very troubled people who apparently wanted salvation in the Church but who couldn't conquer their sexual demons. Sad, but at least perhaps they found some mutuality in each other.

That was the last time I ever saw Henry. We never did speak about what he had done in front of a little girl half a century earlier. He took his secret to his grave. I put mine in these pages.

Do I wish I had confronted him? Yes, certainly, and if this age of #MeToo had existed in the '60s I'm sure I could have found the support and strength to look him right in the eye and tell him what a terrible thing he had done to me a quarter of a century earlier. Back then, families didn't talk about sexual assault — at least mine didn't — and I don't think my mother was any different than others in that respect. Perhaps the thinking was, if you didn't talk about something, you could pretend it didn't happen. As a very little girl in Hollywood, I had been taught by my mother not to speak to strangers. But who was going to warn me not to speak to my own cousin? Even after he violated all the rules of our household and broke the law, I don't think my mother ever spoke of it to anybody — I don't even know if she told my father about it. She handled the situation and pulled a curtain of silence over it. Done. Over. It's private. Don't talk about it. It will only bring shame on everybody. Just move on. Pretend it didn't happen.

In my opinion, today's openness about sex is so much healthier, although in some ways I think it does make childhood more difficult. When children learn so much so young, and the vocabulary of sexual assault and sexually transmitted diseases is taught in the primary grades, what happens to innocence? Is that knowledge acquired at the price of a carefree, idyllic childhood? Are very young children really ready to see what is shown to them every day on both small and large screens? I don't know the answers, but I think today's parents, especially parents of girl children, carry a heavy load.

On a case-by-case basis, and looking at my own case, I can say this: I am glad my mother took immediate action when she learned what Henry was doing, but I wish I had been able to talk to her about it when it started instead of being afraid. I also wish she had been able to talk to me about it after she found out, but she never did. She never mentioned it again; she just handled it with Henry, as though I was no longer involved. But I was wounded by it, and I did heal, but it left an ugly scar of shame and guilt. If she had been able to talk to me about it, to comfort me about it, to understand how I felt about it, perhaps she could have spared me that. And, I think she might have also spared herself from carrying some guilt and shame from the experience too. I will never know whether she felt any shame or guilt for what I had gone through. I think she probably did — but that will only ever be a guess.

# ON BELONGING

CHAPTER 9
## WHO AM I?

# WHO AM I?

When I was a senior at Stanford, chatter with my friends was about what we wanted for graduation. Girls who were engaged started planning their weddings, honeymoons and new homes. Girls who had already been to Europe wanted cars. The rest of us wanted to travel.

My parents agreed to give me a student tour of England and Western Europe, that also went to Morocco and what was then Yugoslavia. I pointed out to them what a good bargain it was. We would stay at hotels used by European tourists instead of the more elaborate accommodations most American tourists preferred. What that meant was that the bathrooms and showers were going to be down the hall, and the rooms would be adequate and not a bit more. But those things didn't matter to me — I was going to see all the places I had only read about until then.

I sent for my birth certificate so I could get a passport. If my mother had known what would be revealed in that piece of paper, she might have wished she had bought me two cars instead. When the birth certificate arrived, it turned out to be a fact checker on a big lie. After I got over my initial shock at the truth it revealed, I confronted my mother, waving the incriminating document at her. "What is this?" I asked, "You've always told us you were all Hawaiian! It says here you're part Chinese."

"Oh, that," she answered in a steely voice. Then she half-closed her eyes as she spat out, "Well, don't worry, it doesn't apply to you.

You don't have any Chinese blood. I kept it all."

I shrank back in disbelief. "Oh, my gawd," I thought, "she creates new biology to fit the lifelong lie with which she has been fooling herself and her children!"

There, in a moment frozen forever in memory, was the emergent tip of the iceberg of confusion I'd been towing behind me from childhood, confusion that had clouded my understanding of who I was, what I was and how others perceived me. Ethnic identity and race are issues that confront all of us, whether we know it or not, whatever color we are, wherever we originally came from. But they loom much larger for people who are black, or brown or yellow and living in a predominantly white culture.

I am Dutch, Irish, Hawaiian and Chinese (as well as Munchkin), although I didn't know for sure about the Chinese part until that pivotal moment. And the revelation certainly explained a lot. I never pursued that topic with her again. It would have been pointless. She had always denigrated Chinese people and taught us "never to trust them, especially Chinese men," a group which now it turned out, included her own father.

I am, as I have said, a multiracial, some of this and some of that. In my childhood, my racial identity felt in many ways like an advantage. Our Hawaiian-ness got my brother and me special placements on the kiddie revues in Hollywood, it got us roles as extras in several movies, and it always got me special attention — all positive.

My mother's ambivalence (or contempt) for her Chinese heritage reveals, in retrospect, what must have been a deep sense of insecurity, all the more mysterious because she was so talented and pretty. She is not the center of any of these stories, but she was certainly a central influence in my life. And I think I am a stronger person because I had to overcome some of her needs and frailties.

She was extraordinarily talented — a gifted singer, attractive with a good figure — but she had such an insatiable need for love and attention that she couldn't share her children — even with her own husband, and even that became a matter of competition. One of my darker childhood memories is what I call, "The Day My Mother Stopped Loving Me."

A big treat on Sunday mornings was Mom reading the funny papers to my brother and me. First he would sit in her lap while she read him three comic strips of his choice; then I got to choose three. One Sunday — I was four or four and a half — I remember being snuggled on my mother's lap as she read the comic strips I had picked, and when she finished, she asked me *The Question*. She had asked me *The Question* several times before, and even though I was a very young child, I knew *The Question* was dangerous and I had instinctively tried to avoid answering it directly. *The Question* was: "Whom do you love more, your Daddy or me?"

Until that Sunday, I had always answered with what, even at that young age, I knew was the answer for survival. It was: "I love you both with all the world."

But that wasn't the answer she wanted to hear, and she kept asking *The Question* — every day, maybe every week, I don't know how often. All I know is, she asked it repeatedly and I didn't like it. It made me uncomfortable and very uneasy. So that Sunday morning I decided to make her stop. That morning I answered, "I love Daddy more."

Her response was nonverbal but there was no ambiguity about its meaning. The arm holding me in her lap loosened and I slid off onto the floor. She didn't say anything, but I knew I was dismissed. She never asked me *The Question* again, and I knew I had made her feel bad, but I also felt she had asked for it.

The interesting thing is, she didn't punish me for it directly. She did not neglect me — she continued to fulfill the contract she had with her gods regarding her duties as my mother. She sewed nice clothes for me to wear, brushed and combed my hair until I was old enough to do it myself. She made sure I did my homework. She taught me how to cook and clean, sew, knit, embroider and play jacks. I cannot claim abuse. People outside the family saw her as a vivacious and charming woman and I certainly was not going to disabuse anyone of that impression. But my relationship with her would always be a difficult one, and I'm sure it somehow influenced my own sense of self.

Another early identity test occurred around the same time, when I was four or five years old. My Texas uncles used to ask me, "What part of you is Dutch, what part is Irish and what part Hawaiian?" I would answer by going down my body, beginning at my forehead (Dutch), then to my chest (Irish) and then to the bottom of my torso when I said, "Hawaiian." My uncles would rock their heads back and laugh, because I pointed right between my legs.

It seemed perfectly logical to me to divide myself up into thirds, but it didn't take me long to figure out what the laughs were all about, and when I realized the joke was at my expense, I stopped designating body parts in my answer. The sting remained however, and for years whenever anybody asked me about my racial background, I tensed up with wariness, vulnerability and the danger of embarrassing myself all over again.

The question of ethnicity was raised and answered for my parents when they first moved from Hollywood to the Hemet-San Jacinto Valley — ("He's a Texan and *she's* Hawaiian.") — but it never came up there for me. Some of my friends nicknamed me "Pagan," but it was a term of affection and we all knew it.

Throughout grammar school and high school, my brother and I were both good students, played in the school bands and orchestras, sang in the school choirs. I was frequently elected class president and never wanted for friends or dance partners at parties and school socials.

Throughout my growing-up years, my mother frequently insisted my brother and I "should be proud of our Hawaiian blood," but she overrode that message when we heard her denigrate Hawaiian relatives and friends. She didn't teach us to speak Hawaiian, but she had a couple of Hawaiian friends with whom she would speak Hawaiian. Since I didn't understand the language, those visits were really boring for me. I had to sit nearby and wait quietly because she was also a strong advocate of the rule that, "children are to be seen and not heard." I was never part of any of her Hawaiian conversations.

The talk about Chinese, however, was purely academic at this point in my life because I didn't know any Chinese people. There were none in Hemet, which was then just a small agricultural town east of Los Angeles. The only minorities in the valley were a few Soboba Indians on the reservation in the foothills, and some Mexicans who lived in a cluster of small houses at the edge of town. Nobody ever asked me about my ancestry.

When I got to Stanford University, I lived among strangers for the first time and questions about my ethnicity came up every time I met someone new who asked where I was from. No one accepted my answer of, "Hemet, in Southern California," and I became increasingly uncomfortable with the question.

Part of orientation for new students was a "jolly-up," a dance where we could all meet each other. The first boy to ask me to dance was Chinese. As he extended his hand to lead me to the dance floor, I recoiled in horror and shrank away from his smiling face. My stomach clutched and my skin crawled. These were the people my mother told me to be wary of and not trust. Furthermore, if my classmates saw me dancing with him they might think I was also

Chinese, and I definitely didn't want that.

As a freshman, I wanted to dance only with *haoles* — white guys. That was *my* group! That's how I thought of myself — mainstream American. I was not a *minority*. Only problem was, I hadn't inherited my father's hazel eyes and light brown hair; I was stuck with my mother's Asian features. I am not proud of having had these thoughts, and I put them down here not to excuse my rude behavior to that nice Chinese boy who asked me to dance, but to help explain why I had to come to terms with who I was. In the wide world outside of Hemet I became increasingly uncomfortable in my own skin.

At Stanford, when I told people I was from Hemet, it simply prompted the follow-up, "No, I mean, where are you *really* from?" I knew they meant, "What *nationality* are you?" But that question made me uncomfortable and I always tried to sidestep it.

I knew if I said I was part Hawaiian, my questioner would follow up with, did I "know so-and-so in the Islands?" or, had I "been to this or that place." I didn't have answers to those questions. I was born in Hawai`i, yes, but we moved away when I was three and a half years old. Since then, I had spent exactly one high-school summer vacation there. I knew nothing about the islands compared with the dozens of students from Hawai`i who were attending Stanford. Most of them were *haole* and graduates of *Punahou*, a private high school in Honolulu from which Barack Obama would eventually graduate. They all knew places and people in the Islands; they knew how to play the ukulele, dance the hula, and could even talk pidgin when they wanted. I couldn't do any of those things.

I did know a couple of hulas, but not the hip, party hulas they knew. I had the looks, but not the culture. My culture was *mainland* not *Island*. Those *haole* kids from *Punahou* had the Island culture, which, even without the looks, seemed to me the better part of the deal.

With each passing year, I became more defensive about being asked, "Where did you come from?" The question was a minefield I couldn't cross without blowing myself up. Maybe I was overreacting, but in those days I was miserable about myself. I'd stare at my face in the mirror, wishing I could change my dark brown, almond-shaped eyes into round, blue ones; wishing I could change my flat, round nose into a narrower turned-up one. I did like my mouth and lips, though, and thought I had pretty — though somewhat large — teeth. But no amount of staring changed anything. The same face just stared back at me every day.

My mother scolded: "Humph, you should be proud to be Hawaiian." How could I be proud of being Hawaiian when I didn't know what it meant? It was just a title, not backed up with knowledge, habit, custom, or language. Although my mother's first language was Hawaiian, she wanted my brother and me to speak only English, because that was the language of success. To her, Hawaiian was spoken by relatives who didn't amount to anything. We didn't hear anything about the wisdom of the ancient Hawaiians, or about physical and spiritual health; we weren't told about their navigational skills, their epic poetry, their long commitment to maintaining balance in nature — something modern civilization has only recently come to value as *sustainable*. The path to success meant thinking and acting like whites, not Hawaiians.

One of my college roommates tried to bolster my flagging self-esteem. "You know, Betty Ann," she said, "people wouldn't bother to ask you where you come from if they weren't interested in you. They ask because they want to get to know you better. They ask because they like you and are interested in you." That explanation helped later, but at the time, I didn't believe it. Until I could find out what being Hawaiian really meant, my insecurity, discomfort and lack of pride continued unabated.

And then, at the end of my senior year, all those insecurities were painfully, horribly confirmed by the man I was in love with. I basically dated one guy in college — a sweet engineering major named Jerry whom I met in Geology when I was a freshman and he was a sophomore. He was from Idaho and, after graduation, planned to return there to follow in his father's footsteps at the mines in Coeur d'Alene. I wore his fraternity pin as the sign we were going steady, and all our friends accepted as fact that we would get married and always be together. He graduated in 1952, the same week my brother graduated from UC Berkeley.

During graduation, Jerry brought his father to Berkeley to meet me. I don't remember much about that encounter except that it was very brief, in the lobby of the hotel where my mother and I were staying. Jerry and his father were on their way back to Coeur d'Alene where Jerry would begin his career as a mining engineer.

Throughout that summer and into my senior year, long and passionate letters flew between Idaho and Stanford, mostly saying how we couldn't wait until we were together again, and making plans for him to come visit during spring break and bring the engagement ring. The day before he was supposed to fly to the Bay Area with the ring, he telephoned. "Betty Ann, I can't come. I'm sorry, but my parents say they will disinherit me if I marry you. I have to break it off. I'm so sorry."

My world fell in. I was devastated. What had I done to bring that about? His father had seemed cordial enough when we met a year earlier. And our conversation had been pleasant enough — I certainly hadn't said anything that could have offended him. The ugly truth was, I realized, that we had met just long enough for his father to see I was not White like he was.

Some painful days of mourning followed that phone call, but fortunately I didn't have a lot of time to mope. My duties as president of the house where I lived with 34 other co-eds, studying for final exams and preparing for graduation, kept me so busy I somehow managed to get through those few weeks. Right after graduation, I left for a student tour of Europe, and by the time I got back home several weeks later, I had received an offer to go to Washington D.C. and work in the personnel office of the CIA.

It was 1953, and in those days racial differences mattered a lot because Washington, D.C. was culturally more Southern than Northern. Although race was not supposed to be a factor in getting a job with the government, interviewers and recruiters put a code in their reports to indicate if the applicant was *colored*. There was no space called "Race or Nationality" on government-application forms, but the information was there for anybody who knew how to find it.

The office I worked in was located next door to a military personnel unit — full of young men in uniform. One day after work, as I was leaving the building one of the soldiers approached me, introduced himself and asked what, by then, had become *The Question*. "May I ask what part of the world you're from?" he said in what he probably thought was his friendliest tone. My response was Pavlovian — anguish, pain and embarrassment. I felt cornered and betrayed. I had always been careful to wear all the right clothes from all the right stores. I always dressed well — high heels, wide belts and the full skirts of the day. But fashion couldn't cover up my skin color or my features, and I knew I wasn't passing as an ordinary American female.

I must have given the poor soldier a withering and reproachful look because he filled the silence by explaining that all the guys in the military wing had a pool about what nationality I might be. "There's quite a bit of money riding on it," he said, "and I've been delegated to find out the answer." I guess he thought that would please me, but the effect was the opposite. I felt trapped.

To me, his question was a knife prying open a wound I was ashamed of and unable to discuss. I stammered something incoherent and hurried away. That evening, when I told my roommates about it, they clasped their hands and rolled their eyes. "What a compliment!" someone exclaimed. "WOW, to be the subject of a betting pool. You must really have caught their attention. Oooh, wow-eee!" As far as I was concerned, it was anything but a wow. My looks were my albatross. I *felt* like mainstream, small-town America, so why couldn't I *look* like it?

Sometimes life deals us body blows that force tectonic shifts. Jerry and his parents certainly dealt me one, but now I can say — thank goodness. I like the me who survived that blow and ultimately thrived by taking another path. I'm not sure I would like the other me so much; I might have turned into a mouse, and that would be a sad, short little book.

At one level, of course, I knew this ongoing identity crisis was mostly of my own making. Other than the profoundly painful breakup dictated by my boyfriend's parents, I can't say I had ever been racially victimized by others. But I did feel branded. And racism is not just Black and White, it's a nuanced palette of colors, prejudices and feelings, expressed in naked aggression or subtle and unspoken rejection.

I know what it looks like, because I've seen it, and I know what it feels like, because I've felt it, deep in my soul. And even though I have never personally witnessed racial violence, I have seen racist hatred, and its image is indelibly printed in my memory. I will never forget a moment in 1955, when I lived in Alexandria, Virginia, the D.C. suburb, when my first husband Russ and I both worked for the CIA. One afternoon I was driving home and stopped for a red light. Two young Black children, each with an armload of books, chatted easily with each other as they stepped into the intersection. I watched them as they crossed the street. I noticed the girl's plaid skirt and wondered if they went to parochial school. When they got to the middle of the street, I caught the expression on the face of a driver coming from the other direction as they crossed in front of his car. He was watching them too, but he was surely not thinking about parochial school.

His face was contorted into such an ugly grimace of hatred and loathing it shocked me. I imagined that his face bore the same expression as faces of the white mob must have had as they murdered hundreds of African Americans and burned down Tulsa, Oklahoma's "Black Wall Street" in 1920. The two Black children in Alexandria, walking home from school in 1955, were so innocent, their demeanor so sweet, it was hard to understand how they could generate hate. But I will never forget what I saw. If I were an artist, I could draw his face today, I remember it so well. The look in his eyes, and the twisted expression on his face as he watched the children pass in front of his car, spoke volumes to me about the nature of racism — intensity of emotion without reason or cause.

A year later, Russ and I moved back to California and were living in Berkeley. I knew I had to resolve my identity crisis because it was ruining my life. I needed to do two things: First, get over my aversion to being part Chinese and, second, find out what it meant to be Hawaiian.

To address the Chinese issue, I accepted a job with The Asia Foundation in San Francisco. It was a good job *and* I would be forced to say the magic word "Asia" whenever anybody asked me where I worked. My hope was that, maybe, by repeating *Asia* over and over again, the discomfort would go away. I might even get to be friends with some Asians.

And I did, but it took a few months of biting the Asian bullet every day. L.Z. Yuan also worked at the Foundation, and every morning

I rode the same train he did from Berkeley to San Francisco. He became my close friend and mentor. During those long commutes, L.Z. and I sat together, so not only was I being seen with a Chinese man, I also carried on a frequent and sustained conversation with him. L.Z. was such an intelligent and lovely man that my discomfort about his race — which was also mine — evaporated. He was so at ease with himself that he made me feel at ease too.

Those commute trips had another practical benefit. L.Z. took me under his culinary wing because he knew I was a recent bride and didn't know much about cooking. We talked about food — Chinese food — that my mother had taught us to love. That's funny, isn't it? She taught us to love Chinese food — but not the people who cooked or ate it.

So, thanks to L.Z. Yuan, my Chinese self became a treasured part of who I am. It took a little longer to fully integrate my Hawaiian self, which in time became the core of my life. That story forms the final chapter of this book, and tells how I met the woman I would call "my Hawaiian mother," a Chinese-Hawaiian, like my real mother, but who was comfortable in her own skin, and showed me how to be comfortable in mine.

1. Cast of the Hawaiian Revue at Bud Murray Studio. FRONT ROW: My brother Everett and me (1930s).

2. Prop in *Hurricane* that broke the stalemate.

3, 4. Shots from the storm scene in *Hurricane* (1937).

5. Everett in our front yard. Background is the side of our dad's liquor store with ad for Uncle Ace's Cafe — plate lunch was 25 cents (mid 1930s).

6. My big nude scene — a moral dilemma for me/nightmare for the director and a two-second shot in the movie *Hurricane* (1937).

**7.** During a break on *The Wizard of Oz* set with Judy Garland. Jerry Maren the Lollipop Kid is on the left. I'm peeking over Judy's shoulder.

**8.** Tap dancing with my brother Everett (mid 1930s).

**9.** Singer Midgets on their way to MGM Studios for the Munchkin Scene in *The Wizard of Oz*.

**10.** Craig with Munchkin Margaret Pellegrini, Chesterton, Indiana (1980s).

**11.** At the Maury Povich Show, NYC (1980s). LEFT TO RIGHT: Karl Slover, Margaret Pellegrini, Jerry Maren, Clarence Swensen, Billy Barty, Jessica Grove', Mickey Carroll, me, and Ruth Duccini. All of us were Munchkins except Barty and Grove' — he founded LPA Little People of America. She played Dorothy in road show of stage musical at that time.

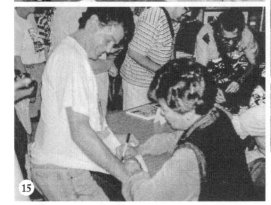

## CHESTERTON, INDIANA (1980s)

**12.** With Munchkin Coroner Meinhardt Raabe.

**13.** Craig and I with Munchkin Ruth Duccini.

**14.** Signing posters.

**15.** ... and T-shirts.

**16.** Craig with Munchkin Jerry Maren.

**17.** At the Hollywood Walk of Fame in 2008 when the Munchkins of Oz got our star..

**18.** Publicity still for 1937 movie. FROM LEFT: Gloria Holden, Bobby Breen, Ned Sparks, Bernadette DeBoalt (Auntie Berdie).

**19.** Auntie Berdie (1930s).

**20.** Uncle Ace at his bar when wine was 10 cents a glass (late 1920s or early 1930s).

**21.** Uncle Ace's "Z card" showing some of the characters he played in the movies.

**22.** The "Cutting Shed" — a corner of the orchard on the farm (1940s).

**23.** Our goat Maggie.

**24.** With Father Mackey (late 1940s).

**25.** In Texas.
LEFT TO RIGHT, STARTING AT TOP:
Earl, Ace and Carl;
Jim (Daddy) and Hughlemma;
Hattie and Ernie;
Grandpa and Grandma Cain.

**26.** With Poochie on my First Communion Sunday (1941).

**27.** Mom as a young woman (1920s).

**28.** As a barber in the army (1920s).

**29.** In his army uniform (1920s).

**30.** Age 12, Wichita Falls, Texas.

**31.** With some of his catch (1950s).

**32.** In his store in Hollywood (1930s).

**33.** By his delivery truck, Hollywood (1930s).

# DADDY

CHAPTER 10

# A LONG WAY *from* WICHITA FALLS

One of my favorite things when I was a little girl was getting to watch my dad shave. He had been a barber as a young man and always used an old-fashioned straight razor that made for quite a show. I was the exclusive audience of one, with a reserved seat on the edge of the claw-footed bathtub to watch the daily ceremony.

Like a good symphony, the shaving ritual began with an overture. Whipping the brush around the inside of the mug to kick up a high lather, Daddy produced a rhythmic tat-a-tat that I would still recognize if I heard it today. Tat-a-tat, lather up, tat-a tat. The shaving soap had its own unique smell, too, not soft and sweet like the Ivory or Sweetheart the rest of us used, but a sharp clean odor that woke up your nostrils. When the lather peaked and started to cascade over the sides of the mug, Daddy painted a mask of thick white suds over his whiskers and, while the suds softened his beard, he sharpened his straight razor on the leather strop hanging from a nail between the basin and the bathroom door. That had its own rhythm, too. Swish. Swash. Swish. Swash.

Then came the part filled with so much danger I always held my breath. My dad didn't seem to realize the slightest wrong movement, the slightest slip of his hand, and that sharp razor edge could ... well, it was just too awful to think about. I didn't want to be chicken, however, so I would sit, clenching my teeth, not daring to breathe, watching my daredevil dad run that perilous razor through snowy drifts of lather. Music played here, too: a kind of rasping sound as the razor mowed down the stalks of coarse hair. Scritch, scra-a-atch. Rinse. Scritch. Scritch. Scra-a-tch. Rinse. What a show.

Pulling his nose to one side, he would open his mouth, stretch one corner downward, and maneuver his razor over elongated cheeks. He even shaved in the cleft of his chin, but I never understood how he could do it without lopping off great chunks of his face. I always marveled at how he could hold the lethal weapon at the precise angle to cut hairs, but not cut skin. But every day, Daddy shaved a flawless shave. I don't think I ever saw him even nick himself. He was always smooth-shaven, with the kind of shave only an old-fashioned straight razor could give.

Two decades later, however, it was quite a different story. In September 1955, I saw him for the first time in two years and, clearly, Daddy's beard hadn't felt a razor for several days. During those two years, I had moved to Washington, D.C., where I met and married my first husband, Russ Bruno. He and I had just driven to California from Washington, D.C. and had swung by Hemet for a few days on our way to Berkeley, where Russ would study law at U.C.'s Boalt Hall, and I would begin a new job that was waiting for me in San Francisco.

We spent a week with the family because Daddy hadn't come to our wedding in D.C. a year earlier, and I had hoped this visit would be the beginning of a good friendship between the two important men in my life. But the week had not gone well. For more than a year, my dad had been in the depths of a depression that had defied treatment, including electroshock therapy, and he had barely said a word to us the entire time we were there.

My mother dismissed his depression as a lack of will to cheer up and, as our disappointing, awkward week ended, she waved us off stoically, her lips forced into a smile. Daddy's face displayed no emotion and hid under several days' growth of beard that told me the extent of his despair. As we pulled out of the driveway, I turned to wave good-bye to Daddy, Mom, and my old dog Putty. And for the briefest moment, I shuddered from a premonition I would never see my father alive again. But I brushed that thought of death aside in favor of anticipating the future we were heading into. A month later, I would recall that shiver of foreboding, and regret I didn't examine it more carefully. At that moment, however, I wanted sunshine, not darkness.

In retrospect, I can now see he had apparently suffered from depression when I was growing up. He was so quiet and reserved I couldn't tell when he was depressed, but every once in a while he would have a couple of drinks. Maybe taking a few drinks was his remedy for depression, but he never got drunk. I don't recall his ever being unable to get up and go to work, or any time when he needed someone else to drive the car. But whenever he had a few drinks, Mom would say he was having a *binge* and would be grumpy and crabby. Sometimes she stayed angry for a long time. My brother and I didn't understand why; to us Daddy never seemed out of control. To us, Mom's recriminations were a lot worse than Daddy's so-called binges. She was an expert at nursing a grudge and keeping it alive way past any usefulness it might have served her.

I painfully remember the year when her anger spanned the Christmas holidays and she refused to open the present my father put under the tree for her. In mid-January, after the tree was taken down and the lights and ornaments put back in storage, Mom's gift remained in the corner of the living room. With its red bow and smiling Santa Claus wrapping, it was a garish reminder of the chasm in the family. The sight of it offended everyone's eyes — except hers. Resisting his gift was strength of character for her and punishment for him for having had a few drinks weeks earlier. One morning, Daddy decided he'd suffered enough. He ripped off the red ribbon and smiling Santa paper, plunked a shiny new toaster on the kitchen counter and declared, "*She* might not want it, but the rest of us can enjoy it." His action didn't help the mood in the household, but it did get us better toast.

Normally, from day to day, my father didn't drink at all. But to my mother, *any* consumption of alcohol was evidence of weakness. That's pretty funny, isn't it, since the sale of liquor was her livelihood and gave her a pretty good standard of living. She didn't seem to mind other people drinking, but she had no tolerance for my father's drinking and made sure we all knew how she felt about that. If she was too strident, my father went out and did the same thing the next day, and sometimes the day after.

I went along on one of those so-called *binges* with him when I was 10 years old. We went to his brother's place in Hollywood – Ace Cain's Cafe – 100 miles away from my mother's scornful eye. Daddy's stay in Hollywood became a little family reunion with all his relatives. He could be a Texas homeboy again and chuckle over old memories of life in the Panhandle. Daddy even bought a cowboy outfit at the Western store on Hollywood Boulevard. I thought he looked very handsome in his 10-gallon hat, riding breeches, cowhide vest, and spurs on fancy stitched boots. I so clearly remember Cowboy Daddy at Uncle Ace's bar — one booted foot on the brass rail, the big hat firmly settled on his brow. He smoked unfiltered Camel cigarettes, drank Lucky Lager beer, ate Henrietta's greasy hamburgers and swapped stories about the old days back in the Texas Panhandle. He was never like that at home. He wouldn't dare. After he died, I kept that outfit, and it was still hanging in my closet when our house burned down half a century later.

Daddy and his younger brother Ace joined the Army Signal Corps because they didn't have bus fare to get out of Wichita Falls, the small Texas town they were born in. They wanted to leave so their futures would not be as colorless as their youths had been. Their dad was a poor dirt farmer in whose footsteps they did not want to follow. Their mother suffered from high blood pressure and sought salvation by listening to radio evangelists. Grandma had zero tolerance for fun. Movies and dancing were off limits. Even card games were strictly forbidden in the house, so her sons went behind the barn and that is where my dad became a skilled poker player, and Uncle Ace a sharpshooter at craps.

By the time they were old enough to enlist in the Army, they were both proficient gamblers. Other young soldiers who played cards and threw dice paved their road to wealth. It was the 1920s — peacetime. After stints at several other Pacific islands, Daddy was stationed at Schofield Barracks in Hawai`i, on the island of Oahu, and had accumulated enough poker winnings to buy a new car and a couple of businesses on the base, including the barber shop. He met and married my mother, who was teaching school in Wahiawa, the town right next to Schofield Barracks. They lived in Wahiawa for a while, but after my brother and I were born they moved to a larger home on the beach. My dad loved fishing and, in Pu`uloa, had his own pier, a boat and a good life.

Uncle Ace, however, wanted more action than he got from pay-day gambling, so he left the Army in 1930 and went to Hollywood, where he found an appealing business opportunity in bootlegging whiskey. Family lore is unclear whether Daddy was a silent partner in the bootlegging business, but as soon as the Volstead Act ended Prohibition, Daddy joined his younger brother in Hollywood and they opened a liquor store and a nightclub. A year later, when I was three and a half, Mom, my brother and I moved to California too. My earliest childhood memory is being on the ship – mostly in the stateroom because Mom was seasick the entire voyage and didn't leave her bunk. I remember people coming in to bring meals and games for my brother and me – including a jigsaw puzzle that had little tiny pieces and seemed as dark and dreary as the rest of the trip.

Shortly after we got settled in Hollywood, Daddy took us all to meet his family in Wichita Falls, Texas. My only recollection of that train trip is the picnic basket of food Mom brought along to keep us well fed. For my mom, I think the train ride had to be more enjoyable than Wichita Falls. In the mid 1930s, Texas was still segregated and my Hawaiian-Chinese mother couldn't go places with my Dutch-Irish father. At the movie theater, my mother was directed to the "other side" of a roped off section, and the local restaurant refused to serve her. I have very dim memories of Wichita Falls because I was so young, but I do remember it was cold, the creek was frozen over and we all had fun sliding on the ice. I didn't go to the movies or get taken out to dinner, but my mother bitterly described those humiliations many years later.

Uncle Ace was my dad's business partner for about five years before we left Hollywood for the clean air of the open countryside. The two brothers remained very close friends, even though they were mirror opposites in personality. Daddy was a modest, quiet and unassuming family man; Uncle Ace was a flashy outgoing womanizer, who decorated the walls of his nightclub with huge posters of himself in various costumes — cowboy, gangster, boxer, rake. Ace Cain's Cafe was a noisy, mildly racy nightclub on Western Avenue next door to the old 20th Century Fox Studios. Daddy could hide out there with impunity and have a few drinks while he visited with his brothers and their families for a day or two, and then he would leave the din of the big city to return to his peaceful little town in the country.

Over the years, Daddy became one of the most respected merchants in the Hemet-San Jacinto Valley because he was honest, generous and discreet. In San Jacinto, his liquor store had a back door opening onto an alley where customers could park and not be seen entering the store to buy liquor. That back-alley door was a blessing for the church-going folks in the valley, who might otherwise have had to buy their spirits in some other town miles away. Daddy gained a reputation as a good guy, a nice guy, who would give you credit and not press for payment. He made points with the locals because he was also a good fisherman and a source of tips about where the fish were biting. He was so successful that, in time, he ventured into real estate and not only helped finance construction of Hemet's new Elks Club, but also supplied all the fish for the fundraising fish fry.

But his last bout of depression kept him from going fishing or to the Elk's Club. He withdrew deeper and deeper into his black hole.

After Russ and I left Hemet at the end of that less-than-satisfying visit with him and Mom, we were temporarily distracted by our new commitments. Russ, as a first-year law student, had to get used to studying again, and I had a demanding new job in San Francisco. But about a month later, one evening toward the end of October, I was suddenly seized with the compulsion to write a letter to my father.

Not my usual "Dear Mom and Dad" letter, but a note only to Dear Daddy "to tell you I know you are suffering. To tell you I love you and I want to help you. To tell you I will be coming home over Thanksgiving and I will be able to help you then. So please hang on, Daddy. Please hang on."

The next morning, as I dropped the letter into the mailbox on my way to work, I knew I was already too late. I knew he wasn't going to get it. About half an hour after I got to my office in San Francisco, my brother called. "Daddy shot himself this morning. He's not going to last much longer. You'd better get down here."

I don't remember much about the rest of that day; my memory of it is a jumble. My brother picked Russ and me up at the bus station in Riverside for the hour's drive to Hemet. It was evening. The 400-mile trip from Berkeley had taken us all day. Everett told us Daddy had died late that morning. Then he proceeded to describe the bullet wound in Daddy's temple with such graphic detail, I stopped him. I couldn't listen. We drove the rest of the way in funereal silence.

The next few days are a blur in my memory. My brother took over the liquor stores and my mother took to her bed, so it fell to Russ and me to make all the arrangements with the undertaker. We selected a cherry wood casket and chose a blanket of yellow roses to cover it. The yellow roses were for Texas. Ever since, I have had a yellow rose bush in my yard.

I felt profound sorrow and guilt. I thought I could have prevented his suicide. Why hadn't I picked up the phone that evening and taken direct action instead of writing him a letter? If only I had called, I might have been able to convince him to hang on for a while longer. Things might have been different if only I had ... Oh, Daddy, I am so sorry. I shrank at the thought my letter would be arriving in the mail. "I don't want to see it," I told Russ. "I won't be able to handle it."

"Don't worry, I'll watch for the mailman."

He did. Each day Russ watched for the mailman so he could intercept that letter, and so I wouldn't have to see my puny, inadequate response to Daddy's last and fatal crisis. When the letter arrived, Russ destroyed it and spared me that bit of pain, but it didn't stop me from thinking about it — over and over and over. In the months that followed, I sought help for my guilt from a psychiatrist, and over time I was able to shift those feelings to my psychological back burner. But they didn't entirely go away.

Twenty years later, on a Sunday afternoon, those feelings boiled up into view again. I was at a Gestalt workshop, run by a wise woman named Barry Stevens. It was the 1970s, the decade of group encounters. I had gone to the workshop more to keep a friend company than with any hopes of self-discovery on my part. The morning session's Gestalt games seemed silly and superficial. I didn't see how role-playing was going to lead to self-knowledge.

At the time, I had a very public job and I didn't want the other people at that workshop — all strangers — to see my vulnerabilities. So I played at the Gestalt exercises, convinced they wouldn't get through to me. I was very guarded about what I was willing to say aloud and then, when I least expected it, during the last exercise of the day, the floodgates opened.

"Get into a comfortable position on the floor," Barry Stevens directed. "Imagine you are a rose bush. We'll take about five minutes. Then if anybody wants to share his or her rose bush fantasy with the group, we'll have time to do that."

I sat on the floor, pulled my knees up to my chin, bowed my head over them, closed my eyes and dutifully visualized myself as a rose bush. I saw myself as a spherical cage of the thickest, thorniest, most forbidding stems you can imagine, and in the center of this thorny fortress bloomed a huge pink rose with perfect and abundant petals. I knew the rose was somehow connected to my father, but I didn't know how. I was sure, however, that I did not want to explore any profound emotion in that roomful of strangers, because I quickly nodded off to sleep. I woke up to Barry Stevens' voice, "Would anybody like to share his or her rose bush fantasy?"

Before anybody else could answer, I heard my own voice describing my thorny pink fantasy. That was on one track. On another track I was asking myself, why was I doing this? I didn't want to reveal anything about myself. Then, losing all control, I blurted out, "I should have been a yellow rose!"

A tidal wave of sobs welled up from deep inside me. I put my head down and struggled against the sea of woe in which I was drowning. The yellow rose, of course, was the Yellow Rose of Texas, the yellow roses I had chosen to cover my father's casket. But why should I have been a yellow rose instead of a pink rose? What did it all mean? I didn't trust myself to say anything else. The strangers in the room might find out something I didn't want them to know, something I kept locked inside my cage of thorns. My distress rendered me totally incoherent.

Barry Stevens didn't press me. She waited a bit, and then said in her soothing way, "I am staying in town through next Friday. If you want to talk to me privately about your rose bush fantasy, phone me." She paused. "And if you don't want to, that's all right too."

"Okay. Thanks," I muttered, head still buried in my arms. And there I remained, rolled up like a ball on the floor, rocking back and forth until the session ended and I could leave.

As each day of that week passed, I thought, "I should call Barry Stevens," but just as quickly I would think of some reason why I couldn't call her at that moment. On Thursday evening, when I was sure she would have commitments for Friday, her last day in town, I called. I was sure she would tell me she didn't have time to see me and I could tell myself I tried. To my surprise she said, "Of course, Betty Ann, I'd love to see you. What time tomorrow can you come?"

That session with Barry Stevens became a turning point in my life. She set up two dining room chairs facing each other, motioned me to one of them and sat down on a third chair to one side. "Imagine your father is sitting in the other chair," she said. "What do you want to say to him?"

What came out of me was not so much guilt over my too-little-too-late letter. What came out of me was anger — a lot of anger. "Why did you leave that day? Why didn't you wait for me? I wrote you a letter imploring you to wait just a little bit longer. I was coming to see you. I didn't want you to leave. I wanted you to know I loved you. I wanted you to know I was really sorry you were so sad. I wanted you to know I wanted to help you. I wanted you to know a lot of things, but you didn't stay to listen to me! Why didn't you stay? You just left me!"

The outburst left me doubled up, sobbing and gasping. I felt as though I was drowning in sorrow, anger and resentment. I felt Barry Stevens' calming hand on my heaving shoulders. "When you can, move to your father's chair and see if there's an answer for you."

That time with her was so compressed I can't tell you how many moments passed before I got myself to the other chair, but when I did, I heard myself speak my father's sorrow. "I couldn't stay any longer. I had to leave. I had so much pain I couldn't think of anything — or anybody else — not even you. I know now you wanted to help. But please believe me when I say there was no way to help. I am sorry I left you. I am sorry if it seemed like abandonment to you. It wasn't. It didn't have anything to do with you. It was only about me! I couldn't get outside myself. I had been in the depths of depression for so many months, I couldn't stand it any longer. Please understand that. Each of us has to bear his own pain and deal with it the best he can. My pain got the best of me and I had nothing left."

The exchange pitched back and forth. I crossed from chair to chair for more than an hour, tearfully, emotionally, until I was spent. Barry Stevens sat next to me patting my back, alternately urging me on and slowing me down, as I groped my tearful way around the abyss of my own despair. She led me to acceptance, truth, understanding, and with it, love. Finally, I sat. Emptied out. Purged. Quiet.

I hadn't expected anything like that, although Barry Stevens probably knew what the outcome of the session could be. She was a very wise counselor and therapist. What was so miraculous was that I now understood why my father hadn't been able to wait for me: he had been deafened by his own screaming demons and believed the only way to silence them was by shooting them out of his head. That afternoon I realized, all those years since his death, I had had all the answers inside myself. That afternoon I understood, as if for the first time. I had known all along, but the knowledge had not found voice before. I had not been able to listen.

But Barry Stevens wasn't through with me. Whether from experience or inspiration, she asked me to put my mother in the other chair and talk to *her* now. How could she possibly know I hadn't been comfortable in my mother's presence for many years. How could she know that every time I took my children to see their grandmother, I suffered a headache that lasted as long as the visits did. How could she know that my husband could always tell when I was talking to my mother on the phone because he said my voice was different. My wariness of my own mother was deeply rooted and automatic, but all that changed that afternoon with Barry Stevens.

My rose bush told me I had some mighty big defenses protecting the flower of myself. I dug them out and confronted them that afternoon and shed my thorny fortress. I accepted the fact I couldn't change who or what my parents were. What changed was me and my expectations.

After that day I understood I could not have done anything to ease Daddy's pain. I was finally able to let him go the way he had chosen. And after that day, I was able to visit my mother without any expectation of her beyond what she could be. I gave up the dream that she would be the kind of mother I had always wanted, or the kind of grandmother I wanted for my boys. That grandmother did not exist, but the one who did was actually a pretty interesting woman who enriched our lives in her own way. Her script was not mine to write.

After that day, I was able to visit my mother and not get headaches. I was able to enjoy her for what she was without resenting her for the things she was not. When you think about it, that's a pretty good attitude to have about all of your friends and associates, isn't it?

CHAPTER 11

# A LONG WAY TO GO FISHING

Several years after my dad died, I had one more visit with him. By that time, Russ and I had three sons and often took them camping on the Northern California coast. We all loved to camp, and Russ, a devoted fly fisherman, had passed his love of fishing along to his sons. Although they were too young to fly fish, they went after trout with worms or lures. I was part of the worm and lure group because I wasn't patient enough to ever get good at fly fishing. Mostly though, I enjoyed watching my sons enjoy the outdoors.

We kept our camping style pretty simple. We slept on air mattresses under starry skies, cooked breakfast on a two-burner Coleman stove and lunched out of the ice cooler. Dinner was ceremonial, cooked over the campfire with everyone participating. I fervently hoped my sons would learn to appreciate nature and the beauty of getting down to basics.

One summer in the late '60s, we set up camp for a few days at Jedediah Smith Redwoods State Park in the northwestern corner of California. We chose a campsite in a redwood grove along the Smith River, and the first day there we explored the trails along the river and let the boys play on a good-sized sandbar. That was good for them but not so wonderful for me. The wind kicked up and blew sand into my hair, ears, eyes and under my contact lenses. In those days, I wore hard contacts and, as anybody who has worn them knows, hard contacts are all your eyes can tolerate at one time — even the tiniest speck feels like a steel splinter.

That windy afternoon, so many grains of sand blew into my eyes they burned painfully and filled with tears. Hours later, after we returned to camp, I rushed to take my lenses out and put them in their case so my poor eyeballs could rest, but a bigger problem showed up.

No amount of poking and searching produced a lens from my left eye. I searched high under the lid, low under the lid and rolled my eyes so I could see in the corners. No lens. It had obviously dropped out on the sandbar. Well that was a sad good-bye. I didn't have any idea what part of the sandbar I was on when my lens came out of my eye. There was no point in going back to try to find a clear plastic contact lens half an inch in diameter. I didn't have a second pair, nor did I have regular glasses. I had refused to wear spectacles for a bunch of reasons. I didn't even own a pair. I knew I would be stuck out of focus for the rest of our vacation. Grimly, I realized I wasn't going to see the forest *or* the trees — at least not clearly. Oh, well. Nothing to be done about that out here.

But *somebody* did do something.

That night — actually, early the next morning while everyone else was still sleeping — I was awakened. It was about 4:30, still dark, before even the birds were up. I couldn't see him, but he was there, waking me up to go fishing, the same way he did when my brother and I were little kids. Fishing days were the most special of all days in my childhood. They were the days when my brother and I had our dad all to ourselves, when he taught us how to put worms on hooks and how to tie the right kinds of knots for leaders and sinkers. If we were lucky, which we almost always were, they were days when he also taught us how to clean and scale the fish we caught.

He always woke us up with the same soft call I heard that morning in the woods. "Four bells. Hit the decks! The fish are bitin'." It was always dark when the summons came because we always had a long drive to where the fish were. But we didn't mind getting rousted early; we always bounced right up because fishing days were such great and happy days. That morning, 20 years after Daddy held a gun to his head, he came calling me to go fishing. And just as I had done when I was a child, I bounced right up out of my sleeping bag without a second thought and got ready for our expedition as quickly and quietly as I could.

Tank top, turtleneck and windbreaker went on in layers because, although it was chilly in that early morning hour, I knew after the sun came up I would want to peel. I packed a sandwich because fishing always makes you hungry. I took one of the fishing creels from the bunch hanging from our camp tree branch, made sure it had salmon eggs and lures, a pocket knife, a pair of pliers (in case the fish swallowed the hook and I had to dig it out) and set aside a rod and reel. I gulped a bowl of granola, wrote "Gone fishing. Back later," to my husband and kids and headed down the path to the Smith River.

It sounds kind of weird, although it didn't seem like that at the time. Daddy was right there, as surely as I am sitting here at my desk writing these words and, like all the fishing trips from my childhood, it was totally glorious. I felt Daddy's presence strongly and with certainty. I couldn't see him. There was no *ghost* at my side. There were no words — simply a warm glow of happiness and joy that filled me through and through. I felt completely secure and loved — much like the joy and excitement around Christmas, or weddings or births. I snagged a lot of fish, had lots of action. I squealed with delight every time I got a strike. I thoroughly enjoyed the outing, winding up the reel and guiding the wriggling fish through the shallows toward my spot on shore. "Look at that one! Isn't he a beaut? Wait till I get this one back to camp."

And so it went, on and on, until the sun was high in the sky. When I finally looked at my watch it was 11 o'clock, and I was way downstream and on the other side of the river. "Oh, my gosh." I exclaimed out loud to my dad, "They'll be worried about me. I'd better get back."

After walking upstream for a short while, I recognized the sand bar where I had lost my contact lens the day before. As I looked at it, I knew if I went over to it I would find my left lens. So I stepped off the path, jumped over to the sandbar, walked directly to the spot, leaned over, put my fingers in the sand and pulled out my left contact lens.

I stood there for a moment. I was relieved but not surprised. It fit with everything else about that morning. It was a parting gift. He had to go, but wanted to leave me with a little something. I stood there on the sandbar, holding the miracle in my fingertips and felt my father return to the heavens of a clear blue northern sky. "Thank you, Daddy," I said. "Thank you. I'm so glad you came."

On my way back to camp I found an unusual stone — small, smooth, shaped like a little papoose with a round face of basalt nestled in blankets of yellow soapstone. It was a talisman marking the day — a small smooth object I could carry in my pocket and feel whenever I wanted to connect with my dad.

I hurried back to camp, washed off my lens and got back in focus. That lens, by the way, was undamaged by its time in the sand and I wore it for another five years. Russ, who pooh-poohed everything he could not touch or see for himself, had to believe my story. The lens was irrefutable proof. How else could I have found that tiny clear plastic object on a large sandbar? When I told my mother about it, she advised, "Keep it to yourself. Don't tell people about it.

These things are best left unsaid."

But I tell anybody who'll listen. I love the story. I love telling it. It's proof my Daddy really did love me. I think he had read my letter and heard my sobs that day in Barry Stevens' living room. Why else would he have come such a long way to take me fishing?

# POLITICS & TV NEWS

# CHAPTER 12

# KIDS *and* CAMPAIGNS

## The Early Years in Oakland

When my second child had his first birthday, I kept the promise I had made to myself a year earlier and joined the Oakland League of Women Voters. I had made that promise after two years of diaper pails, middle-of-the-night bottles, nursings and floor-walkings, with two baby boys born 10 and a half months apart.

I needed a break. I needed to meet women who were concerned with some things beyond child care. It wasn't that I didn't love or even dote on my two beautiful boy babies, it was just that I needed friends and conversation about things other than the latest small grip toy or potty-training tip. I had majored in political science in college, worked for the federal government afterwards, and there was a big hole in my current day that needed filling with discussion and debate about current civic matters.

In the League, I met several other women just like me, women with young children who wanted to be involved in issues of interest wider than their home and family. I liked that the League's meetings were conducted in a business-like manner, and I especially liked the part of the League that focused on getting people registered to vote and analyzing the pros and cons of all the ballot measures. I liked that the League was nonpartisan and was about issues — not personalities. I liked that everyone seemed to do her homework for the discussion meetings and came to them well prepared. And on top of all that good stuff, childcare was provided because, in the mid and late Sixties, most young mothers were home full-time. League moms traded child care. If someone had to go to Oakland City Hall for a meeting, an interview, or give a presentation, someone else in League would take care of her children. We became League sisters and our children grew up as League cousins. League kids often went along when we just had to drop something off at City Hall, or when we set up our ironing boards on the sidewalks downtown to use as tables where people could register to vote. One day, a couple years later, when I was taking care of other League kids while their mothers were at City Hall, I overheard my boys suggesting the game of the day — "Let's have a meeting. You bring the agenda, we've got the cookies!"

On election day, a couple years after that, we were just finishing breakfast when my husband Russ stood up and said, "Well, I think I'll go vote before I go to the office." He started to walk away, but stopped in his tracks when four year old Michael looked up in astonishment and asked in all seriousness, "Dad! Do *men* vote?"

Five of us, who took turns being the President of the Oakland League, became such good friends our families celebrated holidays together. Our kids probably knew more about City Hall than most adult residents of Oakland did, because the dinner conversations they grew up hearing were all about the machinations of the local politicos. When they got to high school age, one of the kids dubbed the five of us "the League Mafia" because they said we knew "where all the bodies were buried." That name has stuck to this day, and now, 60 years later, the four of us who are still around are still close friends, still call ourselves the League Mafia, and still talk politics, although we've stepped back from the front lines of activism.

In the '60s, Oakland's politics were vastly different from what they have been in the decades since then. In those days, what went on in the all-male City Council mostly went on behind closed doors. Councilmen (no one called them Council*members*) did what they were told to do by the real political force in Oakland — a small group of businessmen, most of whom lived in Piedmont, an affluent city completely surrounded by Oakland, but insulated from it by economics and the city limits. Public opinion was molded by ex-U.S. Senator and political power broker William Knowland, owner and publisher of *The Oakland Tribune,* in those days the East Bay's largest daily newspaper. He shaped official policy with his peers in the Bechtel, Kaiser, and Clorox corporations, and half a dozen other businesses with strong but narrow interests in the civic and economic health of Oakland.

In the '60s, those businesses wanted — and got — a quiet Oakland. Los Angeles, Philadelphia, Detroit and other major cities were burning with urban riots, but Oakland stayed relatively calm. Peace marches in the city hadn't amounted to much, and civil rights demonstrations were earnest but polite. I didn't want to see trouble in the streets of Oakland, but would have loved to have heard the City Council debate the issues gripping the nation. But that was not likely to happen with our local officials. They went about their business as though people weren't waking up and smelling their indifference. Several of us in the League regularly attended the City Council and school board meetings, where we heard local activists from the Black Caucus, the Gray Panthers and other community groups describe neighborhood problems and ask for solutions from the city. I watched as the mayor and council members would listen in silence and then go directly to the next speaker or the next agenda item. I can't remember hearing an earnest discussion or even an interested question from city officials in those days. Weekly City Council meetings lasted an average of 10 minutes or less. City policy was decided at the "pre-meeting," a cordial dinner at Jack London

Square's Sea Wolf Restaurant, where the city manager would tell the councilmen what they were going to do that evening. And they always did what they were told.

Neither the school board nor the City Council was responsive to the people who came to them with concerns. At one City Council meeting, I remember seeing a councilman enter the doors of the chambers just as everybody had begun the Pledge of Allegiance, with which all the meetings began. The councilman stood at attention and joined in the Pledge. When it was over, he started walking to his seat and got there just as the mayor announced, "There being no further business, the meeting is adjourned!" That councilman didn't even get to sit down — the meeting had lasted less than five minutes. By the late '60s, I was one of the regular presenters at Oakland City Council and school board meetings, even though the League didn't get any more of a response from our local elected leaders than other groups did.

Community groups also sought help from our local television station, KTVU, located in a converted warehouse at Jack London Square, Oakland's premier tourist attraction. For years, a coalition of local action groups made an annual pilgrimage to the station to lobby for more public interest programming, but our pleas were summarily dismissed by a bored and disinterested head of the Community Affairs Department. But then things changed.

Upon our arrival at the station in 1969, we were ushered into the conference room where the new station manager, Roger Rice, along with all department heads, was seated around the table waiting for us. They welcomed us with carafes of fresh coffee and a huge tray of donuts. I knew immediately this meeting would be different from every one before, but I didn't know why. In two years, I would learn the reason was to protect the station's broadcast license. For the time being, however, our coalition would just enjoy our new and very amicable relationship with our local television station. The agenda of that first meeting was simple and straightforward. Roger Rice asked us what we wanted, listened to our plea for programs dealing with the issues, and told us to come back the following week.

A week later, in the same conference room, again with all department heads in attendance, Roger told us that, in response to our requests, they were going to launch a prime-time political debate show called *Head On*. It would be broadcast on Sunday evenings and moderated by lead News Anchor Gary Park. Then he introduced Ian Zellick, the new head of the Community Affairs Department, who effused about a continuing relationship with our coalition, and invited us to be the station's Citizens Advisory Board — the first such body in the whole country. Before he adjourned the meeting, Roger asked if there was anything else. On a whim, I raised my hand.

"Your 10 O'clock News ends every night with Paul Harvey saluting the flag of the day with a little political observation," I said. "The flag is fine, but Paul Harvey is a right-wing propagandist, and it would be wonderful if he were to go away."

Looking right at me and smiling broadly, Roger said, "He's gone." Then, scanning the whole group, he asked, "Anything else?" Dazzled with the prospects that had just opened up, we just got up, thanked them and left. We had just attended a sea change.

In those days, Oakland held its local elections in the spring of odd-numbered years and, as 1971 unfolded, candidates from neighborhood organizations began emerging to run for every local office on the ballot. People had been talking to me about running for City Council, offering to support my candidacy, and as the filing date drew near, running began to seem like a logical thing for me to do.

So, I became the first woman to run for the Oakland City Council in more than 25 years, and found myself locked in a one-on-one race with an affable white male, a 12-year incumbent named Felix Chialvo. It was a very long shot. Felix Chialvo was regarded as Mr. Nice Guy and hadn't made enemies in his three terms on the Council. He was just another agreeable cipher — like all the other Oakland City Councilmen in those days. He had been anointed, then appointed, then elected and re-elected again and again. He wasn't any worse than the others, but I ran against him because I lived in his district and his third term was ending.

Tom Bates, who later became a state assemblyman and later mayor of Berkeley, offered to be my campaign manager for no fee. He got someone to donate a large downtown storefront for my headquarters. We were off to a great start, and it just kept getting better.

One friend from the League, Shirley Roberson, took a leave from her board position and recruited people from all over the city to host coffee klatches in their homes so I could meet with small groups of voters, precinct by precinct. The coffees were well-organized, and invitations to them were classy and good-looking. The master copy of the invitations was handwritten by Shirley McFarland in beautiful calligraphy. All the envelopes were hand-addressed by volunteers who came to our headquarters every day to copy long lists of names and addresses from precinct lists. Jack Aikawa, a local optometrist, appointed himself my driver so I wouldn't have the stress of traffic and parking, and could relax between events.

Architect Bennett Christopherson designed a flyer of hot pink paper with printed instructions on how to fold it into an origami crane which then displayed brief campaign positions on every surface. The origami cranes were a terrific icebreaker at the coffees. As pink cranes began taking shape from the flat sheets of paper, people would squeal with delight. They enjoyed examining the cranes from all angles and reading the position statements on the wings and sides. It was a very clever piece, and I was proud to have friends who could create such fun in politics. My license plate was simply the word "VOTE" — a gift from my husband Russ. He ordered it for me right after California announced it was going to offer personalized plates. That was late summer, 1970. The plate was supposed to be my Christmas present that year. It came too late for Christmas, but in good time for the campaign. It's still my license plate today — many cars later. I love it, and it gets a lot of thumbs-up signs when I'm out and about.

The coffees were a huge success for the campaign, but when Shirley told me she was organizing 91 of them, I was taken aback. Not by the number of stump speeches I would have to give, but by the 91 cups of coffee I would have to drink. I visualized all those cups in a row and felt queasy at the thought of consuming all that caffeine. It made me so jittery I swore off all coffee, and drank only tea for the entire duration of the campaign.

Other candidates heard about our coffees and began showing up at them, which generated more excitement and interest in the election. Local unions, PTAs, and homeowners' groups held candidate meetings. Huge crowds turned out to hear the new candidates; there was a strong sense of unity and optimism among Blacks, Asians and progressive whites. And I was having the time of my life. I dashed from one place to another every day, giving speeches and answering questions. When there wasn't anything planned, Tom had me go to the Greyhound and BART stations to hand out the origami flyers. My signs and bumper stickers began popping up in windows, on lawns and on telephone poles all over the city. It was a very heady time. Everywhere I went, people greeted me with words of encouragement. "Time for a change! We're with you! Good Luck. You've got my vote!"

It was, as the old saying goes, the best of times before it became the worst of times. The best of it was the strong campaign. The worst of it was, I didn't win. Although I came close — very close — it wasn't good enough, and there was no second prize. The forces of *The Oakland Tribune* and entrenched interests at City Hall won — if only by a hair.

Two weeks before the election, Bill Knowland went through the motions of interviewing me at his office in the Tribune Tower so they "could decide whom to endorse." The interview was a farce and we both knew it. At one point he leered at me and said, "Well, this is politics and you'll either win or you'll lose."

I knew he was going to do everything in his power to make sure I lost and, as publisher of the only daily paper in town, he had considerable power. The *Tribune* refused to print any of my press releases or campaign statements. It didn't cover any campaign news about me or the other candidates running against the incumbents. The *Tribune* simply ignored us until the very last week of the campaign, when it ran its endorsements on the front page, as had been its custom for decades. And of course, no surprise, it endorsed all the incumbents. And then there was the icing on their cake, further proof of the old saying "Timing is Everything." The city of Berkeley held its election one week before Oakland's, and in 1971 Berkeley voters threw out the majority of City Council members and replaced them with a slate of reformers, a self-proclaimed "radical slate." The word "radical" was all the *Tribune* needed. Every day in that week between Berkeley's election and ours, the *Tribune* ran a front-page story with a single theme: Radicals have taken over Berkeley City Hall. Don't let it happen in Oakland too.

The fact that the challengers in Oakland were not a slate, but were from totally different backgrounds and community groups, did not make any difference to Knowland and the old guard. Congressman Ron Dellums, State Senator Nick Petris and Assemblyman Ken Meade had endorsed the Berkeley radical slate. They also endorsed us, and we all became radicals by association.

Actually, I was about as *un-radical* and middle class as anybody could get — a Stanford graduate, former CIA employee, married to another former government employee, mother of three young children, president of the local League of Women Voters. How mainstream can you be?

What made me dangerous was the fact that the Berkeley slate had won, and it looked like I might win too.

Those *Tribune* headlines did their work and when the votes were counted, Felix Chialvo was re-elected and went on to serve a fourth undistinguished term.

I went into grieving. The day after the election, I managed to retain my composure and stayed upbeat through some radio and television interviews. Then I went home and pulled weeds in my garden the rest of the afternoon. A steady stream of friends dropped by with flowers, hugs and words of comfort about what a great campaign it had been and what a shame we hadn't won. I smiled on the outside but inside I was really hurting. There was a lead ball in the pit of my stomach. I kept putting on the brave front of a good loser, and I actually was very proud of our campaign. I felt we had laid the groundwork for other challengers in the future. Or maybe, maybe I would run again. People told me that's the way it always was. Run. Lose. Run again. Win. That was the popular wisdom, and it made sense to me.

A week after the election I went to a meeting at City Hall and, when the mayor saw me, he headed in my direction. He stood in front of me, grinning, shaking his head saying, "What a waste, what a waste."

"What do you mean, Mayor Reading," I asked the owner of Red's Tamales.

"What a waste," he repeated. "All that paper, all those flyers, all those posters. What a waste." And he grinned again, but I could see his grin was really a sneer.

I turned and walked away, smarting from the nasty little encounter with someone I thought should at least be a gracious winner. Reality was setting in. It wasn't going to be fun to be on the losing end. It seemed that now the mayor might treat me as a joke. I began to wonder if I could be an effective spokesman in the community again. The mayor would be rude to me again, surely, and maybe people would not take me seriously. The scenario wasn't at all appealing. For a while, I stayed away from City Hall.

Other people reacted in the opposite way. The State of California and the County of Alameda both invited me to join various boards and commissions. Local nonprofits invited me to help them: the Oakland Museum Board, the local society that worked with disabled children. Everybody, it seemed, wanted to help me fill the void left in my schedule. But I had no heart for any of it. I just wanted to stay home and suck my thumb.

I remember making a lot of soups and stews during those first few weeks after the election. The process of slow cooking in a big pot was homey and comforting. I also remember bursting into tears once in a while as I stirred those pots. Not unlike the heroine in *Like Water For Chocolate*, whose tears flowed into her cooking and made people do crazy things after they ate her food. I didn't notice any changes in my family's behavior though. Everyone was very kind and did everything they could think of to help me get through my grief.

I was sad and depressed until mid-July when I began to feel better and decided to make some changes in my life. I knew I had some marketable skills and knowledge. I also felt more volunteer work wasn't going to fill my needs. Validation is what I needed. I wanted to be paid for my work. I needed a real job. And that's exactly what landed in my open arms a few weeks later.

I went to the TV station one August afternoon because Community Affairs Director Ian Zellick had asked me to drop in to meet with him and Roger Rice. It wasn't an unusual invitation because, for two years, as president of the Oakland League of Women Voters, I had been helping the station with its political debate show and special election coverage, and I thought this meeting was about another show they had in mind. After shaking hands all around, Roger got right to the point and caught me totally by surprise.

I heard what he said, but could hardly believe it. The general manager of KTVU, the largest independent TV station in the country, had just offered me a job.

"It's yours if you want it," Roger Rice said, smiling broadly. "We have decided to expand the Community Affairs Department and hire a full-time producer. When we heard you were available, we both agreed you'd be perfect. So what do you say?"

In 1969, when Roger Rice became KTVU station manager, his assignment was to make whatever changes were necessary to avoid attracting a lawsuit that might put the station's broadcast license in jeopardy. During that time, some TV stations across the country were being sued for not following all the requirements set out in federal regulations governing use of the public airwaves. Roger Rice's job was to make sure KTVU dodged that bullet. The lawsuits not only threatened stations' licenses, but cost huge amounts of money to defend. Roger decided Channel 2 needed to change both programming and hiring patterns, and the job offer to me was part of those changes.

The lawsuits grew out of the political activism of the '60s, and were based on regulations passed when the FCC was created — regulations requiring stations using the public's airwaves to "serve the public interest" with news and public interest programming on issues of importance to each station's audience. The regulations laid out in fine detail exactly what that meant, but until that activist decade, no one had paid much attention to those details.

The station did follow a couple of the better-known FCC requirements: Equal Time whenever political candidates were on the air, and the Fairness Doctrine for dealing with controversial issues. The trouble was, according to the lawsuits, other regulations were being ignored. For example, each television or radio station was supposed to ascertain the top 20 issues of its viewing or listening audience by annually interviewing leaders — both political and business —and then report to the FCC all the programming and news coverage the station had done regarding those 20 issues. If that requirement had ever been followed, it wasn't in the collective memory — or records — of the station. The public affairs programming of Channel 2 had long consisted of a half-hour program at midday on Sundays, on which local philanthropic and civic clubs — like Kiwanis, Easter Seals and the Lions — talked about their good works. There was no grappling with the top 20 issues facing the community because the surveying wasn't done and the 20 issues were anyone's guess.

Now, suddenly, upstart community groups were dusting off those old regs and asking the courts to enforce them. This was a whole new experience for the broadcast industry, including Channel 2. Station department heads had been free to focus their attention on the bottom line, and in that they were extremely successful. Word was that, in those days, KTVU sent a sweet $50 million in yearly profits to the owners, the Cox sisters back in Atlanta, Georgia.

Since that amazing 1969 meeting with all the department heads and our community coalition, the Oakland League of Women Voters had become an unofficial arm of the Community Affairs Department, and good friends with Ian Zellick. As the League's president during those years, I was in and out of the station and on the phone with Ian practically every day, but I never dreamed of being part of the staff.

I didn't feel part of the world of television. My field was local politics. I knew all the players in all the local issues, but nothing about the technical requirements or protocols of television. What the League did for the station was identify issues to debate on air, and recommend people to invite as guests on a panel. It was the same as setting up political debates in local auditoriums, which was routine for us. Ian and Roger also launched election shows and candidates nights, and the League of Women Voters helped out with background information and phone calls. Again, the same things we had done for every election, except now we were on the air reaching thousands of people instead of the 50 or 60 we would get to a local auditorium. So, when they offered me the job of producer, I didn't even try to hide my astonishment — I looked wide-eyed from one to the other and said with disbelief, "But, I don't know anything about TV! How could I be a producer?"

Roger leaned back in his leather executive chair, chuckled and clasped his hands. "We know what you know. After all, you have been popping in and out of this office for the past two years with ideas about what we ought to be putting on our air. We want what you know on our staff, and we can teach you what you need to know about TV."

Dumbstruck, I smiled faintly and murmured, "Of course, I'd love to work here."

"Good," said Roger. "Then the only other question is, how much pay do you want?"

I hadn't given much thought to what I wanted to be paid; I was more concerned with the kind of work I could do next, and had just started looking for a job the week before. I thought I could do political research, issue development or constituency work for a state legislator, so I had started looking for work as a political consultant or legislative staff. The one job I had applied for (aide to a state senator) paid $14,000, so that was the answer I gave to Roger's question.

Both men fell silent, and their smiles vanished. "Give me some time to think about it," said Roger flatly. "Let me see if I can work something out and I'll call you in a couple of days." I had no way of knowing that no other woman in an administrative job at the station got even close to that salary. According to the Census Bureau's figures for that time, women with five years of college made $10,581 a year. Minimum wage was $1.65 an hour. And translating $14,000 into 2020 dollars, it amounts to about $90,000.

I did not know those facts, but as we shook hands all around, I realized my salary request had destroyed the festive atmosphere that had prevailed just moments earlier. I drove home feeling like I had really blown that opportunity. I would have taken less than $14,000. That was just a figure I came up with because it was what the legislative job paid. It had nothing to do with what I really needed to earn or what I would have accepted. When I got home, I felt as though I had just lost my second big contest that year.

I didn't think I could handle another big loss, so for the next few days I didn't answer the phone. I didn't want to hear Roger or Ian saying, "We're really sorry, but we just can't meet your salary request. Thanks anyway." By not answering the phone I could at least delay the bad news. But on Friday afternoon, when the phone rang, I took a deep breath to face the music and answered. "Where have you been all week?" Roger Rice's voice boomed over the phone. "I've been calling you every day; we want you to start Monday morning! Can you be here at 9?"

Roger had somehow found the $14,000 a year. I learned a couple of years later that was the highest salary Channel 2 had paid any woman employee except for news reporters — who were a different breed of animal anyway.

"Oh, my gawd!" I blurted. "Sh-Sure I can. Thank you! See you Monday."

I was so happy, I hung up the phone and danced around the house, all tingly and excited. I set two alarm clocks that Sunday night to make sure I'd wake up on time. I didn't really need to set any alarm because I didn't sleep a wink all night. I just lay in bed as the hours ticked by, worrying about how I was going to get through my first day in my great new job.

# CHAPTER 13

# HOW I GOT ON TV

KTVU'S Community Affairs Department was the perfect place for me to land in 1971. My boss, Ian Zellick, was one of the brightest, most enthusiastic people I have ever known. He needed to be because, despite a very small budget, his department had the big responsibility for making sure the station wouldn't get sued for violating Federal Communications Commission regulations. Until I joined them in August, Ian and his secretary, Maggie, were the entire department. What he lacked in money and staff, however, Ian made up for in energy, brains and chutzpah. Tall, imposing and bald, with a meticulously waxed mustache, Ian would storm up and down the halls talking loudly to everybody or nobody and, when he found the department head he was looking for, his pleas would begin. "Tell me you can do this, just this once! Now, don't shoot me, but could you … just this one time! Oh, Thank you! I'll be forever indebted!"

It seemed he was always trying to convince somebody in the station to repurpose a set made for another department, or tape an interview that wasn't scheduled. Ian fought most of his battles on behalf of some heartbreak group, like the Home for Unwed Mothers, or the School for Disabled and Abused Kids. But sometimes, and just as passionately, for a celebrity or VIP.

"This is the only afternoon we can get him, and if we don't do it now, we won't have anybody to represent … and you know what the FCC says. It won't take long, can't we just … ?"

Ian asked for the impossible and usually got it, because it was hard to say no to a tall, bald man with a waxed mustache who was trying to be the Tooth Fairy to the entire community.

Before Ian joined the department, however, Community Affairs had been the graveyard for KTVU's tired executives, a place to spend their last few years when they couldn't hold their own anymore in sales, news or programming. Community Affairs existed solely because the federal government, through the FCC, required it. Historically, stations all over the country had gotten away with paying lip service to FCC regulations. They observed the equal time and fairness requirements, but could pretty much ignore other regulations that involved surveying and responding to civic and political issues important to their viewing or listening audiences. That was true, at least, until the political fervor of the '60s began targeting the broadcast industry. In the late '60s, some activist groups filed lawsuits against radio and television stations, alleging they were not following all FCC regulations. Defending those lawsuits not only cost a lot of money in legal fees, but losing one of those suits could mean losing your broadcast license. Ian cited those regulations daily, or maybe even hourly; he was the guard at the door of the station's compliance efforts. He was protecting the station's very existence.

Station Manager Roger Rice turned programming inside out. Roller Derby and Wrestling, which had been the station's biggest programming attractions, were phased out. The Film Department was upgraded with better movies, and the ebullient Ian Zellick became the head of Community Affairs. The News Department was expanded, and began looking for women and minorities to put on the air to fulfill the FCC requirement that staff should reflect the demographics of the viewing audience. For Bay Area stations, that was the end of the era of all-white-male news teams.

This was the wave on which I rode into my job at KTVU, and I was not the only beneficiary of the new attitude. Dennis Richmond, a young Black man who had been working props and scenery, was called out of the back room, sent to broadcast school and trained to be a news reporter. Dennis had such good presence, he became an iconic news anchor, his name almost synonymous with KTVU. Latina journalist Ysabel Duron was hired to do *Minority Report* in a 7 o'clock weekday morning slot, and soon became a staff reporter on *The 10 O'clock News* because she, too, was good.

The Community Affairs programming eventually expanded to include more than half a dozen shows, including a woman's show, a Latino show and an Asian show, some of which were even bilingual. Minority employees came, but they also went if they couldn't cut the work. The '70s were the years when everyone got at least a chance. I got mine, and stayed until I retired 22 years later.

Initially, my main responsibility in Community Affairs was to produce *Head On*, the weekly debate show the station launched after meeting with the coalition of community groups that had asked the station to do more local political programming, as laid out in FCC regulations. That was easy because I knew the show well. Ian had been producing it since its inception two years earlier, but with an education and experience in set design and costumes, he had arrived in Community Affairs with not much more than a positive attitude and a quick mind. He often got stuck on details and called for help. "Hey, Betty Ann, got any suggestions about what we could debate for *Head On* next week, and who would be good on the panel?" He knew I always enjoyed brainstorming with him, and would even make the calls to potential panelists or candidates. That was what Roger had alluded to when, in my job interview, he reminded me I had been popping in and out of the station for a good while.

After I joined the staff, I found out there wasn't much more to producing programs for the Community Affairs Department than what I had already been doing on my kitchen telephone: Picking one of the burning issues of the day and finding people willing to come to the studio to talk about it. The News Department, with a much, much bigger budget, sent reporters and camera crews out to film their stories "on the scene," but Community Affairs couldn't afford to do that. *Head On* was able to attract panelists because it aired in prime time — 9 o'clock Sunday evenings, and News Anchor Gary Park was an excellent host. We were allotted two hours in the studio on Thursday afternoons to record the one-hour show "as live," which meant there was no editing. If someone goofed during the tape session, the goof went on the air. Our community coalition, however, was thrilled with the fact we were on the air at all. It was a lot better than debating the issues in school auditoriums.

Six months after I started working at Channel 2, Ian and Roger called me into Ian's office with another proposal. "We would like to put on a second weekly Community Affairs show," Roger said. "We think you can handle the new show as well as *Head On*, and also, if you want to host the new show, it's yours."

Were they kidding? Of course, I would love to have my own show. Ian and I developed the format together, and Ian's background in set design really came through. He suggested a set to look like a sidewalk cafe on Jack London Square, which is where the station was located, and then, to reflect the straight talk we wanted in the content, we named it *On the Square.*

They told me it would be "a fat 58:40," which meant a one-hour show with no breaks and, like *Head On*, would also be recorded "as live." It would air at noon on Sundays — known as 'ghetto time' in the biz — but I didn't care. It was my initiation into another dimension of television. As the producer, I booked all the guests and as the host, I interviewed them. It was so much fun. I had a few regulars, like Peggy Stinnett, a local muckraking reporter who talked about the latest shenanigans at City Hall and the school board. The Lawrence Hall of Science was always good for some flashy experiments and showy inventions. I always had a school segment to showcase kids, and I also interviewed an author each week, because book publishers sent me every new book that came out. To my delight, I also discovered live theaters in the Bay Area liked the free advertising that came from TV interviews with their stars, so I got to see all the shows.

I didn't think a job could get any better. And then, it did.

"Betty Ann? This is Cynthia Rose, from the Sturdy Little Devil's Dress Shop on 17th Street, downtown. Would you be interested in letting me provide the wardrobe for your show, in exchange for a screen credit? I have tentatively explored the matter with Paul Maris, one of my suppliers in San Francisco, and he's interested, too. He suggests you and I go to the Maris showroom once a month and pick out your outfits. He'll do it for a credit too, and you could keep the outfits because Paul doesn't want to bother processing them back into stock."

So, there I was, getting boxes of books, theater tickets, and the latest clothes. Plus, they were paying me. When I began hosting *On the Square,* I joined the union, and every time I did a show I got an on-air fee of a couple hundred dollars.

After two or three years, though, the wardrobe deal blew up. Organized crime came between me and my clothes connection. One day, when Cynthia and I arrived at the Paul Maris Company, a guard at the front door directed us to Maris's office instead of the showroom floor. "This is strange," we murmured to each other, "What's going on?"

Before we could speculate any further, another guard at the office door stepped in front of us. "Who are you and what are you doing here?" he demanded. We told him who we were and why we were there. He disappeared inside the office, and a couple of minutes later he came out and beckoned us inside. Seated behind Paul Maris's desk was a husky blond man with short-cropped hair. Perfect model for an FBI agent, I thought to myself.

"Mr. Maris has had to leave suddenly and won't be back. I'm trying to carry on with this business," he said in what was probably his friendliest voice. I thought, "He even *sounds* like the FBI. What *is* going on?" Once again, we explained our arrangement with the company. He told us to go ahead with our clothes selection, but advised us this might be the last time. He told us the company was making some big changes and he couldn't guarantee any deals Mr. Maris had made would hold up in the future.

It turned out that Paul Maris was in fact Gerald Zelmanowitz, an organized crime figure from New Jersey, whose testimony in court had helped the FBI put some other Mafiosos behind bars. In exchange, the FBI had given him and his entire family new identities, relocated them to San Francisco and hidden them in the Witness Protection Program. But as his clothing business became more and more successful in the 1970s, Maris/Zelmanowitz couldn't resist flashing his new wealth around. He spent so lavishly, his investors became suspicious because they weren't getting any returns on the money they had put into his very successful company. The investors hired a private detective who discovered some inconsistencies in Maris's newly invented personal history. The detective also got some unintended help from the FBI itself. As part of the Witness Protection Program, the FBI had given Mr. Zelmanowitz and everyone in his family — from his grandmother to his grandchildren, all seven of them — a new social security number. And they were all consecutive numbers. This looked pretty fishy to the private detective, who then tracked down Maris's real identity. The investors were about to call a news conference and blow the whistle on him when the FBI got wind of it and swooped in to relocate the entire family. Cynthia and I had just happened to walk in right in the middle of the flap. All those new guards — even the guy in the president's chair — were FBI agents doing major damage control that day.

As the producer of community affairs programs, I met all kinds of people on both sides of the law. It was my job to put discussions together dealing with drugs, racism, prostitution, prison reform, juvenile delinquency and other issues of the day. I met with and interviewed people who had broken the law or were enforcing the law. Some of the nicest people I met were former addicts running rehabilitation programs, and many others trying to cobble our society back together again after the civil strife of the '60s. I got to know the folks at Synanon before it turned into an abusive cult. The Rev. Cecil Williams of Glide Memorial Church became one of my mentors about issues of poverty and the Black community. In those days, Black Panthers Bobby Seale and Eldridge Cleaver were on the lam in Cuba, and Elaine Brown ran the Black Panther school in East Oakland. What I saw of it was impressive, so she and her students became frequent guests on my show. I also did a series of interviews with the local businessmen who were creating the first East Bay cable TV franchise, and with the men who were suing AT&T to break its monopoly and deregulate the phone industry. It seemed everybody with an agenda came through the Community Affairs Department and — once in a while — with bizarre results.

One evening, I went to an open house sponsored by the Women's Health Collective in Berkeley, one of the first women's clinics in the country. Clinics for women were as much about stretching women's consciousness as they were about providing health care. "How many of you have doctors who warm up the speculums before they stick 'em in you when they do a vaginal exam?" a speaker asked. Those of us who were first-time visitors just raised our eyebrows and exchanged glances with each other. I wasn't quite sure I knew what a speculum was, much less whether my doctor warmed it up before he used it.

"Well, you don't have to put up with cold speculums! Tell your doctor to warm them up! Or even better, get acquainted with yourself. Learn how to examine your own vagina. We'll teach you how, and you can buy your own speculum, a nice plastic one that never gets cold, for only $5, right here after our presentation."

She illustrated her lecture with slides of various vaginas, and followed with a demonstration which we were all invited to observe. We took turns holding a flashlight and peering into a live vagina. I went home that evening with my own personal speculum. The next day, I told Ian about the meeting, although I decided not to mention my new equipment, which was in a dresser drawer at home waiting to be tried out. "Invite the Collective to lunch," he shot back, "I think this is something all the department heads should hear about."

A few days later, the Women's Health Collective delivered its illustrated lecture over crab and shrimp salads in KTVU's executive conference room to about eight department heads, who were, of course, all middle-aged males. Just as the speaker got to the part with the slides of various vaginas, the sales manager's secretary came in to tell him he had an urgent phone call. The conference room had been darkened for the slide show, so the screen was the most prominent object in the room. When the secretary saw the bigger-than-life, spread-eagle picture of a two-foot-high vagina on the screen , where she'd only seen sales charts before, her eyes popped out like *Boinnng*! The women from the Health Collective didn't miss a beat. They talked to people every day about vaginas and were used to bug-eyed reactions. If the department heads were nonplussed, they didn't show it, or they might just have been catatonic over the slides and unable to react. Anyway, after the sales manager left the room, the meeting continued.

Ian decided KTVU should do a show with the Health Collective that would air late at night because of the adult content. The station's FCC lawyer said the photo slides could not be shown on the air, no matter how late at night it was. After much discussion, it was decided drawings of vaginas would not violate decency statutes and therefore could be used on the show. So, Ian had the Art Department make line drawings of the vagina slides. But just because you work in the Art Department doesn't mean you're an artist. The drawings were terrible. They were supposed to look like sketches in a medical journal, the logic being a medical journal equals education, which equals Community Affairs, all points on a public service continuum.

That might have been a good theory, but the execution left a lot to be desired. The drawings looked more like little dirty-joke cartoons than sketches in a medical journal. Nevertheless, the Women's Health Collective got their hour on the air, more than they'd ever had before, and they were happy. Roger Rice was happy because vagina slides didn't evoke a single letter threatening to complain to the FCC. Ian was happy because he had just proved his department was on the cutting edge of community awareness. And I was happy because, with politics as my beat at Channel 2, I was able to accomplish some things I never could have on the City Council.

The '70s and '80s were great years for local broadcasting in the Bay Area. They were the years when, thanks to the kick in the pants from those threatened lawsuits, television stations took seriously their roles as public watchdogs. Some days I could not believe people were paying me to do things I had been doing as a volunteer. There were times when I felt guilty taking my paycheck. I found out broadcasting was a very powerful tool, sometimes more powerful than a vote on the City Council. My son Michael nailed it one evening when, after listening to me talking about my day at Channel 2, he asked, "Hey Mom! Aren't you glad you lost that election? Look at all the fun you're having now."

I had been in Community Affairs for five years when the News Director invited me to do a special, five-part series for *The 10 O'clock News*. He said he wanted the story behind the scores of prostitutes who were crowding West MacArthur Boulevard in Oakland. In those days, hundreds of women stood shoulder to shoulder from Broadway all the way out to San Pablo Avenue, wiggling and yelling at men in cars driving by. Some were so bold they took their customers into the nearest hedges or driveways, bypassing the cheap motels that had drawn them to the MacArthur strip.

People who lived in the neighborhood were outraged. I dug around and found the familiar story of Pass the Buck. The police claimed they were making a lot of arrests and blamed *liberal* judges for letting the prostitutes back on the streets after paying measly $50 fines. The judges blamed the laws and said their hands were tied. We called our series *The Prostitution of Justice*. I didn't realize it at the time, but it was the audition for my next career change.

"Have you ever thought about auditioning for the News Department?" Ray Jacobs asked me one afternoon. He was acting KTVU News Director, and the question sounded vaguely indirect. What did the News Department have to do with my life, I wondered.

"Well no, actually, I haven't, Ray," I said, expressing surprise he would even ask such a silly question. "Why would I want to exchange two hours of airtime every week for 90 seconds a day?" I didn't tell him the *real* reason I had never thought about trying out for the

News Department, which was that I had yet to meet anyone in that department who showed much interest in what I thought news was about — the use and abuse of political and economic power.

"Two reasons," Ray said. "First, every night *The 10 O'clock News* reaches an audience many times greater than all the community affairs audiences put together. And second, I know you are now a single mom with three kids, and a reporter in the News Department gets paid twice what you are getting."

Suddenly he had my attention. My financial situation was okay, but not wonderful. During the five years I had been working for the station, my first husband Russ and I had separated, and I was now pretty much on my own. He had signed over our home to me and I was getting by, but the prospects of earning more money sounded very good. The larger audience, the camera crews and the bigger budgets also sounded appealing. If I could do my own stories and reach more people, that was attractive.

There were drawbacks, though. People in the News Department seemed so frazzled, I wasn't sure I wanted that. Besides, I didn't know the first thing about how to put a news story together. As though he could read my thoughts, Ray said something that echoed what Roger Rice and Ian had told me when they first invited me to work in Community Affairs. "We wouldn't put you on the air right away. You'd need time to learn the ropes. You could spend a couple of weeks riding with the crews, watching the editors, getting used to the way we do things. It's a little different than Community Affairs," he said with a knowing smile.

"Thank you very much, Ray, I'd like to think it over, talk to Ian about it, and get back to you. Okay?"

"Sure. Let me know when you're ready."

Ian's reaction was swift and almost scornful. "If you decide to do this, let me give you my Bowie knife as a going-away present, because you'll need it to protect yourself from all the backstabbers up there." Wonderful. I knew the people in News were different than the community types I was used to and comfortable with. I wasn't sure if I could get along with people who seemed to be most passionate about themselves. Ian offered me a way to have a trial period.

"Okay," he said. "If you want to try it out, I'll produce your shows for a month, and you continue to host them. If you don't like the News Department, you can come back to Community Affairs and nobody out there in viewing land will be the wiser."

There was no way I could lose on that, so I accepted Ray's offer. He told me to start the following Sunday, generally regarded as a slow-news day. I could watch the other reporters and just stay on in the evening and do my live Community Affairs phone-in show at 9 p.m. It all sounded good to me.

While I was getting ready to go to the station that Sunday morning, for what I thought was going to be my first day of training, the phone rang. An urgent sounding assignment editor on the other end of the line said, "Betty Ann, we need you in here as soon as possible. The reporter called in sick and you're going to have to cover her schedule today. Your first story is the Glomar Explorer. The cameraman will meet you here at 8 o'clock to take you over to Hunters Point. Thanks." Click.

So much for my two weeks of riding around, observing and training. Fortunately, I knew something about the Howard Hughes spy ship that had succeeded in recovering part of a Soviet ballistic missile submarine — the K-129 — that had sunk in the Pacific, in some 16,000 feet of water, somewhere north of Midway Island. The famous ship, financed by the CIA, had been brought to the San Francisco shipyards to be prepared for mothballing. I was excited about getting to see it in person, so I sped off to Channel 2 without a thought about the fact that I still didn't have a clue about how to put together a news story.

Craig Scheiner was the cameraman assigned to me that first day. He was a soft-spoken, good-looking hunk, who was known around the station for making beautiful handcrafted jewelry. Just about every woman at the station had a ring, a necklace, or a pair of earrings Craig had made. Months earlier, I had asked him if he would like to make a setting for a black opal that had belonged to my grandmother, but he declined, saying he only made jewelry for friends. Later he told me he was just expressing the way people in News felt about Community Affairs. "Community Affairs is the *downstairs*," Craig explained, "News is the *upstairs*. News made money. Community affairs didn't and was like a poor relation."

Recalling Ian's comment about the Bowie knife and the news, I realized neither department had much use for the other. As soon as I transferred upstairs to News, however, attitudes toward me among the staff changed. I was now part of the News family — someone to be helped and protected if need be. I no longer belonged to the 'downstairs-poor-relation' crowd.

I would not have gotten through that first day without Craig's coaching and advice. I think he was a better teacher than even another reporter would have been. Until that Sunday, I had never regarded local news programs as sources of information and had never analyzed or even thought much about what went into a news report. That's what I was supposed to do during my two-week training — which didn't happen that day, or any other day.

It was 1976. News crews were still using film. Expensive and awkward to handle, film came in 400-foot rolls, which would take about 10 minutes of sound and pictures before having to be changed in lightproof black bags that field crews used as portable darkrooms. News reports ran from about 90 seconds to two minutes on the air, and were supposed to be shot on no more than one roll of film. That included interviews, pictures (known as B-roll) and the stand-up. Everything was fine with the Glomar Explorer story until we got to the last bit of field production. "Ready for your stand-up?" said Craig.

"What's a stand-up?" I asked, not realizing the question put me at the bottom of the class. Even interns knew what a stand-up was. I didn't understand why Craig was now looking at me as though I had lost my mind. Or maybe he was trying to figure out if the News Director had lost his. But he just took a deep breath and proceeded to explain to me, patiently, the elements of a news story.

"That's the closing line at the end of the story, when you see the reporter standing in the field with an appropriate picture behind him or her, saying a short blah blah blah and then, 'This is so-and-so for *The 10 O'clock News*.' You need to think of a sentence or two to end your report, and then sign off with the line, 'This is Betty Ann Bruno at Hunters Point, for *The 10 O'clock News*.'"

"But how am I going to write the last two lines when I haven't written the first part of the report yet?" I bleated. Again, the look. Again, the deep breath.

"It's just the way you have to do it in News. You can write the beginning and middle of the story when you get back to the station. But we have to shoot the ending right now, here in the field. Let me know when you're ready to try it."

My first several attempts were total and utter failures. I just couldn't get it into my head how to write the end of something before I had written the beginning and middle of it. I failed miserably and, after more than a dozen bad *takes*, Craig muttered, "Well, I guess we can close on film," and began packing his gear into the trunk of the car. I didn't even know what "closing on film" meant, but, judging from Craig's expression, I guessed it was like getting measles.

"No, I think I can do it. Just let's try it again. I'll get it. I know I will."

"Okay, but we have to be careful. I'm almost to the end of my second roll of film on this. I only have 20 seconds left."

I had used an entire roll of film — 400 feet, 10-plus minutes — just trying to get an acceptable stand-up. Unheard of. It was really awful, but I finally got something that would pass as a stand-up for the broadcast that evening. Fortunately, we were sent on another story immediately, so I didn't have time to brood about how terrible I had been.

Before I staggered into the studio that evening to meet the guests for my 9 o'clock Community Affairs show, I had been sent on two more stories. Next was a jumper off the Golden Gate Bridge. For that, we went to the Coast Guard Station at Crissy Field — the park just below the bridge — where the body lay under a white tarp. I avoided looking at it when the Coast Guard spokesman lifted up a corner to show it to the other reporters. That was just the first body I avoided looking at. Over the next many years, I covered dozens of murders, fatal accidents and suicides, and only once looked at the body. That time, it was to see the remains of an elderly lady who had died of smoke inhalation from a fire in her home, and the only reason I looked was that Craig, who was the cameraman then also, promised me it would be more interesting than grisly. He was right. The result of the smoke was that she looked like a wax figure, unreal, more like a sculpture than a corpse.

My third story of that frenetic first day was a report on a CB club. The Good Buddies and the Citizens Band radios were still a novelty in those days and, in the opinion of our assignment editor, warranted a report on *The 10 O'clock News*.

I will never forget that day. It was the most confounding, stimulating and exhilarating day of my first five years at Channel 2.

I discovered a lot about myself that Sunday. First, I really enjoyed the rush of adrenalin that comes with chasing a news story. Second, I loved being in the middle of the action. And finally, I found I really could sift through a lot of information in a short time and come up with the essence of the situation. After that, I decided I was going to stay with the News Department, make the best of my 90 seconds on the air each day, and never look back at my two hours a week for Community Affairs.

# CHAPTER 14

# THE 10 O'CLOCK NEWS

B y the time I moved from KTVU's Community Affairs to News, Ted Kavanau, who in two years would leave to become CNN's first news director, was sitting in the corner office upstairs. He was a lean man who wore a trimmed mustache on his upper lip and wide, bright red suspenders on a white dress shirt, with sleeves rolled up to his elbows.

Ted was restless, driven by nervous energy to *get the big story*. He seemed to have a sixth sense when it came to sniffing out a good story, but he also often missed. He was always in trouble with the station manager because, on any given day, a reporter, a cameraman or an editor would complain about Ted — he was working them too hard or changing his mind about which stories to cover or where to play them in the broadcast; basically that he was driving them nuts. They complained he would have news crews chasing down one lead in San Francisco one moment and then hurtling to San Jose the next moment on a different and unrelated but, in his view, *better* story. Sometimes he was right. Sometimes he was wrong. When he was right, the reporter or cameraman took the credit, but when he was wrong, they made sure he got the blame. His misjudgments became grist in the daily gossip mill. Field crews dubbed him "Mad Dog Kavanau," and spun out taller and taller tales for crews from other stations about wild goose chases he orchestrated in the name of beating the competition.

Before he had logged his first six months as news director, several veterans in the News Department had resigned to seek more stable management in other newsrooms. This was the atmosphere in News when I transferred from the relatively tranquil and serene Community Affairs department. Kavanau pushed me as hard as he pushed the rest of the staff, but he pushed me where I wanted to go — digging into my own investigations. He was very supportive of my efforts to follow up on tips people gave me. "Go find out what's behind that," he'd say. "Go get'em, Betty Ann. There's a story there. Dig it out and get the bad guys!"

One day, the assignment editor sent me to cover a snail race at one of Oakland's elementary schools. Obviously, a snail race was a story not to be taken seriously, so I treated it with the same spirit in which it was held. It was a light story, in which all the kids had fun, the teachers giggled and most of the contestants were stomped under kids' feet during the cheering and jumping around. When I saw it on the air that night at home, I thought the editor had done a nice job with the pictures and the report had turned out well. I had enjoyed that day's work, which was relaxing compared to the stories I did most of the time. I went to bed that night pleased and content.

The next morning when I got to the newsroom, however, I found a scowling news director; he was not amused. He summoned both the assignment editor and me to his office and bellowed, "That was the worst report on the newscast last night!" Turning to the assignment editor, he unleashed his fury. "She is never, *never* to be sent on a silly assignment again. She is to do only tough reporting. I want people to tremble when they hear Betty Ann Bruno is on the line. You cannot develop a tough reporter with an investigative report one day and then give her a silly feature the next. Do you understand?"

"Yes sir," muttered the assignment editor as we both slunk back to our desks. I wasn't sure what I was supposed to do. I didn't always want to be a warrior. I didn't always feel like going after bad guys. I didn't always want to do the hard stuff. That snail race had been like a day off for me. Sure, I got a lot of news tips. People in the community knew they could call and tell me the latest skulduggery in the school district or city hall. Those stories, however, were not only difficult to put together but were also a hard sell in the newsroom — upstream all the way, starting at the assignment desk. The conversation usually went like this: "Hey, I've just gotten a call claiming (blah blah) and it sounds pretty interesting. How about I phone some folks to check on it and line up a story? What do you think about my seeing if I can get anybody to go on camera?"

"That sounds good, Betty Ann, but here's something in the *Chronicle*. Go out and get that story for tonight's broadcast and then maybe you can follow up on your leads."

The established pattern was to take the morning paper and turn some of the articles into TV reports by setting up interviews with the main players and shooting some pictures. Most of my leads were for stories about political issues and didn't come naturally endowed with exciting images. The producers and the assignment editors lectured, "This is television, Betty Ann. Your story would be a great newspaper article, but where are the pictures? We've got to have pictures! Think visuals! They are what drive this medium. Your information may be important, but if it doesn't have pictures, it's not TV!"

That's the way it went — week in and week out. Some weeks, of course, were better than others. If one of my tips resulted in a good story, that success led to more freedom to follow other leads. If I hit a stone wall — like no one willing to go on camera — then I was back to following the newspaper stories for a while.

For the most part, the Channel 2 newsroom was a very good place to work. The news staff was a lot like the bumblebee which, according to weight and aerodynamics, shouldn't be able to fly. Our news staff was about one-third the size of the network stations across the Bay in San Francisco, but *The 10 O'clock News* show competed head-to-head with them in both ratings and awards. Morale was high, and everybody was encouraged to come up with story ideas. We all shared pride in our broadcasts, and consistently won more than our share of Emmys — not just individual awards but also for the coveted Best News Show.

The late 1970s and early '80s were salad years for Channel 2. They were also great years for me, despite the fact I never got over wanting to report stories I felt were important even if they didn't have action pictures. I always *tried* to find pictures for stories lacking action and good visuals — with uneven success. Here's an example: One day I learned three out of four departments in Oakland's city government had no department heads. For several months, top executives who resigned had not been replaced. I don't remember now what the reason was for all the vacancies, but one day I realized most city departments were running themselves. The city manager was there, but the next tier down — department heads who reported directly to him — existed only as a line of empty squares on the organization chart.

The story itself was interesting; the news director and assignment editor both agreed on that point. The problem was how to turn it into a TV story. You can't take pictures of managers who aren't there, so we decided to take pictures of the only things we had — unoccupied desks. Throughout the report, we showed shot after shot of executive offices all over city hall — bare desks and empty black leather chairs. Assuredly not the most exciting pictures in the world, but they made the point. That kind of story is a hard sell to a TV producer, and you can't do it every day. I did understand that eventually, but it was a constant struggle to balance what I saw as social or political significance against television's inherent need to show the viewer pictures.

For another story, not only could I not get a picture or an interview with the central figure, but I had to use a code name when I called my source. It was the late '70s and someone who worked at Fairmont Hospital in Oakland told me that sheriff's deputies had brought in an elderly lady, *in handcuffs* that afternoon, because she had resisted the Sheriff's deputies when they were evicting her from her house.

Even though I could not interview her, I was able to put together a report on her from the arrest record, and from interviews with the deputies and her neighbors. I found out that Grace Malone had disregarded tax notices for a couple of years. They were found stacked up inside her house, along with a big pile of empty vodka bottles. In effect, Grace Malone was an angry, drunk old lady who didn't have any use for the tax collector or any other official, and didn't bother to open letters from the county.

She had no close relatives or friends to watch over her or take care of her affairs. The deputies said, when they came to evict her, she kicked and clawed at them, so they clapped handcuffs on her, took her to Psych Emergency and put her in locked detention. The next day her house was sold at auction for back taxes.

My report set off a storm of protests to the Tax Collector's office. He called me personally to assure me he really was not a monster, that his office was only following procedures as set out in the regulations, but he agreed it didn't look good. He told me he had been inundated with calls from viewers who were incensed at his office, the deputy sheriffs and everybody else involved, including the man who had bought her house.

There was so much fallout from our news coverage that, although the County of Alameda could not reverse the sale of the house and reinstate Grace Malone in it, they set up a special trust fund for her and she spent the rest of her life in a very nice convalescent home in Oakland. And the Tax Collector's office changed its procedures so notices of seizure and sale would no longer be done solely by mail, but would include personal visits to investigate the situation with the homeowner.

My source for the story could leave messages for me at the newsroom, but when I called him back I couldn't leave a message for him saying who I was because that might have jeopardized his job. We both agreed I should go under cover. The undercover persona I created for that story came in handy many other times over the years when my sources — whistleblowers, if you will — needed anonymity in their workplaces. When I called those sources I would use a fake name, disguise my voice with a bit of drawl and assure whoever took the message that the person I was calling knew my number and didn't need it again.

One of my wildest news adventures was just the luck of the draw. It was October 29, 1983, and that morning, as I did every morning, I listened to the news while I drove to the station. The top story was about a massive earthquake that had just struck Idaho, causing widespread damage. The 6.9 quake was also felt in four neighboring states and Alberta, Canada. Its epicenter was the small town of Challis, about 200 miles northeast of Boise, Idaho's capital city. Two young children walking to school were killed instantly when a brick wall collapsed on them. I felt painfully sad, thinking about those two children's lives ending so suddenly and violently. My heart went out to their moms and I started thinking about how precious my own kids were as I pulled up to the station and opened the back door that led directly to the newsroom.

As I walked down the corridor past the edit bays toward the main room, I could see News Director Fred Zehnder and Assignment Editor Jay Martinez standing at the desk. Both of them were watching me and smiling. "Good morning and congratulations, Betty Ann," Jay began, "you've just won a trip to Idaho today! John MacKenzie is your cameraman and he's ready to roll. A plane is waiting at the Oakland General Aviation airport to fly you both up there. Get going right now, because this is the lead story tonight."

"What did I do to win?" I asked feeling a little off-balance at the idea of going halfway across the country on the spur of the moment.

"You're the first reporter to come through the door this morning," Jay answered, and with a chuckle he handed me some printouts from the news wires and wished us both *Good Luck*.

Fifteen minutes later, John and I boarded a twin-engine plane and took off for Idaho. The two pilots said our flight would take about four hours, but two hours into it they informed us the large airport close to Challis had just landed its maximum number of planes and couldn't take any more. News crews from all over the country had flown in to cover the biggest earthquake in the history of Idaho, which had torn a 25-mile-long rift in the Lost River Range. The network stations from San Francisco had all chartered jet planes, which made the trip in half the time it was taking us. Thinking we were going to be the last ones to get there did not make us happy, but we could understand why we were in a more economical prop plane instead of a jet. The network affiliates all had 6 o'clock newscasts and our broadcast was not until 10 that night, so initially we weren't terribly concerned. As the day played out however, we found we had plenty to worry about. Where to land was only the first problem.

The pilots said there were no other airports close to Challis and the best they could do was a landing strip in a field 70 miles away.

The terminal and control tower were a farmhouse, we learned, the door of which had a note tacked on it saying, "Please come in. Back soon. Nursing the baby."

Seeing no alternative, we settled in the farmhouse to wait, but we began to feel the pressure of time. It was about 1:30, which meant we had three and a half hours to get our story, because we had to start back no later than 5 p.m. if we were going to get to the station by 9 to edit our piece and have it on the air by 10. Three and half hours to drive 70 miles to Challis, find people to interview, shoot pictures and drive 70 miles back. We were waiting for the nursing mom to come back and rent us a car so we could hit the road, when the pilots informed us it would take more than four hours for our return flight because they would have to stop and refuel.

"There won't be time!" I said, suddenly feeling very anxious. "We have to be back in Oakland by 9 or the story won't make it for *The 10 O'clock News!*" Then I suggested maybe they could go refuel while we were in Challis. I expected a little pushback, but they immediately agreed.

"No problem," the pilot said happily. "In fact, we'll even bring back a couple sandwiches for you two so you won't starve to death before we get back to Oakland." That was wonderful to hear because it meant the pilots were totally on board with our mission and our pressure-cooker schedule.

Nursing Mom came in, apologized for keeping everyone waiting, and revealed two other problems. "First, we don't have any rental cars here and second, the roads have all been damaged from the quake and I doubt you can get through to anywhere from here."

John and I both went into overdrive. He got on the phone to check the road conditions and I explained to the mom why we were there, what our deadline was and begged her to rent us anything that had four rubber tires and a steering wheel. She was very sympathetic, and eventually admitted they had an old station wagon that was not in great shape but said it would probably get us to Challis and back as long as the roads were open. That was good enough. A few minutes later, we were on our way and really feeling the pressure of the clock. Fortunately, all 70 miles of the road to Challis were open and clear.

Challis was — and still is — a very small town, and I think that day there were more news people than locals walking around inspecting the damage, especially the building that had collapsed on the children. Several local residents eagerly told their stories to reporters. The problem was how to get our story back to the newsroom. It was 1983, BC (Before Cell Phones), and we were way out of range for our two-way radios. There was only one working pay phone in the town, and the line to use it was so long, I was afraid I wouldn't be able to talk to the station before we had to leave to go back to meet our plane. And then, the strangest thing happened.

While I was waiting in the line for the phone, a man came up to me and asked if I was a reporter. When I told him I was, he said, "You might want to go up to the lake outside of town, because the governor is there now with state inspectors looking at the dam to make sure it wasn't damaged in the quake. Because, if it breaks, it will flood this whole town."

Without hesitation John and I jumped out of the phone line and raced the couple of miles to the reservoir. Just like the stranger had said, Governor John Evans was there, walking the lake with some of Idaho's engineers. No other reporters seemed to know about that yet, so I got an exclusive interview with the governor. I have no idea who the man was who gave me the tip about it or why he picked me out of the long line of reporters who were waiting for the telephone, but I certainly thank him and will always remember that very special act.

On that day in Idaho, I knew a lot more about how to do a TV news story than I had seven years earlier — my first day in the field on the Glomar Explorer story, when I struggled through 18 or 20 retakes trying to get a stand-up for my report. This day, after our interview, as the governor and his party resumed their tour of that endangered lake, John and I ran ahead of them and, with the gubernatorial group in the background and coming toward the camera, I rattled off a standup in one take.

Whereupon, we called it a good day's work and raced the 70 miles back to the little farmhouse with the landing strip, where our plane, loaded with fuel, sandwiches and sodas, was waiting to zip us back to Oakland. You could almost hear the William Tell Overture playing as we sprinted from the station wagon to the plane. The pilots seemed to be enjoying the excitement of it all and made our deadline their own. When we hit some headwinds, they shouted out they were gunning the engines full throttle to make sure we would get back in time. During the flight, I wrote my report so it would be ready to go for the editor the minute I walked in the door of the station.

When we got close to Oakland, John's two-way radio connected with the newsroom so he could tell them exactly when and where we were going to land. The newsroom must have called the control tower and gotten special permission because, as our plane touched down and taxied along the runway, the news car drove out on the tarmac and was alongside the plane the moment it came to a stop. One of the pilots popped the door open and, to my surprise, our messenger was standing there with outstretched arms. "Betty Ann, I'm taking you and the tapes back to the station. John will come in his own car, but you've gotta go right now." I jumped into his car and we raced back to the station where he pulled the car right up to the back door. The editor, Leslie Donaldson, was standing in the doorway holding it open. I grabbed my stuff and we both ran inside to put the piece together.

What followed was like an exaggerated scene in a movie about a newsroom, except this was real. We worked at what felt like lightning speed. Fortunately, I had had enough time on the plane to log every sound bite and every picture Leslie would need for the piece, so it went together quickly and easily. She was extremely fast, decisive and competent. At one minute to airtime, she grabbed the video cassette from the edit machine, ran through the newsroom, down the hall to the control room and handed it to the engineer who rolled it just as Dennis Richmond was opening the broadcast and reading the lead into the story. It had to air on time, and it did. There was no way we could have missed that deadline, because missing a deadline simply was not done in News and, apparently, also wasn't in the lexicon of any of the good people who made that day come together for us.

Sometimes the news stories I chose to cover got me in trouble with management. One day, my muckraking friend Peggy Stinnett gave me a tip that *The Oakland Tribune* was about to pull an end run around City Hall. "There's an item on the agenda for the next City Council meeting to approve a proposal for a federal block grant so the *Tribune* can build a modern printing plant out by the airport," she said. "And there has to be something fishy about that, so why don't you see what you can find out."

Peggy had a good nose for political shenanigans and insider deals, and I was good at digging in and finding out who and/or what was behind them. I made some phone calls and found a story that needed telling — a story people were never going to read about in *The Oakland Tribune*. What I found was that the *Tribune* had been working on getting a multimillion-dollar federal block grant for itself. The groundwork had been done over a period of several months in Washington, D.C. and was a well-kept secret. The only thing left for the *Tribune* to do was to get City Council approval. No one else even knew about these particular grants, that were part of the federal government's anti-poverty program, although there were plenty of marginal businesses in Oakland that could have benefited from a jump-start from the feds.

Joseph Knowland had bought the *Tribune* in the early 1900s and unapologetically used it to advance his conservative political agenda. His son William became a U.S. Senator and when he took over the paper, it was the most powerful political influence in the city. In the late '70s the Gannett corporation, a huge media company, acquired the *Tribune*. The newspaper's original plant, housed in the Tribune Tower in downtown Oakland, was outdated and inefficient. Naturally, Gannett wanted to modernize.

The question was, why did a wealthy corporation like Gannett need a federal grant to update its presses? Certainly, it could qualify for a regular commercial loan. The publisher agreed to an interview. His answer to the question was simple and probably too honest. Looking right at me with the camera rolling, he said, "Why would we want to pay interest on a loan when we can get the money for nothing?" And then he smiled, obviously pleased with the prospect of all that federal money he thought was about to head his way.

But the mayor, who saw the report on *The 10 O'clock News*, was not pleased by either the smile or the answer. He was furious, and the City Council not only turned down Gannett's request for approval, but publicly castigated the publisher for "trying to pull a fast one."

Peggy and I also found out there was a limit on the amount of money any one city could request. Since the *Tribune*'s request was for nearly all the money Oakland was entitled to under the program, there wouldn't be much left for the small businesses in West Oakland or along East 14th Street. Those districts had suffered from the exodus of white merchants moving out of Oakland, and were now filled with struggling Black shopkeepers, or worse, boarded-up storefronts. The *Tribune* had counted on getting its proposal in first, and just before the deadline. It would then be too late for anyone else (read Black mom-and-pop entrepreneurs in East and West Oakland) to submit their own proposals. And it might have worked if my story hadn't shone a very bright light on the big corporation that appeared to be stealing money intended for the poor and needy.

Peggy covered the story for *The Montclarion,* a small neighborhood paper, but the *Tribune* maintained its silence. The San Francisco papers, which got most of their information about Oakland from the *Tribune,* started covering the story after my reports went on the air. Eventually, all the major news outlets in the area, except the *Tribune,* covered the story, but the *Tribune* publisher did not give another interview. His only comment to all the other news outlets was, "no comment." In the end, Gannett did not build its new printing plant in Oakland. In fact, a short time later, the Gannett corporation left Oakland altogether. Talk around town was that Gannett gave the paper to Black editor Robert Maynard.

That may or may not have been the case but what eventually became painfully clear was that the *Tribune* had even more serious problems than outdated machinery. Beginning in the '60s, white flight to the suburbs had moved most of the *Tribune's* readership from the city of Oakland to Contra Costa County, and *The Contra Costa Times* was growing about as fast as the *Tribune* was shrinking. I think even a new printing plant could not have stemmed the tide against the *Tribune.* Perhaps it could have become the regional newspaper and served both Oakland and Contra Costa County, but that didn't happen. Bob Maynard's heart lay with the city of Oakland and its people. He was less interested in the suburbs, and he wanted so much for Oakland to prosper. He focused his paper on the efforts and institutions within the city; his horizons did not extend to nearby Walnut Creek. He put a team of reporters and columnists together that did the best it could, and even brought scholarly distinction to the paper, but he was not able to hold back the loss of subscribers and advertisers. Eventually the *Tribune* abandoned its old plant downtown and became just one part of a consortium of East Bay papers. It might have happened anyway, but once in a while I can't help wondering if the story would have had a different ending if Gannett had gotten the federal grant, or just spent some of its own multimillions, and built a new printing plant.

The story also had an impact on my own success at the station. At the time the story broke, a man named Bill Schwartz was the general manager of KTVU. Beyond the fact he and Roger Rice held the same title, they had little else in common. Rice enjoyed using the station for the community, and I think he almost welcomed the pressures for better local coverage because it gave him an excuse to do things he might not have otherwise been able to justify. Schwartz was a very different breed of cat —the first of the bottom-line managers at KTVU whose goals were all about making money and building power.

Roger Rice met every activist in the Bay Area through his Community Affairs luncheons in Channel 2's conference room, whereas Bill Schwartz joined all the downtown business groups, including The New Oakland Committee. He got to know other CEOs in town, including the top two or three execs of *The Oakland Tribune* who, of course, were not happy with the disclosure of the block-grant story and apparently told him KTVU exaggerated the importance of the block grant and there was no story there. Every day, during the week I was reporting the latest revelations about it, our news director got a call from the general manager asking, "What is the big deal about this, anyway? Why is she doing these stories?"

Fortunately for me, this happened in the late '70s, before television was deregulated. The FCC regulations originated in the 1930s, when the agency was established, and they were based on the belief the airwaves belonged to the public and therefore, radio and television stations using them had to operate in the public interest. One of the regulations said a station's news department was independent from the rest of management, which meant not even a general manager could censor the news. As long as the news director thought a story was newsworthy, it stayed in the lineup.

My reports about the *Tribune's* grab for the federal grant stayed in the lineup, but that didn't prevent Schwartz from telling me directly how he felt about it. In this same time period, Channel 2 had a groundbreaking ceremony in a vacant field on the shores of the Oakland Estuary where it was going to build a $20 million, state-of-the-art plant. All the city's leaders were there and made nice speeches about "KTVU's vision and its commitment to Oakland's future." The news director had asked me to do a piece on it for the evening broadcast, so I was there doing a couple of interviews for my story. But I took a break when General Manager Schwartz said he wanted a private word with me. I walked beside him as he maneuvered away from the crowd. I was so busy navigating the rough terrain of the vacant lot we were in, I didn't notice the expression on his face until he stopped and looked at me. I knew in that instant he had not called me out there to give me a raise. His face was dark, his eyes narrowed and steely. He glared at me, saying, "I am not going to ask you to stop the reports on *The Oakland Tribune.* I can't do that. But I do want you to know your pursuit of that story is an embarrassment to me. I am trying to make this station a part of the workings of this city, and you are not helping. That's all I am going to say on this subject." He turned abruptly and went back to the celebration, leaving me standing in the middle of the field.

Good to his word, nothing more was ever said to me directly about the story by Bill Schwartz, or by anyone else. But I knew at that moment in the field, my future was sealed. I would not be offered a personal services contract, or the raise that would come with one, nor would I enjoy the crumb of prestige the title "Correspondent" gives a reporter. I got my corporate stripes on that story, and they crossed each other in a big *X* right over my square on the station's organization chart.

The general manager couldn't have that story pulled from the news lineup because of those federal regulations protecting News from the station's commercial and political interests, but that's not the way it is any more. Today, general managers can tell news departments what they want to see on the air and what they don't want to see. Deregulation has meant news no longer has to be fair or balanced. We've even managed to blur the line that once distinguished news from commentary, so viewers might think they're getting the news, but they're really hearing political opinion.

I feel very fortunate to have been a part of the news industry while it still had to present all sides of political issues, while we still operated under the credo that anyone using the public's airwaves had an obligation to serve the public interest — before the public's airwaves became just another item to sell to the highest bidder.

CHAPTER 15

# THE HOLLYROCK CREW

*"You Bitch! I'm Gonna Get You!"*

One afternoon in 1986, a flyer addressed to me in the newsroom arrived at KTVU's reception desk in a plain manila envelope. An unsigned note in the margin said simply, "How about some news coverage on this drug gang?"

I called the number on the flyer and got the Oakland Vice Squad. "Hmm," I thought, "someone thinks putting this drug gang on the news is going to help get rid of it. Well maybe … In any case a drug gang might make a good story!"

I read the flyer, then read it again. It said The Hollyrock Gang was an evil menace that had taken over the streets in West Oakland and was terrorizing the residents. The flyer asked people to come forward with information that "could restore order by helping the police arrest the gang's leader, James Lorenzo Holloway, a career criminal."

The vice squad officer who answered the phone told me that the point-of-contact for the Hollyrock Gang was a grocery store at the corner of 34th and Grove streets. So I drove out there and left a message that I would like to talk to the gang leader. Police described him as having diamonds implanted in his front teeth, and said he drove a gold-trimmed, candy-apple red Mercedes Benz.

Several days later, an invitation to meet with him came via an anonymous phone call to the newsroom. The voice said I should come to the street corner at 4 o'clock the next afternoon. I could bring one other person, but no camera or notebook. Mark Richardson, an assignment editor who had grown up in Oakland, agreed to go with me.

When we arrived at 34th and Grove, a young Black man greeted us with an inquiring once-over, and then went inside the grocery store and made a call on the pay phone. A few minutes later, a candy-apple-red Mercedes cruised up to the curb, and suddenly about 15 young Black men with metal baseball bats emerged from nowhere and from everywhere and formed a circle around Mark and me.

If I had not been so disquieted by the menacing presence of so many metal bats, I might have admired the choreography of it. The entire chorus of young batters was leaning forward on the handles of their bats with joyless grins on their faces, as their unmerciful eyes searched us.

When the Mercedes' driver-side door opened, a young man with diamonds in his front teeth stepped out and sauntered toward us. He was a light-skinned Black man with hazel eyes, short, of medium build, with brown, straight, shoulder-length hair. He was wearing a baggy jacket over an old sweatshirt and rumpled pants, certainly not the decked-out look of storybook drug-lords.

There must have been times however, when he dressed to the nines because his nickname was Iceman, street lingo stemming from "iced," or "dressed to kill" — although that phrase may have been a little too literal in his case. I also thought the name could refer to his incisor diamonds. Later, after I learned more about him, I wondered whether Iceman referred to what ran through his veins.

Mark and I introduced ourselves and explained we had seen the flyer and were interested in getting his side of the story. We said we wanted to do a profile on him, and spend a day with him, just like we had done with the vice squad. I tried not to show my unease or think about the threatening baseball-bat fence that enclosed us.

What struck me most was Holloway's manner — he was quiet, soft spoken and young. Only 20-years old, he headed a criminal enterprise, was allegedly awash in money and dominated an entire section of a large city. I wondered how he had done that, and thought if he would be even half candid in his interview, our viewers would get a great story. The question was how would I convince him to be a feature on *The 10 O'clock News?*

Based on his car and his teeth, I decided to appeal to his vanity. We heaped praise all over his car. I admired the custom 14-karat-gold door handles and the deep, rich finish in candy-apple-red lacquer. "Wouldn't it be fun to do the interview," I suggested, "while riding around West Oakland?" The image seemed to intrigue him.

Holloway then turned to one of his escort cars and opened the trunk to reveal a bank of pulsing, Pyle Driver speakers. I felt a physical impact from the decibels pouring out of the open trunk. Our introductory meeting lasted about 10 minutes. Then he said he'd think about doing the TV thing, walked back to his car and drove away. "I'll be in touch," promised his aide-de-camp before getting into the Pyle Driver car and speeding off after his leader.

The aide did call, and we made arrangements to do the interview the following week. Craig, his camera and I, spent two days with the Hollyrock Gang. We told them we needed pictures and more pictures of the Hollyrock crew. And while we took them, we witnessed countless contradictions.

A group of young men gathered in the parking lot next to the grocery story. The Pyle Driver car was there with the trunk wide open so Craig could shoot the pulsing speakers and record the blow-away, louder-than-loud music. They told us the music being played was the Hollyrock theme song, and members of the gang — teenagers, women, even an older man or two — did some really great dancing right there on the asphalt. Hard to believe these agile young dudes were the same ones the police said had tortured, beaten and robbed.

As we cruised around in that candy-apple-red Mercedes, Craig was more successful in taking pictures than I was in getting Holloway to discuss his business. He kept insisting he was just a regular Joe who liked to hang out with a bunch of good friends. He denied having much money or being involved in anything illegal.

"How about all the stories about you, including how you dump $20 bills on the floor of the back seat of this car and then invite school children to ride around barefoot so they can rub their feet in piles of money?"

"Well, I like kids. I give them rides once in a while."

"What about the piles of $20 bills?"

"You know how kids like to talk."

"What I've heard is, that's how you get kids to work as look-outs for you. Is that true?"

"Why would I need look-outs? I don't do anything wrong. I'm just a regular guy."

"There are a lot of stories on the street about you. One is that you have a five-gallon-water jar stuffed with $20s, $50s and $100s. Is that true?"

"Well, umm, my wife and I have a jar where we keep our lunch money."

An Oakland police officer later raided Iceman's apartment at 34th and California streets, found the jar and counted $8,000 worth of lunch money.

"Tell us about how you got this car."

"It ain't mine. It belong to my little sister."

"What does she do?"

"She go to school."

"How does she get enough money to buy a car like this if she's going to school?"

"I dunno ... she just does."

"How do you support yourself?"

"I have a job. At a car repair shop right here in West Oakland. You wanna go there and meet my boss?"

"Yeah, let's go there."

He took us to the ABC Auto Repair shop nearby which, interestingly enough, had one of the contracts with the city to maintain official cars. The owner of the shop confirmed that Holloway was on the payroll, but became very vague when asked about Holloway's work schedule, and just grinned silently in response to my request for specifics.

I subsequently learned that Holloway had managed to get probation despite dozens of arrests, and that a condition of probation is employment. At least on paper, Holloway did have a job. But, mechanics in the shop claimed, although he was in and out of the shop frequently, they never saw him do any work there.

I also learned that Holloway's rap sheet began when he was a child and had never stopped growing. When we printed it out on continuous-roll computer paper, it stretched 15 feet across the room and included robbery, assaults, and even murder charges or investigations.

Craig shot video as a police officer read from it — inch-by-inch, charge by charge. It made an impressive visual for the report. At the time, Holloway was scheduled for a court hearing on two additional felony charges and the county was recommending probation.

James Holloway was born in West Oakland to a prostitute and a petty, alcoholic drug dealer. He told us he didn't know where his mother was, or whether she was even alive. We located his father, who was living in a cheap hotel in San Francisco's Tenderloin district, but he refused to talk to us about his notorious son. Holloway, however, told us he had grown up along San Pablo Boulevard in West Oakland with winos and prostitutes as his only role models.

Most people who lived in West Oakland had heard of him, but very few were willing to talk to us about him and nobody would go on camera. They were all afraid of getting beaten up — or worse. We met a couple of people who had been beaten because they had displeased him or one of his henchmen.

The Hollyrock Crew was known for its brutality. We found one little boy who described his ride in the back seat of the red Mercedes with the pile of money, but we didn't dare ask that young witness to go on camera. We began to understand the problems the district attorney's office had in getting convictions for the numerous arrests. People were afraid to testify in court, and charges couldn't stick without prosecution witnesses. As a result, the Hollyrock Crew operated with impunity, suggesting there was another problem that wasn't just in the streets.

I noticed that the officer involved in many of Holloway's outstanding arrests was a Sergeant named Michael Yoell. I asked him for an interview and to comment on the county's recommendation for probation. He seemed genuinely surprised — and angry.

"Are you kidding? Probation for that gangster? With his past convictions, and he's facing new ones now? How can the County even think about probation? Well, that's the problem. We keep arresting the bad guys and the rest of the system keeps letting them go." Yoell was outraged that so much field work by the police department would go for naught, and he said so right to our camera.

At that point, I had covered enough drug and criminal cases to notice that most drug cases ended up in the same courtroom — that of Judge Stanley Golde, a former criminal defense attorney and highly respected jurist among his peers who, nevertheless, had a reputation for being soft on drug offenders. Years earlier, I had suggested that the grand jury should investigate the county's record on drug arrests and convictions, but the deputy district attorney, who ran the grand jury, just laughed.

Perhaps there were good reasons that some large, notable criminal gangs operated in Oakland and avoided prison. Best known were the Hell's Angels, who ran a methamphetamine manufacture-and-sales business out of Oakland for years, and whose leaders all lived in the upscale Oakland Hills. Another drug-lord, named Felix Mitchell, ran a multimillion-dollar enterprise out of East Oakland's housing tracts for almost 20 years before he was finally convicted and sent to prison. During his heyday, Mitchell was featured in *Forbes* magazine as an "outstanding businessman with an organization run as skillfully as a Fortune 500 company."

Many Oakland observers felt that Hollyrock was just the latest example of a too-casual relationship between Alameda County's criminal justice system and organized crime. I felt all I could do was point it out, get some outraged reaction, and then maybe — with public pressure — the system would do what it was supposed to do.

But unless KTVU was going to provide a full-time-investigative staff and clothe us in bullet-proof vests, I didn't see any way I could go any further than writing a straightforward news story. So that's what I did. But I didn't count on what Sgt. Yoell would do after he finished commenting on Holloway's recommended probation.

Craig and I had a little bit of shooting left to do on the story. Then he went home while I finished writing and recording the script. The report was scheduled to run the following week as part of a special series on gangs and drugs.

It was a Friday evening, and Craig and I were flying to Tahiti the next day for a long-awaited, three-week vacation. I had just walked through the door at home when the newsroom called to say Sgt. Yoell had notified them that he had busted Iceman and put him in jail.

Craig and I piled back into the news car and sped to the police department. Yoell told us that he was so angry at the idea that Iceman was going to get probation again, that after he finished the interview with us, he went to the streets of West Oakland, stopped the red Mercedes, searched it and found several large rocks of cocaine. It was enough to put Iceman behind bars.

We crossed the street to ask the local bail bondsmen if they had arranged bail yet. One already had. Iceman was back on the streets, and was free again pending his scheduled court appearance — which now had one more felony charge added to the previous ones.

It would have been interesting to see if the probation department was going to stick with its lenient recommendation. But no one would find that out because when Holloway's court date arrived, he did not appear. He skipped bail and ran.

I didn't know that had happened, nor did I see my report when it first ran on the air. I was having the vacation of my life in French Polynesia, and the Bay Area's drug gangs didn't enter my thoughts.

Three weeks later, upon returning to the newsroom, I found a stack of messages from the Hollyrock Crew — none of them friendly. I picked up my ringing phone.

"Channel 2 News. Betty Ann Bruno here."

After a pause, a low voice with a definite edge said, "You bitch. I'm gonna' get you. You f- - -ed me, you bitch. You sicced the cops on me!! You should fry in hell!!" It was Iceman, rumbling like a volcano about to blow up.

"I didn't sic anybody on you. What are you talking about?"

"That cop, you told him he should arrest me!"

"Good grief. I did not. Why would I do that?"

We went back and forth for a few minutes, but he was carrying a giant, three-week-old grudge and was not about to be calmed down.

When he finished venting, he hung up. I doubt if he had heard anything I said. I sat there holding the phone as the dial tone pulsed. I was scared. The baseball-bat demonstration when we first met had been scary enough, but that was just a ceremonial dance, a show of strength. This was different. This was a declaration of war. Holloway's rap sheet whirred through my brain — beatings, shootings, murder. I had no doubt that he'd done all those things. And now I was on his short list.

I called Sgt. Yoell. "Don't worry," he said, "that's all bluff. He isn't even in town anymore. He skipped bail, you know. He never showed up at that court hearing because he was going to go to prison on all those counts he had. I don't think he'll act on his threats. These guys are all basically cowards. He won't come looking for you."

Fine. Easy for him to say, I thought. He, with his guns and his bulletproof vest. Well, I didn't like it. Over the years, I had done a lot of stories that presented the subjects in their own true light. They looked as bad as they really were. But before I met the Iceman, nobody had ever blamed *me* for the trouble they had gotten themselves into. This guy, obviously, was different.

I went to News Director Fred Zehnder, and told him what happened. He came up with a plan to keep me a little safer while I was at work. He alerted the station's head of security and advised him to tell all the guards that if anybody asked for me, not to let them in the building unless I gave permission. Then he gave me a key to the secure area in the parking lot reserved for the News Department's microwave trucks.

As far as I knew, my car was the only private vehicle ever to be allowed to park in that special area. About six months later, I felt comfortable enough to park in the general lot again, but even then I always parked close to the building and looked around carefully every time I entered or left the newsroom.

Eventually, Iceman was arrested. It happened in Stockton, 85 miles from Oakland. He was washing a car with a bunch of hoodlum buddies with whom he had been hiding out. He was no longer driving his candy apple red Mercedes. I don't know what happened to that.

I do know that Holloway was finally convicted and sent to prison.

Update, 2004: Sgt. Michael Yoell had been promoted to lieutenant in the Oakland Police Department and was head of the Special Victims Unit. When I called him to check on some of the details for this story, he told me he had recently run into Iceman on the streets. Iceman, he reported, complimented him on his good police work and told him, "You always had someone in my organization! Every move I tried to make, you were always there to bust me."

Yoell added that Holloway has been in and out of prison over the years and that the good-old-boys club in the county's criminal justice system was, in his view, still operating as strong as ever.

It has to be said that the Oakland Police Department had had its own problems, including a 2003 federal consent decree putting the department under the authority of a federal judge in response to rogue officers robbing suspects and excessive use of force. There was even a subsequent threat to put the department into federal receivership. Yoell, now retired, has been highly praised by his peers (he was voted the 1995 OPD Officer of the Year, the same year he was suspended for shooting an unarmed robbery suspect).

In thinking back over these events, I can hardly believe I jumped into the Hollyrock story the way I did. I can't picture myself doing so today. My feelings have changed, as has the criminal justice culture over almost two decades. I remember in those days having a sense of immunity from harm and, therefore, from fear. I also felt that the streets of Oakland were my streets too. I had lived in that city for more than 20 years when I did the story, and I was familiar with the neighborhood. I knew the people in City Hall, I knew the merchants, I knew people in the streets; it was where I lived and worked.

Now that I have been away from Oakland for almost 30 years, I no longer have that sense of familiarity. Oakland is not my town anymore. I only know what I read in the newspapers or what my friends tell me about what's happening there.

It is no longer part of my own experience and I think that makes a difference. I look back on those days with a bit of awe. Did I carry a sense of bravura when I went out to 34th and Grove to talk Iceman into appearing on television? Even though I didn't say the words, did I give out the signal to Sgt. Yoell that I wanted him to go out and arrest Iceman? Was I moving events along just by the act of covering them?

It is generally accepted that people often go to extremes in order to attract the attention of the news media. Early on in the civil rights movement, people learned that crowds of marchers seeking justice were not enough to get on the front page. They had to break the law to make the headlines: occupy the dean's office, sit in the mayor's office, lock directors in a board meeting, shave their heads, take off their clothes. Activist organizations gave training sessions in how far to go in breaking the law and how to behave if you were arrested. It's all stimulus/response, back and forth, until the two are fused or "con-fused."

I know I was a link in that chain when I did stories like Hollyrock. On the one hand, you could say that seeing the gang members dancing in the parking lot, telling stories about the sea of money in the back seat of the red Mercedes, was free advertising for the drug gang, glamorized the criminals and possibly helped them recruit new gang members. On the other hand, shedding the light of day on a lackadaisical, flawed justice system led to some improvements.

There is also a moral issue in this story, but I don't think that was my motivation. I wish I could say that I did the piece because I wanted to be part of the forces that were getting the bad guys off the streets. Actually, I think the truth was simpler and not so moralistic. The stories were fun to cover. It was exciting. Riding in a patrol car with the siren blaring and lights swirling overhead was an adrenalin rush. It made great pictures and put me in a special category because no ordinary citizen, not even many reporters, got to do those things. So, I have to confess, I did the stories because they were immensely interesting. They set me apart. I had a good time and, given half a chance, I'd probably do it all over again.

There's another moral issue, too — the huge loss of talent and energy because of the underlying problems manifested in the story of the Hollyrock Crew. And it's an issue echoed across the country, in cities large and small, in the lives of all the James L. Holloways and the Felix Mitchells and all the other big and little drug dealers. While I was writing his story, I fantasized about the What Ifs of Holloway's life. What if there had been adults in his growing-up years who had been able to teach him math, science, art, music and philosophy; adults to take him to museums, the theater, the concert halls. What if he had adults in his life who took him on camping trips to the country, who taught him how to cook over a campfire under a starry sky? What if he had adults in his life who played catch with him when he was a little kid, and later taught him how to kick the ball between the goal posts? Would that have made a difference in how he lived his life and how he used his leadership skills? What difference would that make in the lives of the other young men who followed him?

That story plays out in our schools, churches and synagogues, and government agencies all the time. That story is not one the newsroom can write.

# LIFE AFTER LIFE — AFTER LIFE

How I Met my Husband Before I Met My Husband

The 1960s saw a renewed interest in spiritual matters, and in the '70s that interest spawned a fascination with spirits and psychics. Interest in psychic phenomena exploded, and I wanted to capture the story for our KTVU viewers. Elisabeth Kübler-Ross's books (*On Death and Dying, On Grief and Grieving, On Life After Death*) were on the best-seller lists, so in 1976, when I proposed a series on *Life After Life*, the news director enthusiastically said, "GO!"

I figured if the "after-death experiences" described by Kubler-Ross were for real, somebody in the Bay Area must have had them. I began looking for psychics, medics and patients who had stories to tell. The first psychic I called was Sylvia Browne, whom I had met the year before. She had done a "reading" of me — an impressive one — and some of her predictions about me were still unfolding.

That first meeting in 1975 was long before Sylvia became a network star. At that time, she was doing psychic readings out of her home in Campbell, near San Jose. Anita Bryant, another producer in the station's Community Affairs Department, had set up an appointment with her, and at the last minute asked me to go with her, saying she was too nervous to see the psychic by herself. I had always been fascinated by ESP and psychic phenomena, so I was glad to tag along. My arrival at Sylvia Browne's office was a surprise

204    *The Munchkin Diary*

to her, so I don't see how she could have known anything about me. But when Anita asked Sylvia to demonstrate what she could do, Sylvia looked right at me and said, "I'll demonstrate my readings with you," referring to me. "You're like an open book."

She then proceeded to describe my first husband, and our marriage that had ended the year before, our children, our house, our dog, the man I was involved with at that moment, and she went even further. "This man is not good for you; he has too many scars. He will be gone by Christmas. But there is a husky, dark-haired man who will come into your life next year. The man you're with now will want to come back, but by then you will be able to tell him to keep on going."

When she said the words, "husky, dark-haired man," the image of one of the guys upstairs in the newsroom came to my mind, but I didn't know anything about him, except that his name was Craig Scheiner and he made beautiful, handcrafted jewelry in his spare time. I didn't realize his image flashing through my mind in that split second was a sneak preview of what would happen over the next several months.

The next spring, I was a news reporter making my first production calls for the *Life After Life* series, and Sylvia's predictions began to come true. Jack and I had indeed broken up just before Christmas, and by spring the chemistry between Craig and me was undeniable.

I still couldn't believe it, however. Falling in love with him broke all my main rules: 1) he was still living with his first wife, albeit very unhappily; 2) he was years younger than I was; and 3) I really did not want an office romance — they're just too complicated and tend to be more public than private.

But all that reasoning didn't make the butterflies go away whenever Craig walked near me, and it didn't make my head stop spinning when he accidentally (or not so accidentally) brushed against me when we worked together. In fact, Craig and I worked together every chance we got. We were falling in love, although neither of us had spoken of it, nor had we done anything about it up to that point. This was April, almost a year after Sylvia had turned to me and said, "I'll demonstrate by reading *you*."

Everything fell into place for the production of a strong five-part series. Doctors and nurses at Alta Bates Hospital in Berkeley not only had witnessed many technical deaths and then revivals, but they also willingly told their stories to our camera, and then put the resources of the hospital at our disposal. Craig smeared Vaseline on his camera lens to shoot mystical-looking re-enactments of deaths and returns in the operating and emergency room. They even had Craig lie on a gurney with his camera shooting up at their concerned faces as they rushed him down the hospital hallway from the ER to the OR.

Sylvia put us in touch with ghost-chaser and author Antoinette May, who set us up for a shoot at an old home in Atherton where one of the previous owners had died last century and allegedly still hung around. We took Sylvia out there and filmed as she located the spirit and talked him "over to the other side.'"

The series was fun for some of our friends and co-workers at Channel 2, and they eagerly volunteered to participate in both a séance and a past-life regression, two psychic phenomena I wanted to include in our series.

The séance went very well — people validated several *hits* Sylvia's spirit guide reported to her during the half-hour session. But the regressions bogged down. Sylvia managed to hypnotize a couple of associates from the station, and even got them to travel back to their moment of birth, but they were not able go through the "tunnel" and into their previous lives. We spent a couple of frustrating days taking people all the way from Oakland to Campbell and filming the first stage, but we weren't able to find anyone who could regress into a previous life. The news director was getting anxious about the amount of time we were spending because time was money and he began worrying about his budget. I felt strongly that in order to have any credibility for me or our viewers, the subject in the regression had to be someone I personally knew, not someone Sylvia found for us.

On our third trip to Campbell for the regression, and our third failure to get past the moment of birth, I was ready to dump the regression from the series. Then Sylvia said she had the solution to the problem. "You do it," she said, looking right at me. "You could do it," she added confidently.

"But Sylvia," I argued, "I'm the reporter, not the story. And I don't want to be the story. That's not my style. This is not a series about Betty Ann Bruno experimenting with psychic phenomena."

Sylvia insisted, "You could tell the story of a regression from the inside out. Your other option is to let me regress one of my staff members. I could arrange to do that. But I think it would be very strong if you did it yourself. It would also *make* the series, because a regression to past lives is usually very dramatic."

I agreed to do it, although I still had no idea what to expect since I hadn't witnessed one yet. Sylvia turned out to be right on all counts. I was an easy subject to hypnotize, and I went sailing right past the moment of birth into another world. Craig shot the whole thing on film — two hours of my visit to not *one*, but *two* previous lives.

Both episodes were sad, but the first also involved Craig. I didn't want anyone to know Craig and I were having, or were about to have — or in another life, *had* had — a relationship. I certainly didn't want to say anything about it on TV. I didn't even want anybody in the newsroom to know, so I didn't say anything about it at the time.

But I can tell the whole story now.

Sylvia placed me in a comfortable lounge chair in a reclining position with my feet up. She sat in an upright chair to my right just behind me and operated an audio tape recorder of the entire session. Craig moved freely around the room, shooting and recording from whatever angle he wanted.

"Now Betty Ann," Sylvia began, in a soothing, monotone, "I want you to relax, empty your mind of thoughts and concentrate on the black and silver pinwheel you see on the table in front of you." A few minutes later, I entered the strange state of hypnosis, a state in which I was aware of being in the room with Sylvia and Craig but also felt my mind drifting back in time.

She talked me all the way back through my life until I was a baby about to be born, and then I found myself going through a tunnel and emerging in bright, clear air on the other side. I was definitely flying.

"Do you see anything?"

"Yes, I see some woods and a wagon being pulled by some horses going through the woods."

"Who is in the wagon?"

"Oh, my children. They are my children. Three or four of them. They are all very young, and they are all dead. I'm also in the wagon. No, I'm floating along just above the wagon, looking down at all my dead children. I think I'm dead too, or maybe dying. Sometimes I float above the wagon, and sometimes I am lying in the bed of the wagon. I feel so sad."

"Do you know what happened to your children?"

"They were all killed by the Indians. And the Indians burned our cabin. We had a cabin in the woods."

"Who else is there?"

"My husband is driving the wagon, taking me and my children

to safety or at least to a place where he can bury us."

I realized my husband in the regression was Craig Scheiner, grimly and stoically facing ahead while pressing the team of horses down the road to the West. He was wearing a dark brown buckskin jacket with fringe on the shoulders and sleeves. Oddly, however, part of my brain told me not to say that out loud. This is where those two areas of consciousness seemed clearly defined: I knew I was in Sylvia Browne's office under hypnosis, and I knew Craig was filming everything I said. I did not want to say he was my husband in the regression because I did not want the people in the newsroom to hear that. I didn't even want *him* to hear that. Mainly for that reason, but also because that life was one of such a heavy enveloping sadness, I didn't want to stay there. Sylvia sensed it and asked me if I wanted to leave that life and look for another one.

"Yes, let me go from here." And I went up into the clear blue air and felt again the sensation of flying quite high above the ocean.

"Do you see anything?"

"Yes, I see an island down there."

"Do you want to go there?"

"Yes, it's a beautiful green island in the tropics. There's a tall, sharp mountain peak, all steep and green, and I am going to land at the base of it."

"Are you there now?"

"Yes, I am here at the base of the mountain."

"Can you describe yourself?"

"I am a young girl, my clothes are very dirty and ragged and oh, my arms hurt. Oh dear, my arms are gone from just below my elbows. They're both gone! And I've been brought here to die, away from the village." Again, I had the sensation of two separate consciousnesses. One in the present with Craig filming everything I said, and the other there, on that tropical island. The *me* on the tropical island knew I had leprosy, and that I had been exiled from the village and sent to the foot of the mountain to die. An old man from the village walked by on the edge of the clearing and looked over at me. I knew in that moment he was my father in this life, even though he didn't physically look like my dad. He was checking up on me — although he didn't speak to me, nor I to him — but I knew he was concerned about me and didn't want me to suffer. I was also not willing to say the word "leprosy" out loud on film — on TV that would be odd, I thought, but that's what was going on in my head. Two stories playing at the same time.

"How old are you?"

"I'm 14. My name is Mele. Oh, my arms hurt a lot."

"Can you go forward in time. Can you go to the next year?"

"Yes. Oh, my dress is all beautiful and white, and I'm not dirty anymore. And my arms don't hurt! I'm still here at the foot of the mountain, but I'm all whole and perfect. I think I died and now everything is perfect, but I'm still here."

"Do you want to go to the village? Can you fly?"

"Yes, I can fly. I can go to the village." The next instant, I was hovering over a small fishing village on the shore of the island. There were people in the waves on their canoes, their backs glistening with droplets of ocean water and they weren't aware of me. I could see my mother taking care of several other children, my brothers and sisters. Life was just going on in what seemed like a very normal way on the island. Nothing dramatic was happening.

"Would you like to come back now, or do you want to visit another life?"

"I'd like to come back now. "

She brought me out of the hypnosis. I had been under for almost two hours. I was exhausted. Craig went into the other room to change film. I seized the moment to have a private word with Sylvia.

"Sylvia, in the first regression I couldn't say it out loud, but Craig was my husband in that life! What does that mean?"

"Well, you have been together before."

"But he's married, Sylvia! He still lives with his wife!"

"Yes, I know, but they haven't really been married for more than a couple of years. They are only married on paper. Don't be afraid of him. He will make you a very good partner in time, when he outgrows a few things. Don't worry, you're not breaking up his marriage. It has been gone for a long time."

Oh, my gawd. Now I had all these threads in my life, or *lives*, and just what I did not want to happen was happening. How was I going to sort all these things out to get something on the air, and still maintain a level of honesty and candor about my experience? I needed some time to think it through.

In the meantime, I felt more strongly attracted to Craig than ever. Now there was something cosmic about it. Was it possible we had been together in previous lives? Was it true our souls were traveling through time together, intertwined in such a way that each of our lives here on Earth would always involve the other? Was there any validity even in the regression? Was it just an illusion? Did that mean we were destined to be together? That was a romantic notion, and I am nothing if not a romantic. In my heart of hearts, I believed we did belong together. Otherwise, nothing made sense.

We spent that night —- our first — together. Craig apparently had been anticipating it, because he had a candle that he lit by the side of his bed. He was young, virile and very romantic, and I was ready for romance. The night passed quickly, uninterrupted by thoughts of how in the world I was going to put together a piece that could go on *The 10 O'clock News*.

I decided to let the regression percolate for a few days so I could sort out exactly what had happened, but I found I couldn't really figure it out by any scientific method. There was no way to search for documentation of either of my *past lives,* and I didn't want to use the pioneer life on the air anyway. It was just too profoundly sad. It had no entertainment value.

In thinking about the other one, I couldn't decide if that was the way a previous-life regression was supposed to go. It had certain dream-like aspects because it involved people from this life (my father, for example). And what about the sensation of knowing I was under hypnosis at the same time I was experiencing the other life. My arms continued to ache for some time after I woke up from my 'leprosy' affliction. Ultimately, the experience was immensely interesting and powerful, but I couldn't say with certainty whether I had really visited previous lives, or had simply had a couple of interesting dreams under hypnosis.

The *Life After Life* series ran in five parts, with a segment playing each consecutive night. The pieces were breaking the rules for local news stories because they were running for about five minutes each, when the broadcast rule was no more than two minutes in length. The formula for the news show included the long-established pace — stories of up to 90 seconds, with 10- to 20-second introductions by the anchors. The belief was, if you inserted a five-minute or longer piece, you would break the pace and ruin the show. It simply wasn't done. Producers were adamant and unanimous in their protection of the pace.

Ted Kavanau, the news director at the time, had his own rule: If it holds up, run it for as long as it needs to run. Try as I did, I couldn't fit the regression into even a five-minute slot. Certain phases were mandatory. I had to have Sylvia Browne explaining what to expect in a regression. I had to have her putting me under. I had to have me going through the tunnel to the other side, finding the island, identifying myself, describing my arms, moving forward in time, discovering I was dead and flying to the village.

Each one of those elements took time because, under hypnosis, I spoke very slowly, in a little girl's voice, and the precious minutes ticked by. The editor and I hacked and hacked away at the film and finally couldn't find any more to cut out. Anticipating his response with dread, I went to the news director with the bottom-line timing.

"WHAT!" he thundered. "Eleven minutes! Are you kidding? Eleven minutes is an entire section of the broadcast. You can't have that. Nobody has ever had an entire section before. It's not possible! It'll ruin the pacing. Cut it DOWN!"

He roared past me, swooped through the newsroom, grabbed up Anchorman Dennis Richmond and marched to the editing bays. On the way, Dennis agreed it was absurd to even consider an 11-minute report. What in the world was I thinking? Both of them huffed into the tiny bay and announced they were going to cut the story considerably. Making myself as small as I could, I squeezed into a corner so I could take notes on the parts they would order cut.

With a practiced hand, the editor cranked the film reels while Ted and Dennis watched in silence. I kept waiting for something to write down, but neither one of them said anything. They watched the entire piece without uttering a word. When it was over they stood in silence, still staring at the small viewing window that was now just a square of light.

"You can't cut it," said Ted. "It holds up. It's an amazing report. Run it."

So, it lived — for a record-breaking 11 minutes. The following spring, the series won an Emmy for best feature series on the news.

Craig and I became a couple and four years later, a married couple. I have listened again to the audiotape of the regression a few times over the years, and I am still not sure what it was. But I am convinced it was more than just a dream.

Craig and I had been together about 10 years when he decided we should take a trip to Tahiti. "You have to go there," he announced. "It's where your Hawaiian ancestors came from."

"But Craig, look at the prices in these brochures. It would cost a fortune. We can't afford a vacation like that."

"Yes, we can," he insisted. "Just leave it to me. I'll make all the arrangements. I want to take you there." So we went to French Polynesia for three glorious weeks, the best vacation I have ever had. It was the *most* in all ways: definitely the most expensive, but also the most luxurious, the most fun, the most relaxing, the most spiritual, and the most astounding.

As our plane turned and banked in its descent for landing on the island of Bora Bora, I pressed my face to the window and got my first glimpse of Otemanu, the volcanic peak that forms the steep center of the island. I was so excited my heart was pounding and then I gasped, "Oh, my God! I know that mountain. That's the same peak that was in my regression 10 years ago. That's where I was, at the foot of that mountain. That's where I died of leprosy. Oh, my God!" The realization literally took my breath away.

Craig had reserved a cottage at the luxurious Hotel Bora Bora, right on the sandy beach that stretches the length of the island's picturesque lagoon. The geography of Bora Bora is simple. The island is very small, a few miles in circumference via the main road. Otemanu rises sharply in the approximate center. It is what remains of one of the sides of the volcano that rose from the ocean's depths long ago. Otemanu, with its rich lava soil, is now covered with lush trees, shrubs and vines, and its lower slopes form a wreath of land upon which Tahitians and French residents have built houses and small settlements. You can see both Otemanu and the ocean from every point on Bora Bora.

Every day, we would bicycle into the little town to buy fresh papayas, mangoes, cheese and bread for our midday picnic on the beach, and every day I would look up a side road seeming to lead to the foot of the mountain. Each time, I would think, "While I'm here, I really ought to go up there to the foot of that mountain and meditate upon my past-life regression, see if I can get in touch with the part of me that emerged in that session." But the days went by, pleasantly and sweetly, and I didn't seem to get around to making the trip up the road to the foot of the mountain.

When we weren't sightseeing, I was either lazing in one of the hammocks that swung between the coconut palms on the beach, or swimming with the colorful fish living amidst the rock and coral formations in the clear blue water of the lagoon. I spent so much of that week underwater, I recognized several individual fish and knew where they hung out.

A young French couple, who had lived on the island for many years, befriended us and made us feel very welcome. Alan and Linda owned a boutique where they made a comfortable living selling beautiful, hand-painted clothes Linda designed and created. We met them our first day on the island, and Linda immediately took us under her wing.

"You're part Hawaiian, aren't you?" she asked, as soon as we walked into the shop. "I really like Hawaiians. Tell me about yourself. Would you like a cup of coffee? Come on in the back and let's talk. I really like Hawaiians."

We sat in her workshop in the back, surrounded by bolts of sheer white fabric and shelves of textile paints and brushes, while I tried to answer her questions about the Hawaiian Islands and my ancestors.

"We really don't like tourists," she said. "They're all so boring. They never know anything. Poor Alan has had to deal with them so much because he ran the Club Med here in Bora Bora for a while. And before him, his father managed the Club. Ugh. Tourists. But you're different. You're Hawaiian. That's good."

She invited us to tour the island with them the next day. As we circumnavigated Bora Bora in their Jeep, they told us stories of the people who lived in that island paradise. At the end of the day, when they dropped us off at our hotel, they invited us to dinner at their home so we could meet the friends they had told us about.

"Betty Ann, you have to meet Miriami. You will just love her. She is a real Tahitian. Her family has been here for generations. You will really like her. I can't wait for you to meet her."

The dinner party was lovely. It was a hot sticky night, but the iced rum drinks went down easily, and everybody was dancing. We had a good time, and I met Miriami, an attractive woman, tall and brown, who I guessed was about 50-something. She had a head full of curly black hair pulled back from the strong features of her face. As she talked with us and the other guests, her eyes — deep-set and dark — seemed to see right through any protective mask or artifice anyone was hiding behind. "Before you leave, you must come and visit me," she said, but left it vague. It seemed like a comment only out of courtesy. It wasn't a specific invitation with time and place, so I didn't think much about it.

Our last day on the island, I swam to all the now-familiar rocks and coral formations and said goodbye to the yellow tangs and angel fish I had gotten to know that week. Packing was the only other thing on our agenda that day. As I was coming in from the lagoon, I saw Craig up on the beach. What *had* been on my mind was, now we could go back to the cottage and start packing. But when I got to Craig, what I said was, "Craig, I have to go see Miriami."

Without hesitation or question, he said, "Okay, you go ahead. I can start packing. I can see you need to go."

I didn't know what he could see, but I accepted his offer, exchanged my wet bathing suit for a dry *pareau*, jumped on one of the hotel bikes and headed out to the road. Then it hit me — I had no idea where Miriami's house was. But I quickly thought Linda and Alan must know where she lived, and I wanted to say goodbye to them anyway, so I went to see them. They gave me directions to Miriami's house, which — surprising on one hand but not on the psychic level — was at the foot of Otemanu, up that road I had seen the first day. But that's not all.

Miriami lived in the house I had drawn plans for when I was 20 years old — a sprawling, one story home with light, airy rooms around an inner courtyard full of orchids, ferns and ginger. As she took me around, I could hardly believe what I was seeing. It was my dream house in real life. I loved everything she had done in the house and garden. She showed me all around and I took it all in. And then we walked way out, deep into the back yard.

"That's where they filmed the re-do of the movie *Hurricane* in 1979," she said, pointing to the corner of her five-acre property at the foot of the mountain.

"Are you kidding? *Hurricane?*" I asked, totally astounded. "Miriami, did you know I was in the first *Hurricane* with Dorothy Lamour and Jon Hall?" I was almost giddy with the coincidences, and then Miriami led me to my third big surprise.

We went to the most ancient and sacred part of her family land, the *marae*, or Tahitian place of prayer and sacrifice. It was a small plot, bare of foliage, rectangular in shape and defined by a border of lava rocks.

"It used to be all rocks," Miriami explained, "but they took most of them to build the road out front. They only left a few to mark the place. At least they left the main stone." She pointed to a vertical rock, like a headstone, sticking out of the dirt on the far side. It was very much like the large *marae* Craig and I had visited on other islands, so I was curious about this one and wanted a closer look at the altar stone.

I stepped over the border of lava rocks separating the *marae* from the surrounding garden and started walking toward the stone. I didn't get far though, only a couple of steps, when I was seized with a horrible and frightening sensation. I felt I was being drawn downward into the earth. My legs suddenly got very heavy, leaden, and I had to cross my arms over my chest to protect myself against an intense chill. I had felt this sensation before, at an amusement park in the centrifugal machine that spins you round and round and pins you against the wall, and you can't move your arms or legs. You're just suspended there, feeling pressure in every part of your being. That's exactly the way I felt now, except the pressure was downward instead of backward. I felt if I didn't get away from there right away, I would be pressed downward into the earth and might never be able to come back up again. I felt my breath leaving me. I was getting dizzy. "Miriami!" I yelled, "I'm sinking! Help me!"

"Get off that! Come back here!" she shouted as she grabbed one of my arms and pulled me off the *marae*.

"Oh my God, thank you!" I said, as I rubbed my arms back to warmth. I looked down at them to see my skin covered with goose bumps. "That was really scary. Thank you."

"Let's get away from here! Let's go have a cup of tea." Mariami had my upper left arm in a strong grip, steering me back toward the house.

Suddenly, I felt the need to tell Miriami about the past-life regression. I wanted to tell her about how I had leprosy and had been exiled to this place to die. I wanted to tell her about how I had lived in a fishing village not far away, and that I had roots here too, just like she did.

But, as I began describing the past-life regression, Miriami just frowned and shook her head. "No, no. I don't believe in any of that stuff. That's all a lot of hooey. But you know, you should tell Linda.

She believes in all that kinda' stuff. Tell Linda."

"Tell Linda," I repeated dully. Thoughts raced through my head trying to connect Linda with Miriami, with me, with the little girl in my past-life regression.

"Maybe that's why Linda wanted me to meet you. Do you think she sensed something? Do you think she knew something? And if it wasn't connected to that other life, what was it? It was something real. I didn't imagine it. I really felt the pull into the earth."

"Well, it might have been Henry."

"Who?"

"Henry — my husband. He's buried right over there, and sometimes he comes out and bothers people. Don't pay any attention to it."

We went into the kitchen and had a calming pot of tea. She didn't want to talk about spirits or ghosts. I thought it was pretty strange for her to say she didn't believe in the spirit world, and then tell me her dead husband pops out and pesters people every once in a while. But I was her guest and wasn't about to start an argument, so we just chatted about flowers and gardens some more and, when I regained my composure, I took my leave. "This has been very special to me," I told Miriami. "You can never know how much this visit to your home has meant to me. I will remember you always."

"And I, you. You know, you are my sister." And she gave me a warm hug.

"Thank you. I've never had a sister, but if I did I would want her to be you. I hope we see each other again."

Both Miriami and Linda came to the airport early the next morning to see us off. We all smiled cheerily and promised to send each other lots of letters. The conversation did not touch on what I considered the most significant event of the week.

I don't know if they thought about me afterwards. I hope so. I wrote to each of them a couple of times but didn't get a response, and it is true what they say about time and distance. One goes on with other things in life but, every once in a while, I reflect upon that time and place. And I think, yes, that was real. That past-life regression was real, and Craig knew to take me there so I could prove it for myself. He had been in the other regression, and he is in this life, but how did he know about that one?

I have wondered what would happen if I went back to meditate at the foot of that mountain? Would I find out some answers if I did?

But I haven't gone back, and I probably won't. If it is a memory from another life, I think it belongs with that other life. And I belong here in this world, in this time. This is where I need to concentrate on being. Still, I feel extremely fortunate to have had a peek through a tiny window to another time, to another experience, which now I know was not just a dream.

# CHAPTER 17

# AUNTIE MARIA'S MIRACLE

## DID THE SHARKS DO IT?

T his story may be hard to believe, but I know it's true because Auntie Maria told it to me herself, and Auntie Maria never lied. Besides, I saw the newspaper clipping about what happened, and right there in the article was a picture of her while she was still in the hospital after the rescue.

Auntie Maria (pronounced Mariah, like the wind) lived with Uncle Tony in a ramshackle homestead in Hilo, Hawai`i. Good and honest folk, they raised their own kids, plus a large number of foster kids who flowed through the household over the years. From the street, the funky old house with its galvanized tin roof didn't hint that it was a haven, a cultural center and the heartbeat of a family. The living room had long ago given up its role as a place to entertain guests — too many kids needed beds. After the bedrooms filled up with cots and bunks, the dining room and living room got second careers. No one slept in the kitchen, but when the small kitchen inside could no longer contain the food preparation for so many people, kitchen functions moved outside, under what was originally the car porch. The family cooked, ate and hung out together in the back, around two or three Formica-topped tables surrounded by two dozen chairs that didn't even pretend to match each other.

Auntie Maria and Uncle Tony never had much money, but that

didn't stop them from always having enough food for anybody who stopped by to visit. A big pot of something was always cooking on the big cast iron stove, poi was in a big bowl on the table and rice was always ready in the cooker.

Auntie Maria greeted everyone who entered her home with, "Come, sit, eat," as she ushered a visitor to the table. A plate would appear from nowhere and you would find yourself enjoying pork neck and cabbage soup, or chicken and luau. Meals were simple but always enough to feed whoever dropped in. After the mandatory meal, and talk about how you and your family were, Auntie Maria's ukulele would come out and she'd start the sing-along. She had a huge repertoire of songs — campy *haole* songs as well as Hawaiian. She knew hundreds of lyrics by heart, although I don't remember ever seeing a songbook in her house; she seemed to absorb songs from the air she breathed. Mostly she sang ballads, but once in a while she'd toss her head back, wink, and sing a wicked little ditty. One of her favorites was about the "*Rubba ele ele.*" She only grinned and wagged her finger at me when I asked her what a "*rubba ele ele*" was, so I can't tell you exactly what it means. You'll just have to imagine it for yourself, like I did.

Uncle Tony kept pigs on some land, thankfully away from the homestead. He fed them with the stuff he picked up on his route as the local garbage man. Uncle Tony was proud of the way he fed his pigs. In the farthest corner of the homestead, he set up a big cauldron he had created from a 50-gallon oil drum. It sat on a stand of rocks and rebar high enough to stoke a fire underneath — a fire hot enough to boil 50 gallons of nourishing, germ-free swill soup for his sows. "Always boil your pigs' swill," he told me as he stirred the odoriferous stew with a long two-by-four. "That way, they won't get sick. You never know what's in other people's garbage!" I nodded in agreement and wondered what was there about Uncle Tony that gave dignity to stirring hot swill.

I first met Uncle Tony and Auntie Maria when I was 14 years old. My mother took my brother and me to Hawai`i during summer vacation to introduce us to the Hawaiian side of our family. It was her first time back to the Islands in more than 10 years. She had left with two toddlers and returned with two teenagers. As far as our Island cousins were concerned, our 10 years in California had turned us into "mainlanders" or *malihini*. "You talk different, Cuz," they pointed out, "more like *haole*." They put up with us anyway, took us surfing and taught us the pleasures of eating sugar cane right in the field where it grew.

During our month in Hilo, we stayed at Tutu Maria's house. Tutu Maria was Auntie Maria's mom and lived in a two-story gray house on Kino`ole Street. The job of taking us around to see the sights fell to Uncle Tony and Auntie Maria because all the other relatives were tied up with regular 9-to-5 jobs.

Auntie Maria and Uncle Tony drove us all over the Big Island in their ancient Woodie station wagon. Its creaks and groans accompanied our singing as we bounced along the mostly-gravel roads on our way to the Black Sands Beach, the Parker Ranch, the volcano, the City of Refuge and Rainbow Falls. Uncle Tony and Auntie Maria knew everybody everywhere and caught up on all the local news as we stopped here and there to buy treats — fresh coconut pies, sweet potato fritters, sushi cones and shave-ice with sweet black beans. Actually, what I wanted most was a mango, but they told me June was a little too early — that mango season started in July.

The day we were at the Black Sands Beach, however, Uncle Tony spied a ripe mango high up in a tree, and he shinnied right up that mango tree to bring back the most beautiful orange fruit with a red blush over one fragrant side. "If she wants mango, she should have a real Hawaiian one" he explained to my mother as he handed me the prize. "Better than you can get in the stores." And was it ever! As I slurped through it, the juice ran through my fingers, down my hands and arms and then dripped into the sand. It was the mango of a lifetime, chewing was optional. I can still taste that flavor, though more than six decades have passed since that day on the beach.

Several years later, after I had married and had kids of my own, Uncle Tony and Auntie Maria visited us in Oakland. Their trip was a gift to them from friends all over the mainland who took turns hosting them, a kind of payback for all the hospitality those friends had enjoyed at the family table in the back in Hilo.

It was Uncle Tony and Auntie Maria's first visit to the mainland, and it turned out to be the only trip they would ever make here. My husband Russ and I felt privileged to take them sightseeing in San Francisco. At Fisherman's Wharf, we ate shrimp salads at Grotto #9 while we watched the fishing fleet. We inhaled steaming crab pots, wound down Lombard's crooked curves and rode a cable car. We had a long list of places to take them, but on the second morning of their visit we had to cancel our *holo holo* because, during the night, our hot water heater had burst and flooded the basement.

"Oh!" I wailed "What are we going to do? We just can't show you around today. We've got this mess on our hands."

Russ and I went to Sears and spent the morning picking out another hot water heater. It was past noon before we were back home with our new heater in the back of our pickup truck. For the rest of the day, Uncle Tony, with a pipe wrench in one hand and a beer in the other, helped Russ dismantle the old heater and install the new one. Actually, I think Russ was more the helper, because Uncle Tony was the experienced plumber.

That evening, as we barbecued chicken in our own back yard, we apologized again for the emergency we were sure had spoiled their vacation day. Uncle Tony grinned and said, "Not a bit. This has been the best day of our trip so far. For one month now I have felt *useless*. No one has let us do anything. Everyone has waited on us as though we were *cripples*. Today, I finally feel again I'm good for something. Thank you! I'm sorry about the flood in your basement, but for me it was a great day."

The last time I saw both of them was in 1981. Their lives seemed pretty much the same as they'd been before. In fact, Uncle Tony was still driving his 1960-something Pontiac station wagon, except now it had 300,000 miles on it, maybe twice that. Its springs were shot, and the upholstery was a faded "uncolor," but the engine purred and no one doubted the car would get you where you wanted to go and back again. "It's changing the oil every 1,000 miles," Uncle Tony confided. "That keeps it running smooth."

Craig and I were in Hilo that spring to do some filming for Channel 2 on *The Aloha Spirit*, a five-part news feature on Hawaiian culture. Hilo's Merrie Monarch Festival included three days of dance competition and seemed like a good way to look at the hula as a force for revival of Hawaiian culture. We also wanted to include a segment about Auntie Maria and Uncle Tony, because their lives epitomized the Aloha Spirit of giving without needing to get anything in return. This loving couple, though living on the edge of poverty, had enriched so many lives. They gave freely and endlessly gifts of time and love. That is real aloha. Auntie Maria, in her soft, calm voice, shared her philosophy of raising so many foster children. "All they have to do is their little chores, pick up their things and make their beds. That's all. We are all family. This is home whenever they need it."

Another powerful force on the Island of Hawai`i is Pele, the volcano goddess. Myths and legends about her are still vivid and powerful today because they provide explanations for the inexplicable.

We wanted to include stories about Pele in our feature series, and show the influence she still exerts over the lives and beliefs of people with Hawaiian blood.

Auntie Maria knew all the Pele myths and was also a good storyteller. She knew where and when the volcano goddess had appeared and to whom, and she could tell you what fate they met if they didn't treat Pele well, or were stingy, mean or disrespectful. One of her stories was about a popular band that refused a request for a certain number from a raggedy old lady who suddenly appeared at one of their concerts. "Within a year," Auntie Maria told us, "every member of that band was dead. Uh-huh. Every one of them!" She nodded her head, affirming the facts of her story. "One got sick, another had an accident, something happened to each one of them. All gone. No one left. Hard to explain. It could be a coincidence, but a lotta Hawaiians say it was because they showed disrespect for the *Lady*. People say she was Pele. You know, Pele comes sometimes dressed in rags, like a poor old lady."

Auntie Maria also told stories about other gods, and *aumakua* (guardian angels) who watch over Hawaiians. One of Auntie Maria's favorite *aumakua* subjects was sharks, and she had many stories of rescues by sharks. To be clear — that's *by* sharks, not *from* sharks.

One of her stories was about some promoters of a shark shoot in a bay famous for a high shark count. Their plan was to chum up the sharks by floating cow carcasses in the water. The shark hunters could sit on the shore and fire away. All the promoters had to do was get the hunters there. Nature would provide the shooting range and the live targets. Easy. And it might even have worked had it not been for *aumakua*.

According to Auntie Maria's story, on the day of the shark shoot, dozens of *haole* hunters who had paid a lot of money to the promoters for the privilege of this "unique opportunity," arrived at dawn to stake out their vantage points on the shores around the bay. Several cow carcasses were towed out to the middle of the bay. All the hunters had to do was wait for the sharks to come in for the feeding frenzy, and — BAM, BAM — the fun would begin. The hunters popped some beers and waited. Then popped some more. And waited some more. The sun rose higher and higher in the sky. The cow carcasses bobbed up and down like so many navigational buoys. Midday was hot and the beer wasn't helping much anymore. The sharks did not show up. As the sun began its afternoon descent, the shark hunters started shooting at the cow carcasses. Not as much fun as shooting at live sharks would have been but then — what the heck, it was better 'n nothin'.

No one saw a shark at all that day in that bay. Not a single dorsal fin. The hunters riddled the cow carcasses until the beer and ammo ran out. Then they left, grumbling, "Paid good money to come and shoot sharks. They promised us sharks and all we got were dead cows! What a gyp!"

The distraught promoters, beset with demands for refunds, tried to figure out what had gone wrong. This *was* the right bay. They had come here themselves to verify these waters teemed with sharks that came in by the hundreds twice a day to feed. Where then were they today? What had happened?

What the promoters did not know was that the sharks were the *aumakua* for the Hawaiian families who lived around the bay — that is, the sharks were their protectors — and everyone could recite the times when sharks had rescued kids caught in treacherous currents, were in danger of being pulled out to sea or dashed on the rocks.

What the locals knew, and the promoters didn't, was that the day before the shoot, an old man from the village had sat on the shores of the bay and told the sharks all about the promoters. He told them about the cow carcasses, he told them about the hunters and their high-powered rifles with the telescopic sights, and he told the sharks, "Stay away, no matter how tempting the smell of cow's blood in the water is." And that's exactly what the sharks did. It seems only fair the power of *aumakua* works both ways.

Auntie Maria said she didn't know if sharks were the heroes in the story about her own rescue at sea, but they might have been. That rescue happened on March 6, 1972, when Auntie Maria went fishing on the other side of the island at Malama, in Kalapana district. She wanted a particular kind of fish that could only be found offshore there, more than an hour's drive from Hilo. Sheer cliffs formed one side of an area of ancient *ponds* in the sea, the only place where this small fish thrived. Hawaiians highly prized this delicacy and, in the old days, village fishermen could reach the sea ponds by boat. Auntie Maria and Uncle Tony, however, did not have a boat, so they had to use the only other access — the cliffs. The cliffs were steep and dangerous and rose straight up from the rocky shore below. The area is on the south shore of Hawai'i, inside the national park that surrounds the island's volcanoes. In the 1970s, there was no guard rail at the edge of the cliffs, so the park service posted the cliffs off-limits. Park rangers would have liked everybody to stay away from the cliffs, but local Hawaiians were exempt from the rule so they could catch their traditional little fish for special occasions.

To fish those cliffs, you had to stand on the edge and drop a very long line down to the surf more than a hundred feet away. Auntie Maria went with her daughter and her son. Uncle Tony didn't go with them because he had business in Hilo that day, but the expedition started out well and the ice chest was filling up nicely.

After a couple of hours, the daughter realized she hadn't seen her mother for a while. She thought maybe her mother had gone back to the car to rest. But, when her brother told her the car was empty, they both began to worry. They called out for their mother but got no answer. They put down their poles and began running back and forth along the edge of the cliffs and then to the car. "Mom! Mom! Where are you? Ma-ahm. Ma-ahm." No answer. Over and over again and again. They searched and called some more. Nothing.

There was no phone booth near the cliffs because people rarely went there, and in 1972 cell phones did not exist. Choking back tears and panic, the two concluded their mother had fallen over the cliff. They jumped in the car and sped to the ranger station 20 long minutes away. A call to Hilo Search and Rescue immediately put a fire truck on the road and a helicopter in the air. Uncle Tony went racing out in his Pontiac station wagon, but many precious minutes ticked by before any rescue vehicles arrived at the cliffs.

After another hour or so of anguished and futile searching and calling, the family reluctantly and mournfully concluded Auntie Maria was gone. There was no point in their staying any longer at the cliffs. No one had ever survived the fall from the cliffs into the surf below. Totally despondent, Uncle Tony and the two kids sadly and slowly got back into the cars and headed back to Hilo. When they got home, the phone was ringing. "She's safe," the caller told them. "The helicopter crew picked her up and they're headed to the hospital right now." Later that evening, when the family saw Auntie Maria at the Hilo Community Hospital, she had a broken toe and was a bit soggy, but otherwise was unhurt. The chopper crew had found her more than a mile south of the cliffs from which she had fallen.

**This is the rescue team's story:**

> We searched up and down the shore from the point on the cliffs where the lady had been fishing. We scanned the shore and the water, looking for any clue of her fate. We didn't see anything, but very gradually we became aware

we were being accompanied by a flock of white birds. The birds were not following us, but seemed to want to direct us. The birds would fly south, and then come back to the chopper. The birds would fly south again, and then come back, as though beckoning the helicopter.

Eventually, I (the pilot) decided to follow the birds. As I stated in my official report, about a mile down the coast, the birds disappeared into a cave in the cliffs. The helicopter hovered a short distance from the entrance of the cave, although we had no idea exactly why we were there. Then a woman emerged from the cave, smiled and waved. She began carefully picking her way along the boulders from the cave to the water's edge. I turned on the loudspeaker system and instructed her to swim out a little way from the cliffs so we could drop a basket to her and haul her up.

She kept shaking her head, no. At first I couldn't understand why, but finally, through gestures, I understood she couldn't swim out to a basket because she didn't know how to swim. She was the one Hawaiian who had never learned.

A crewmember got into the basket and the helicopter lowered him to the water. He paddled over to the rock, helped the lady in and they were reeled up together to the helicopter. We couldn't figure out how she got to the cave if she didn't know how to swim. Even if she survived the fall, she couldn't have walked to the cave because there's no shore to walk on; the cliffs dropped straight down into the rocks and waves. So, she could not have walked and she couldn't swim. But there she was.

### And this is Auntie Maria's story:

I remember falling, falling and then being caught gently. Something held me and carried me, but I don't know what. Maybe sharks cushioned my fall and took me to the cave — maybe dolphins. I don't think the birds carried me, although the birds were the only animals I remember seeing. I just know I was very wet when I arrived at the cave.

I gradually became aware that I was inside a lovely earthen room and white birds were flying all around me. It was warm and cozy and there was a golden glow, maybe from the birds, or maybe from the walls of the cave itself. I didn't analyze it — I just accepted it. I didn't hurt, but I looked at my clothes and thought, 'Oh, how messy, dirty. I need to wash them. I can't have anybody see me looking like this!' So I took off my clothes, rinsed them out, put them on a rock to dry and waited.

After a while the birds all left, and I just kept waiting. I don't have any idea how long I stayed in the cave, but eventually the birds came back. Then I heard the pocketa-pocketa of the helicopter engine outside. My clothes were dry enough to put back on, so I got dressed, went outside, waved to the crew and you know what happened from that point on.

**Conclusion:** So, what really happened? Why? How? Who caught her? Auntie Maria tried to figure it out and came up with, "Maybe my work here isn't finished, yet. Maybe there's something else I have to do."

If she did have more work to do, she said, she was never able to identify it as such. She died in 1984, a dozen years later, and as far as I know those years were just like all her others. My own thought is, maybe her entire life was her work here, and her miraculous rescue was just a way of Somebody saying, "Thank you for a job well done, a life well-lived. Have a few more years, on Me."

1. League (of Women Voters) Mafia. STANDING: Shirley R. Kaufman, me. SEATED: Jan Kaufman, Charnee Smit, Susan Duncan (2004).

2. Origami Crane Campaign "flyer" for my run for Oakland City Council (1971).

3. Campaign flyer showing family. CLOCKWISE FROM TOP: Steve, Russ, me, Michael, Dan.

4. Reporting from San Francisco for KTVU Channel 2.

5. On *The 10 O'clock News* set with Anchor Dennis Richmond (1980s).

6. Craig ready with his news camera (1970s).

**7.** Aerial view of Otemanu on the Island of Bora Bora.
Bora Bora (16542797633) wikicommons)

**8.** Our cutter *Ka Hale Kai*.

**9.** Craig and I looking for wind to fill our sails.

**10.** Oakland burning (October 21, 1991).

**11.** Michael *Kalani* reads his essay at our family ceremony saying thank you and goodbye to our home.

**12.** Jar of "memento ashes" that we gathered at our family's farewell ceremony for our home. Craig and I included the burned remains of his grandad's pocket watch and the end of the hose I used trying to put out the fire.

**13.** Our family looking through the ashes of our home.
LEFT BACK: Dan, his dad Russ, Michael *Kalani* looking in the safe.
FOREGROUND: Susanne (Russ's wife) and me.

**14.** The eucalyptus tree in the big intersection that became a neighborhood bulletin board after the fire. These signs were the first of many generations of signs after the fire.

**15.** Charred pages from Craig's "babybook" that son Steve found after the Firestorm.

**16.** Family photo of Dan and his two brothers to remind me "of the things *not* lost in the Firestorm." A wonderful lesson in priorities.

**17.** Four "insurance warriors" at the State Capitol in Sacramento to lobby for homeowners' reform bill (1994).

**18.** STANDING LEFT: State Senator Art Torres, author of the reform bill with homeowner-lobbyists for SB1355. FRONT: United Policyholders co-founder Amy Bach and me (1994).

**19.** Ina deLong, co-founder of United Policyholders, Sacramento (1994).

**20.** Mom and Dad on a picnic in Hawai`i (mid 1920s).

**21.** FROM TOP: My brother Everett, Auntie Maria, Uncle Tony, me and cousin Andrew (1945).

**22.** Mom in her eighties.

**23.** Auntie Maria (1945).

**24.** Ida Namanuokawa`a Wong Gonsalves in the 1950s. Pre-eminent hula dancer in Hawai`i during the 1930s and '40s, she toured with Bill Lincoln throughout the US. After moving to California, Ida taught hula in the East Bay and her troupe the Hulamanus performed Hawaiian shows throughout the state until she retired in the 1980s.

**25.** Pages of choreography from Ida's classic hulas.

**26.** In my Tahitian costume (1950s).

**27.** The Hulamanus, Ida's Dance Troupe. STANDING ROW: Ida and husband John in the center. FRONT ROW: Ida's son who sang with the group on the right, and me in the center (late 1950s).

**24.** Dancing in San Francisco's Golden Gate Park (late 1950s).

**27.** In one of Ida's shows (1971).

# HO`IKE

**30.** Blowing the conch shell signaling the beginning of Hula in the Plaza, our annual "gift of aloha" to the community of Sonoma.

**31.** Part of the lineup for *Kaulana Na Pua*, Hawai`i's protest song: LEFT TO RIGHT: Becky Zyskowski, Pam Gilberd, Wendy Shepard and Gail Ford.

**32.** Dancing *Aia La O Pele*. LEFT TO RIGHT: Celina Hall, Gail Ford, Kim Douma, Becky Zyskowski, Lynda Morley-Mott, Karyl Carter and Ava Burk.

**33.** Hula Mai dancers with *pu`ili* (a split bamboo implement). LEFT TO RIGHT: Linda Bodwell, Kim Douma, Ava Burk, Wendy Hayes, Karyl Carter, Becky Zyskowski, Pam Gilberd.

**34.** Kim Douma takes center stage in a Maori hula twirling *poi* balls. STANDING: Becky Zyskowski and Gail Ford.

**35.** Dancing *Kauohikukapulani* .
**36.** Wendy Hayes dancing *Pua Hone*.

**37.** Finishing touch to the Hawaiian War Chant with *Uli Uli* (feathered gourds). CENTER: Linda Bodwell STANDING FROM LEFT: Wendy Hayes, Gail Ford, Wendy Shepard, Becky Zyskowski, Pam Gilberd, Karyl Carter, Stephanie Brucker. KNEELING: Celina Hall and Kim Douma (faces hidden by the *Uli Uli)*.

**38.** Hula class on our deck: "masked and distanced"in the Age of Covid (October 2020).

# FIRESTORM

# CHAPTER 18

# BURNING DOWN THE HOUSE

BETTY ANN — YOUR ROOF IS ON FIRE!

Saturday, October 19, 1991, broke clear and sunny, which was not what Bay Area residents wanted to see. After five years of drought, people scanned the morning skies looking for signs of rain. But there wasn't a cloud in the sky as Craig and I packed a picnic basket and headed to the docks of the Oakland Yacht Club. Our boat, *Ka Hale Kai,* was in her slip, and our son Dan and several friends were loading provisions, getting her ready for a day on the Bay.

Soon we were all settled in the cockpit, our thermal cups brimming with hot coffee, as we motored slowly down the estuary that separates Oakland from the island of Alameda. We chatted easily, catching up on everyone's news, enjoying the calm of the protected waterway before thrusting ourselves out on the mercies of the fickle winds and currents that challenge small-boat sailors on the open waters of San Francisco Bay.

We moved past the Port of Oakland, the Army Base and Alameda's Naval Air Station. I never tired of the view of port activities and always thrilled at the sight of the tall cranes hoisting railroad-car containers from ship to shore, or vice versa. The winds remained still, and we motored around the Bay vainly searching for a breeze to fill our sails. As we chugged along the San Francisco Marina, we noticed a small column of smoke rising straight up in the air from the East Bay hills.

"Look, there's a fire over there!" Craig pointed, as he grabbed the binoculars. "Appears to be on the hill just north of the Caldecott Tunnel. Good thing there's no wind today! That hillside is like a tinderbox after all these drought years. But without wind, maybe the firefighters can get it under control fast."

"Yeah, bad for us there's no wind," I said, as I squinted to see the plume of smoke, "but good for everybody else. So, let's be thankful for that."

We spent the day motoring, drifting and basking in the sun. We were relieved when the column of smoke disappeared and the hills returned to green, interrupted only by the grays and whites of houses and a few red tile roofs.

*Ka Hale Kai*, Hawaiian for "Sea Home," was part of our retirement dream — a 37-foot, full-hulled, ocean-going cutter that was going to take us first on a test run to Mexico and then, if we liked the sailing lifestyle, we were going to cruise the Pacific Islands for a while. We had spent the previous several months refitting her for life at sea. She was looking very pretty, and we spent every free day and weekend on her.

That weekend was the middle of our two-week sailing vacation. We had just spent six days in a leisurely sail around the Bay — Richmond, Belvedere, Sausalito and South Beach in San Francisco — and were looking forward to six more days. But it was not to be. That Saturday would be our last sailing day, and our comments about fire and the wind would take on tragic meaning within the next 24 hours.

Sunday morning, October 20, we woke up to a long list of errands and chores. We had planned to sail to the Delta for a week and needed to get more supplies for the boat and get our house ready for vacating. Craig took the outside errands — tires for the car and grocery shopping. I took the inside list — laundry, watering houseplants and packing. We were full of anticipation. Even though we had sailed the Bay for more than five years, and had ventured out to the ocean several times to anchor at Half Moon Bay, Monterey and Carmel, we hadn't yet been east to the Delta, the confluence of the Sacramento and San Joaquin rivers. For sailboats and other pleasure craft, the Delta was a gigantic aquatic playground, where the joint forces of nature and man had built hundreds of miles of canals, rivers and sloughs, and we were looking forward to exploring it.

While Craig and I embarked on our day's chores, fire crews returned to the site of the previous day's fire to make sure all embers in the five-acre area were out. In wooded areas, fires can travel undetected underground, feeding on duff — layers of decomposing leaves and pine needles. As the firefighters hosed stumps and sifted through duff, a news crew from KTVU was shooting video for the evening's *10 O'clock News*. The footage would be forgotten in the horrific drama that was about to begin, but one year later that videotape would be given to me to use in the first anniversary story of the event that changed the rest of Craig's and my lives.

Up to that moment, October 20, 1991 was just another sunny day. The 49ers were going to play at Candlestick Park and their game looked like the big story for the day. A follow-up on Saturday's fire was going to be a nice little report on the mop-up, and the opportunity for yet another warning that the drought had pushed fire danger into the red zone.

Channel 2's Reporter Rob Roth and Cameraman Nick Soares arrived at the mop-up location to interview Fire Captain Donahue, who was in charge of the work. His words echoed ours from the day before. "Good thing the winds are down. If the wind were to kick up and take a spark from the duff into one of those trees, we'd have a blaze that wouldn't stop until it reached the shores of the Bay."

Thirty minutes later, dry Santa Ana winds from the east pierced the still air, picked up a swirl of sparks, threw them into a dry Monterey pine and set off what, at the time, became the worst urban wildfire in United States history. The fire would claim 25 lives and 3,000 homes before westerly winds from the Golden Gate would kick in and turn the blaze back on itself. The Firestorm would overpower everything the army of firefighters could throw at it. Oakland and Berkeley firefighters, helpless in the face of the inferno, would suffer their first humiliation of defeat, and make them realize they had to set aside petty turf battles over where the city limits were. The Firestorm was no respecter of boundaries drawn by mere mortals.

About the time Capt. Donahue was talking to Rob Roth, Craig was turning the key in the ignition to get on with his list of errands. He headed north on Highway 80 to the Price Club (now Costco) 10 miles away in Point Richmond. I went down to the basement and put the first load of dirty clothes into the washing machine. When I got back upstairs, the phone in the kitchen was ringing. Craig was calling from a payphone. "The fire from yesterday seems to have kicked up again. There's a lot of smoke on the hill — a lot of smoke. Turn on the radio to see if there's anything on the news." It was about 11 a.m. I flipped the dial to 740 AM but only heard babble about the weather and heavy traffic ahead for the 49er game.

I called our newsroom and talked to the assignment editor. "Jay, Craig just called to say the fire from yesterday looks like it's kicking up. If you need us to help out today, let us know. Even though we're on vacation, we're still in town. Call if you need extra hands!"

"Thanks, Betty Ann. We're okay. Rob and Nick are up there already and have it covered. It's a slow news day — nothing much going on except the 49er game. We're fine. Thanks for the offer though."

At 11:30 Craig called again to say he had just pulled into the store's parking lot and could see the smoke was much thicker.

Obviously, the fire was spreading rapidly. "Do you want me to come home now? I haven't gone inside yet and could head on back if you want."

"Naw," I assured him. "The fire is on the other hill, up near Grizzly Peak Boulevard. That's gotta' be five miles from here. I'm fine. Just finish what you have to do. I talked to Jay in the newsroom, and he says things are under control."

But that was no longer the case. In the half hour since I had made my first call to the newsroom, the fire had spread both up the hill and down toward the Parkwoods, a huge apartment development in Hiller Highlands. The sky was darkening, churning with yellowish-brown clouds of smoke. The winds were picking up and gusting to 60 miles per hour. I called the newsroom again. "Jay, the fire is looking pretty bad. Are you sure you don't need us to come and help? Have you got enough crews?"

"Yeah, Betty Ann. I've sent another camera up to the Parkwoods complex and Rob and Nick have hitched a ride with one of the engine companies. If I need you, I'll call you, but right now we're fine. Thanks." Within the hour Jay would call everybody on staff to come to the newsroom, but not us. We had become part of the story.

I had a good friend who lived at the Parkwoods, so I dialed her number to tell her if she needed a place to go, she could come to our house. The line was busy. I didn't realize it at the time, but that busy signal meant the lines were down. My friend, and the other 1,000 Parkwoods residents, were running for their lives as the fire swooped down the canyon toward their buildings, incinerating everything in its way. The sky was very dark and ominous now. There was a huge, deep roar everywhere. Both Oakland and Berkeley fire departments responded to the fire because the Parkwoods is close to the border separating the two cities.

I stepped into our front yard and saw a stream of cars heading down the hill from the street above ours. I thought an awful lot of people were going off to see the fire. "Voyeurs!" I snorted. I ran into Judith, my next-door neighbor, who had also come out to see what was going on. We joked about our fire-chasing neighbors. We had no idea the fire was on the other side of our hill, and that our uphill neighbors, like the Parkwoods residents, were also fleeing for their lives.

By 11 that morning, the strong winds had spread the fire's leading edge for five miles west and south from its point of origin — across an eight-lane freeway — knocked out a power substation and pushed the flames into the park around Lake Temescal. When the flames reached the steep hillside on the far side of the lake, they were fed a giant vertical scoop of dry pines, which let the deadly fire race up the hill as though roaring up a chimney.

Unaware the fire was now on our side of the freeway — and was devouring trees and homes on the hill we lived on, I went back in the house and noticed the light on our answering machine blinking. There was a message from Earl Frounfelter, the producer of *The 10 O'clock News*. He and his wife lived about six blocks down the hill from us. "Just checking to make sure you guys are okay. The fire looks nasty and now looks like it's moving in your direction. Give me a call."

Before calling him back, I ran to the dining room window and looked at the houses on the street below ours. One was on fire. I rushed back to the kitchen and dialed 911: "We are aware of the fire and have units in your neighborhood. Thank you," said the operator.

Then I started to dial Earl's number, but didn't finish because my across-the-street neighbor was yelling urgently, "Betty Ann! Betty Ann! Your roof is on fire! Betty Ann! Betty Ann! Are you there?"

I threw the phone down and ran out to the front. "Damn," I thought. "We should have moved faster getting the roof re-shingled.

Now look what's happening. Why did we go so slow?"

Angry with myself and with Craig, from the front yard I could see flames licking at our shingles. Two days earlier, we had received the third and final bid on a new roof. Ours was about five years past its life expectancy, and in that moment I believed our house had caught fire because we hadn't taken care of it. I felt terribly guilty and angry. I had also just told Craig he didn't need to come home, but that was before I knew our house was on fire. We didn't have a cell phone, and there was no way to reach him now. God. Couldn't I do anything right?

I felt scared. I didn't know what to do, but I guess I went into automatic reaction because I grabbed a garden hose, forgot my acrophobia, and climbed up onto the roof. I no sooner got up there when, suddenly, a young man appeared behind me. "Let me help you," he shouted over the roar of the wind. "Have you got a couple of crowbars? We should pull off the burning shingles and toss them into the yard, then water down the roof. Here, let me take the hose while you go look for crowbars."

I had never seen him before. I don't know where he came from or why he climbed up on my roof, but there wasn't time for explanations or introductions. I dropped off the roof, found a couple of crowbars in the garage and then remembered we had another hose on the deck off the dining room. I threw the crowbars up to my new friend on the roof and rushed out to the deck, turned the faucet on and tossed up the end of the second hose.

We worked valiantly but vainly. Our shingles were as dry as the Monterey Pines in the woods. They caught fire faster than we could pull them up and toss them into the yard. With dismay, I saw flames move along the whole west side of the roof. It was like watching the jets in a gas oven light up. We could not save the house.

My anger and disgust with myself just increased, but there

really wasn't time for self-pity, blame or anything else. People were yelling at us. We had been facing west, away from the wind. I turned around and looked in the direction of the voices. I saw a wall of fire. All the houses across the street were ablaze. A small group of firefighters was standing in the street near the corner fire hydrant. I could hear them shouting, "Lady! Get off the roof. Get out of the neighborhood! Lady! Come down!"

The words slowly registered. The good Samaritan who had been helping me jumped off the roof and disappeared. I never saw him again. I felt a clutch of panic in my stomach as I took in the rapidly spreading flames on my roof. I climbed down and ran inside the house to gather things to take with me. I moved quickly through the living room, down the hall to our bedroom, still unable to believe our house was going to burn up and I would never see it again. Stage one of grief, they say, is denial.

The small suitcase we had brought from the boat was on the bed. I opened it and carefully put my jewelry box in it, a small koa wood bowl that had been my great-grandmother's and the wooden box that held Craig's cufflinks and tie tacks. Then I carried it into the other rooms, looking for more things to take. I went right past the hall closet where we had stored a lifetime's worth of color slides and didn't even think about them.

I went into my office, looked at my computer and saw immediately it wouldn't fit into the small case. I didn't think about just taking the disks. I looked around the walls, decorated with framed photographs I had taken and was proud of but thought, nope, also too big. Next I dashed into our TV room and paused in front of the shelves containing my opera CD's. I really wanted to dump them into the case, but I thought people would laugh if they learned I rescued my opera collection and didn't take other more important things.

I left that room and rushed into the living room. Surely there were *important things* in the living room. I looked around. Paintings on the wall were important, but they were way too big to fit in the small case. The beautiful antique straw duck I had bought in China was one of my favorite things, but I thought, this was the living room for heaven's sake, the fire wouldn't dare come in here. So I left the living room without picking up anything.

"Do something, Betty Ann," I muttered as I ran back down the hall to the bedroom. I grabbed one armload of clothes from my side of the closet and one armload from Craig's side. With the half-filled case banging against my legs, I ran out to the garage to put my things in the car and leave.

It didn't occur to me to go downstairs to the secret closet where we had a safe filled with Craig's antique coin collection and my grandmother's jewelry. We had the closet built behind one of the walls in the extra guest room downstairs. We called it the secret closet because the door was hard to see in the knotty pine paneled walls. If you looked closely you could see the lock, but there was no knob, no doorframe and no obvious door hinges.

If you lived in the Oakland hills, you guarded against burglars, especially if you worked out of the house all day, which we did. Hence the special room in the basement with a large safe full of our most precious possessions. But I didn't think about going down to the basement closet that day, I only scoured the main floor of the house and went away with just a few things, including my boom box because I didn't want to miss the news!

It was odd later on, thinking about those five minutes or so I had spent gathering things to take. Apparently I was in a state of shock, maybe the same shock that had enabled me to overcome my acrophobia and work on the roof a few minutes earlier. But shock had also blocked clear thinking about what to take and what to leave. In the months immediately following the fire, I was among several Firestorm survivors who were on the service club circuit to give advice about what to do in that situation. If I had been thinking clearly while I was filling my little suitcase, I would never have grabbed the clothes from the closet. Leave the clothes. Clothes are so replaceable. Ditto for the boom box. The jewelry boxes were a good thought but, unfortunately, Craig's was practically empty. His emerald tie tack and his grandfather's gold pocket watch were in the safe downstairs, along with my grandmother's black opal, her jade jewelry and my Mikimoto pearls.

This was Lesson Number One from the Firestorm: the most important things to take from your burning house are your photo albums and scrapbooks, the symbols of your memories. The little clay handprints your kids brought home from kindergarten, and their projects from art class, metal and wood shops. I didn't do very well in saving either the valuables or the kids' art, but one of my sons helped me get through that later. At the moment, what I had to do was get out of the house, which wasn't easy. I almost didn't.

I dumped my clothes and stuff in the back seat of the car, climbed into the driver's seat and started the engine. I pushed the button on the garage door opener and waited for the door to slide up on its tracks to the overhead position. Nothing happened. I pushed the button again. Still nothing. It didn't work because the substation had blown the electricity out all over the neighborhood. But I didn't know that yet. I got out and tried to open the door manually. I couldn't do that either because I didn't know about the little red cord you have to pull to disarm the automatic system. I pushed and pushed against the door, but it just heaved a bit and settled back into a locked position.

I got back in the car and started the engine again. I put the car in reverse and thought, "I can gun the car and crash through the door like Batman." So weird. There I was, a full-grown woman in a very serious situation, and I'm visualizing myself being Batman. I quickly nixed that plan because I realized the garage door had two metal bars that braced it and crossed it diagonally. "If I crash through the door," I thought, 'those metal bars will scratch the car and that'll be a mess. But if I just sit here in this closed garage with the engine running, I'll probably asphyxiate myself!"

I turned the engine off and remembered our neighbor Steve had been on his roof with his hose while I had been on ours. I ran out to the sidewalk and down to his driveway. He was still up there. "Steve!" I shouted over the roar of the blaze across the street. "I can't open my garage door. The clicker doesn't work! What should I do?"

I expected him to yell some instructions to me, but instead he climbed down from his roof, turned his hose off, and dashed to our house. He hurried, but he wasn't panicked, as he told me about the red cord, which he pulled putting the door on manual. Then he opened the door and went back to his house to resume watering down his roof. Very cool neighbor — a computer analyst.

I backed out of our driveway and drove around the corner to the big intersection, where five streets converge around an island with a huge eucalyptus tree in it. The neighborhood newsboys used to gather there to fold *The Oakland Tribune* every afternoon when the *Trib* was an afternoon paper.

A small crowd was gathering, watching the flames work their way down from the crest of the hill. I moved until I had a clear view of our roof. It was totally engulfed now, and threatening Judith's house next door. Steve's house was on our other side and still looked all right. I was overcome with guilt. I couldn't help thinking, "Judith's house is going to burn because we didn't replace our roof in time. This wouldn't be happening if we had gotten rid of those rotten, dried up shingles!"

"Is that your house?" The voice came from a man at my side.

"Yeah, that's our house." I answered hoarsely.

"That's a tough one," he said. "I'm very sorry."

If he only knew how sorry I was. It was my fault. First, my own house, then my neighbor's. I watched in horror until I couldn't stand it anymore. I was there for about 15 minutes, and then the firemen ordered people out of the intersection and off the hill. "This whole neighborhood is going to go!" they shouted as they herded people into their cars. "Get off this hill. Everybody who lives here, evacuate your houses immediately! Go down to College Avenue! We're setting up barricades there and we want everybody on the other side!"

I got back in my car and took one last look at my house. Its flames were now covering Judith's house too. Steve's still looked untouched. Maybe his house will be saved, I thought, as I headed down off the hill to College Avenue and the other side of the barricades. I hadn't gone far before remembering our news producer Earl, and his wife Peggy, lived in that same neighborhood. What luck, I thought. He just called, so I know he's home. Somewhere in my brain I knew I had to be connected with the people in the newsroom, because that's how Craig and I would find each other in the chaos.

I pulled up in front of Earl's and Peggy's home and rang the doorbell. As I waited for someone to answer, I heard Earl's voice behind me. "Betty Ann!" he shouted, "We're watching the fire from the top of the apartment house across the street. How's your house?"

"It's gone, Earl." I shouted. The words sounded strange when I said them out loud. "It's gone. The whole neighborhood is going. What happened?"

Earl must have bounded to the street from the roof because suddenly he was walking toward me. I waited on his front porch. "I don't know much," he said, coming up the steps to the front door, "The fire jumped the freeway about half an hour ago. It's these awful winds. Go on in and rest if you'd like. I need to get back across the street. Come along if you want to, or stay here. Whatever you want, Betty Ann."

"I don't want to be alone Earl. I'll come with you and Peggy."

"Okay, then come with us." He turned around and headed back across the street and I followed, seized by a fear of being left alone and the need to see for myself just how my world was ending.

When we got to the roof across the street, I watched the burning hills for a couple of minutes, but it was too painful. The apartment house we were on was a Mission-style stucco, with a flat tar-and-gravel roof and boxy structures covering chimneys and steam vents. I found a quiet corner and sat — huddled, rather — with my arms around my legs and my face on my knees. I was aware of more people arriving on the roof, people bringing things. I recognized newsroom voices, walkie-talkies, Earl giving directions. I heard the voices, but didn't pay attention to what they were saying. I was numb, trying to digest what was happening to the home I had lived in for almost 30 years.

Then Earl's voice was in my ear. "If you can do it Betty Ann ... you don't have to ... but if you feel strong enough, we're setting up for a live shot. We're hooked up with CNN. Do you think you can go on the air and tell us what's happening on your hill?"

I looked up at Earl's face and then at the face next to his. It was Faith Fancher, the Sunday afternoon reporter. They were both looking at me intently, hoping to see a clue. Was I — or wasn't I? I searched the faces of one, then the other, as though I'd find my answer there. Finally, I said, "After all these years of my asking people to talk to me in their moments of struggle, how could I not? Sure, I'll do it. I have to do it." They both smiled, relieved they were going to get their interview, and probably glad I wasn't a complete goner.

"But wait! Earl. I have a problem," I called after him. But he'd already reached the other side of the roof where the cameraman was setting up the shot. Earl was telling Jay, the assignment editor, I was going to do it, so I told my problem to Faith. "Faith, I look awful! I didn't put on any make-up today. We were having a workday at home. I don't even have any lipstick. Do you have anything I can borrow?"

"Sure," Faith said, all business. "Here let me put it on you." She dabbed some powder, eye shadow and lipstick on my face, all the while thanking me and assuring me I was performing a great service by agreeing to go on the air.

At 2 p.m., KTVU went live with the first televised coverage of the fire, and, through CNN, the report — with me as the principal witness — went around the world.

I would hear about that interview for months afterwards. Someone would say, "I was in … Detroit … Paris … Thailand … Beijing … Portland … and I saw you on CNN talking about losing your house. What a devastating thing! And yet you seemed so calm. You're sure a pro."

I was a pro all right — in shock and on automatic — but I was also with my friends, surrounded by the same people I worked with every day. It seemed quite normal to be discussing the event, but it wasn't a matter-of-fact discussion by any means. Faith's demeanor was that of a good friend, suffering right along with me.

"Tell us what it was like up there?" she asked on camera. "What did you do?" When I told her about going up on the roof with the hose and crowbar, she asked, incredulously, "What did you think you could accomplish, Betty Ann?"

And I looked back at her — surprised she needed to ask. "I was going to put the fire out, Faith." When we finished, I went back to my corner and hunkered down again, but couldn't be quiet because the news cell phone started ringing. The newsroom was flooded with calls from friends offering Craig and me a place to stay. Some of the calls were from people I knew and wanted to call back, but other calls were from strangers who just wanted to help.

Soon Craig arrived on the roof too. It was one of those moments when you could almost hear the music as we rushed into each other's arms. We clung to each other sobbing, overwhelmed by emotions that had been held in check until that moment. In between gasps, Craig explained how he had driven through the barricades and gone up to the house. He wanted to make sure I had gotten out. He told me he couldn't get the car closer than the big intersection, so he had gone the last block and a half on foot. He said he walked between two walls of burning houses. "It was eerie and powerful and — in a strange way — beautiful. I didn't see another soul. No firefighters. No residents. Everybody was gone. Just all the houses, burning. The top floor of our house was completely gone and the flames were boiling up out of the basement. I could see the car was gone, so I knew you had made it out. I turned around and went back down the hill, called the newsroom and they told me you were here."

Then Earl placed his hand on Craig's shoulder and told us it was time for business again. To Earl, Craig was another way to update his eyewitness reports. Not much was coming out of the fire department, its communication lines were totally overpowered. Those still working were being used to deploy firefighters, not to report damage. We later learned the Oakland Fire Department only had three lines available to all its crews, but on that day 30 lines would not have been enough. Craig took his place at the edge of the apartment-house roof, with the burning hills in the background, and told Faith and the world about the devastation that was at its fiercest and deadliest point.

At 4 o'clock, Earl and the crew began breaking down the gear to head out to other locations. By that time, Craig and I had talked to our two sons who were in the Bay Area, Steve and Dan, and we had all agreed to meet at the Oakland Yacht Club. We decided we would stay on the boat. We knew our homeowners' insurance would pay for a hotel room, but the boat — although not as comfortable as a nice hotel — was at least ours, and being on our own bit of turf seemed important at that moment.

Three other families from the fire showed up at the yacht club, where Joan, the manager, greeted us all with brand new sweat outfits and an invitation to her house for dinner. Her hospitality was just the first deed in a long and wondrous string of generous things people — both friends and strangers — did for us in the days and weeks following the disaster. Emergencies bring out the best in people. They also bring out the worst, and we were to experience both, although fortunately much more of the former than the latter.

After dinner, Joan told us she'd leave the club open all night and we could watch the news coverage of the fire if we wanted to. An hour of viewing time was enough, though, because the broadcasts got very repetitive. So we settled down on the terrace. The air was still full of smoke, but we could see across the Estuary to the hills, which looked like they were covered with campfires. The walls of flames that had been there earlier in the day were gone now, and had left behind a huge swath of blackness where houses and streetlights used to be. The blackness was broken here and there by the flickering of natural gas jets continuing to burn.

The sight was hypnotic. The four of us didn't say much to each other. We just sat there and stared into the nothingness. Steve, feeling restless, stood up, rummaged around the clubroom and came back with pencils and paper for everyone. "We might as well be doing something useful. We're going to need an inventory of all our stuff for the insurance, so how about getting started on it now. It'll be better than sitting here doing nothing."

One year later we finished our list: 82 pages of computer printout, listing in detail all the earthly belongings of our whole family; every stick of furniture; every utensil; every piece of clothing, including how many pairs of socks and underwear; every tool for every hobby any of us had ever had and were still using or had stored in the basement; how many pencils, paper clips, or sheets of paper we had lost.

The inventory was one of many onerous tasks fire survivors would face. It was difficult, not only because of the circumstances that made it necessary, but also because the insurance companies used the inventories as weapons in what became a full-fledged war with homeowners. That's another story however, about the second life-changing disaster, and more difficult to bear because it was a man-made, deliberate corporate policy, and weighted by laws on the side of the insurance companies.

# CHAPTER 19

# PLUMBING THE DEPTHS OF TOTAL LOSS

How Much is Everything Worth?

N one of us slept well that first night. Craig and I tossed and turned, beyond fatigue, still trying to absorb what had happened to us. I looked through my jewelry box about a dozen times that evening, looking for my grandmother's jewelry, hoping if I looked one more time I would find my black opal and the Cat's Eye bracelet that was a gift to her from Queen Liliuokalani, the last sovereign monarch of the Hawaiian kingdom. But no matter how hard I stared into the corners of that velvet lined box, I couldn't make her jewelry materialize. My next hope was that, somehow, those boiling flames Craig had described weren't that hot and the contents of the safe in our secret closet had survived so we could find them the next day.

When the next day finally came, we couldn't go up to the house. The fire area was still closed off due to live power lines lying across many of the streets, and houses still burning here and there. Police were holding everybody back. No exceptions.

Craig seized the day to start rebuilding our lives. "First thing we have to do," he began, "is get a mailbox, then, let's go see our insurance agent and hear what he has to say. After that, we'd better look for a place to live. With 3,000 people suddenly dropped into the housing market, we'll need to move fast if we want to get a decent place."

Dan and Steve had their own jobs to go to, so Craig and I set out to get a post office box. That turned out to be unnecessary because, a few days later, the local post office — proving that bureaucracies don't always have to be bureaucratic — told fire survivors it would forward mail to us wherever we were. We didn't have to bother with the change of address cards for magazines, bills, etc. They took care of everything.

Ken Bullock, who had been our insurance agent for more than 20 years, greeted us with a big smile: "I knew you'd be in today. See, I have a list of all my clients who lost their homes yesterday. First thing I want to say is how sorry I am for your loss." He motioned for us to sit down and went on. "Second thing I want to do is to congratulate you on having the best insurance in the world. You have the Cadillac of policies, and State Farm is here to help you get back on your feet right away." From a stack of papers on his desk, Ken pulled out a check and held it out to us. "This will help you get settled in a temporary place while you sort out what you're going to do about rebuilding."

We looked at it and both of us gasped when we saw the amount.

"Fifteen thousand dollars!! Wow. Thank you."

"Go rent a place. You're entitled to a home comparable to the one you lost. Go buy clothes, furniture, whatever. State Farm is here to help you get through this."

We left, feeling hopeful and optimistic. "That was pretty impressive," Craig commented as we went back to the car. "Let's go find a place to live!"

But first we had to go to the bank to make the deposit and pick up some new checks since our old ones had burned. We stopped by the Alameda Branch of the Bank of America because that island community, cheek-to-jowl with Oakland, seemed the mostly likely place to find a temporary home. As we were leaving the counter, the manager called to us. "Let us know if there's anything else we can do for you," she said with feeling. "I know what you're going through, because I lost my house to a fire 18 years ago." She paused, swallowed, blinked and her eyes filled with tears. "It's terrible to lose everything. I don't think I'll ever get over it. Anyway, I just wanted to wish you good luck." She turned and bowed her head.

We stood there and watched as she hurried back to her office. Oh, my god! She lost her house 18 years ago and still cries about it. That's bad. As we headed for the car, we wondered if we would be like that in 18 years. But we couldn't stay with that thought for long — there was too much to do.

We decided we wanted a place near the water. Having spent nearly every weekend for the past five years on our boat, we felt that proximity to the Bay would help heal our wounds. Later that afternoon, we signed a lease for a 3-bedroom townhouse on Bay Farm Island, right on the walking path following the shoreline. The rental agent for the development told us someone else was interested in it too, but he decided that — as fire survivors — we had precedence. There it was again, special treatment for us because we were in the disaster. Everyone seemed to want to help us recover.

We were carried on a pillow of care that got us through those first days and weeks of shock and grief. In those days, cell phones were scarce — not used by the general public yet — but Channel 2 loaned us one of theirs and a local phone book. My memory of those first few days is a jumble of appointments, forms and endless errands. Each day was spent in the car, with Craig at the wheel and me beside him with the phone book open in my lap, calling this place and that to make arrangements for the services and things we needed to restart. Plus, we had calls to return from people all over the country because we had become poster children of the fire. Everyday, people who wanted comments or information from fire survivors left messages at Channel 2 to have us call back. One of the network morning shows asked us if they could send a camera crew to the boat so we could go 'live' in an interview when they went on the air the next morning at 7. "But that's 4 a.m. here in California," I protested.

"Sure, but you have an important message, and of course we're seen all over the country," the producer urged. We thanked her but declined, concluding at that moment in our lives, a couple hours of sleep were worth more than three more minutes of fame.

But we said yes when our own newsroom asked if they could send a crew with us to go to our house the next day. We felt an obligation to share what we were going through because too many other families were going through exactly the same thing. As news people, we wanted to help the public understand.

On Tuesday, 48 hours after the fire, Craig, our sons Dan and Steve and I drove through the police lines with the Channel 2 crew. Even though we had watched the news footage on television, we were not prepared for what we saw as Cameraman Roy Inouye slowly maneuvered the news car up the hill to the fire zone. As the debris and clutter in the streets increased, the color in the landscape faded until we reached a point where there was no color at all, just shades of gray and black ash. It was as though we had entered a black and white film about the end of the world. It didn't feel real. This was where we had lived, but it had been completely transformed.

There were no houses, not even frames of houses. The only structures left standing were the chimneys, and they were black now too, even though some had once been red brick or pastel marble. The chimneys, which had been built to contain fires, now testified in ironic silence to the flames that had engulfed them. Tree skeletons, blacker than the ash in which they stood, broke the flattened landscape, as did a few twisted, agonized power poles.

Here and there were blistered remains of cars still parked on the street or in what had been a garage or carport. You couldn't tell anymore what had been there before. Everything was gone. This couldn't be our neighborhood. For just a millisecond I thought maybe this is Hiroshima.

We came to the big intersection. The eucalyptus tree was still standing — that is, its trunk was there — but its leaves and branches were gone. In the days to come, this tree trunk would become an altar on which fire survivors would tack letters and hand-painted signs. At first the messages would express grief mixed with promises to return and rebuild, and hope that the tree would leaf again. Over time though, skulls and crossbones over the names of insurance companies would replace those words with warnings not to buy from this one or that one. There would be signs shouting that such and such a company lied and cheated. Simple truths from complicated times. The sign and letter phase would come soon; today the intersection was a quiet ruin like the rest of the hill.

Our conversation was singed with emotion, disbelief and wonder. "Oh look, there's where Johnstons' house was. Oh god, and there's Mills'. Jeez. There's nothing. There's nothing!"

"I think I see our chimney."

"Is this our place?"

"Are you sure?"

"How can you tell?"

"See, here's the brick walkway that led to the front porch!"

We had a downslope lot; the front door opened onto the main floor of the house. There were more rooms downstairs, and from that level you walked down more stairs to the back yard. This day, at the end of the walkway from the street, instead of the house, there was a big pit full of ashes and the burned carcasses of furniture. We stood there in mute awe, staring into the hole — eight pairs of eyes searching for something recognizable. I nudged Craig and pointed to a black blister-covered box. "Look, there's my computer."

"Are you sure?"

"Yeah, that's under where my office was! And see, over there's the kitchen." More blackened box shapes covered with blisters. Stove? Fridge? Dishwasher? We couldn't tell.

Steve and Dan climbed down to take a closer look. Suddenly they knelt, pointing to something in the ashes. They asked Roy if he had a shovel in his trunk. They had found what was left of Newt, the family cat, and wanted to bury him. He had apparently been cornered on the kitchen porch which, when it burned, crashed down into the side yard. They dug a grave in his favorite spot, a corner of the front yard. Months later Steve went back to visit and found one lovely flower blooming on that spot.

For a while, we convinced ourselves that Little Sweetie, our black and white lop-eared Dutch bunny, was safe in one of the many holes she had dug in the basement. She had been down there the morning of the fire; it was her cool place for hot days, but we never did find out what happened to her — she was just gone.

Roy moved his camera in and around us, recording our discoveries and reactions. He was like family; Craig and I had both worked with him for years, so we were completely comfortable with him there. We spent more than an hour roaming through the ashes. We didn't recognize much. It took us a while to determine that the tangled heap of metal wires was what remained of our baby grand piano, or that a clear glassy pool was the melted residue of our dining room crystal, a legacy from Craig's grandparents.

We made our way toward the back of our lot and spotted something in the ashes that still had its original shape. "My bathroom cup!" I shrieked. "Oh look, that's my bathroom cup." I reached into the ashes, picked it up, and clasped it to my heart. "I made this cup 30 years ago; it was one of the first things I made in my pottery class. I totally love this cup." I cried and cuddled the cup. Roy's camera moved in close and recorded every tear and emotional syllable.

That night, on *The 10 O'clock News*, the scene with me clinging to my bathroom cup became the central moment in a lengthy report. I learned later that, after Reporter Eric Green finished writing it, none of the editors wanted to work on it. They said they all felt too bad for us. Finally Bill Longen, the supervising editor, said he'd do it himself. Bill was a tough guy and, as a long-time news editor, he'd seen the worst of what the human race endures. Even with all that thick skin, however, Bill told us he couldn't keep his own tears back as he put our story together.

That was the effect the news piece had on everybody, including our insurance adjuster, who was a different person from Ken, our insurance *agent*. The adjuster said he cried for us, but his tears didn't interfere with his ability to do the dirty work for his company. That story comes a bit later though. It took us a few months to catch on to the pattern of cruel games adjusters from most insurance companies were playing.

For years afterward, people would mention that Firestorm report to me. Ten years after the fire, I met someone for the first time and they asked, "How's your bathroom cup?" and then added, "I remember your being in that fire."

That report, and especially that scene, was an intimate, homey look at a horrendous tragedy. On such a large scale, it's difficult for readers or viewers to absorb an enormous event because the totality is often expressed in statistics. But everybody can identify with a story when it's told on the individual level, in terms of everyday life we all share. And it doesn't get much more down-home than a handmade bathroom cup. Several months would have to pass before either Craig or I would be able to watch the report. We knew it would put us in a place we were trying to get out of, so we kept our copy of it on the shelf and didn't watch.

I have never been a good sleeper, and the first few nights after the fire I couldn't sleep more than a couple of hours. I'd wake up, feel miserable and mourn for the things I would never see again, like the lovely jewelry that had been my Hawaiian grandmother's. I didn't think anybody could hear me because I cried as quietly as I could, but boats are small places.

One morning, Dan said he had to go back to his apartment in Fremont for a while. "Be back later this afternoon," he explained as he stepped off the boat. "Catch up with you before dinner." He waved and then walked briskly up the dock and headed to the parking lot.

When he came back, he was holding one hand behind him as he approached with his head cocked to one side. "Mom," he began, looking directly into my eyes, "I've been hearing you at night not sleeping, feeling bad about what's happened, missing all the nice things you lost. Well I thought if you could look at this, maybe it would help you feel better."

He brought his hand out from behind his back and held it out to me. In it was a picture of him and his two brothers, taken one afternoon that summer after one of our customary Sunday brunches, with the whole family and any number of friends. It was a wonderful picture of all three of my sons grinning at the camera, their arms around each other's shoulders.

The sight of those precious faces, smiling at me from a happier day, immediately put everything into a different and much sharper focus. Yes, I had lost all my stuff, but I hadn't lost what was most important in my life. The real treasures in my life were right there in that picture. They were very much all right, and they were very much still with me. And sure, *some* stuff like my grandmother's jewelry is better than *other* stuff — but it's still all just stuff.

I looked up from the picture into the gaze of my first-born and felt extremely lucky. I grabbed him in a big hug. "Thank you, Dan! Thank you for a wonderful lesson in priorities!" Every night since then, that picture has been on the table next to my bed. I take it with me on trips. I am never without it. I want to always remember that lesson.

On Monday, the first day after the fire, a light rain cooled off some of the still-burning home sites. At the marina, the air was damp with a steady drizzle that only reinforced our grim sadness. About 7 p.m., the four of us headed to the cars to find a place for dinner and, as we passed the phone booth, I realized I hadn't talked to my mother yet.

"Grandma might be worried," I said to Craig and the boys as I pulled open the door of the booth. "Give me a few minutes. I'll meet you at the car. No point in your standing around in this drizzle, too!"

She answered right away. "Mom, I just wanted you to know we are all safe, although the house and everything in it went in the fire. I couldn't save much of anything. It's all gone."

"Well, Betty Ann," she said, "You'll be alright — you're a strong person. Do you know what I did today? This is my bridge day and guess what. I made a Grand Slam in Spades!" She proceeded to tell me what cards she held and how she had played them. I felt like I was caught in some sort of time warp.

"Mom! I just told you that the Firestorm destroyed my home and everything in it, and I am standing here in a phone booth in a parking lot. I'm sorry, but I can't listen to you talking about your bridge hand. I feel really bad, Mom!"

"Oh, I'm sorry, Dear. Then you should take a nice hot bath. That will make you feel better."

"MOM! I can't take a nice hot bath. I don't have a bathtub anymore. Don't you get it? I don't have a home!"

"You're a strong person, Betty Ann. You can't let this get you down. You'll get through it."

"Yes Mom, I know I'll get through it. Thanks. I have to go now. Goodbye."

"Goodbye, Dear."

I stumbled away from the phone booth feeling as though someone had clubbed me. Blinking back tears of anger and disappointment, I climbed into the passenger seat of the car where Craig, Dan and Steve were waiting. "How's Grandma?" they asked.

"Grandma is just fine," I answered with perhaps a little too much resolve in my voice. "She bid and made seven spades today at bridge." I swallowed the lump growing in my throat. I wasn't even able to tell them their grandmother had said "hello" to them because she hadn't. I didn't say anything more. Neither did anybody else. We rode to dinner in silence. If the boys had hoped for more from their grandmother, they didn't show it, and Craig knew better than to say, "You mean, she didn't even ..."

The first week after the fire was a grand mixture of things: days brimming with errands, meetings about insurance, interviews with contractors and architects, endless shopping and being amazed at the thoughtfulness and generosity of both friends and people we had never met before. Above all, our job that first week was getting used to our situation. We called it, "Plumbing the Depths of Total Loss," because every so often it would stab at us fiercely and unexpectedly.

Like on the Thursday after the fire. We had been doing pretty well, taking care of business. We had rented a townhouse and furniture to put in it, including sheets, towels and everything for the kitchen. The deliverymen brought our order, titled "Modern Three Bedroom," and had just finished putting everything away — they even hung the rented towels in the bathrooms. When they left, I looked around the living room. It didn't look like our home; it looked like a motel room. I sat on the white leather sofa and cried a good long, bawling-out-loud sob session. Later, when Craig came back from grocery shopping, he showed me something he thought might help us. It was a large campaign badge with the red international *no* sign circling the word "whining." In the months that followed, whenever one of us felt low and overwhelmed, the other would wave that badge and we would giggle, sigh and move on.

There were many generous actions from so many people, including gifts of dishes, towels and clothing, all wonderful and much appreciated, but a few of them need their own stories.

Helen Craddick, whom her old friends called *Bodo*, was a top interior designer with her own home being her major point of pride. The first time I saw her home in the 1950s, she became my standard for home beauty. Our husbands were classmates in law school, and we were all living on the students' poverty line. Their attic apartment had only one real piece of furniture — the rest was scrounged from the Berkeley dump or created out of bricks and boards. The overall effect though was lovely, tranquil and elegant. Over the years, as their earnings increased, so did the value of her furnishings, but her basic touch remained the same — simple understated elegance. Since she had never had children, she never had to make compromises for practicality over beauty. In her home, beauty always came first.

A couple of days after we had settled into our townhouse with our rented furniture, Bodo called us and asked us to drop by. "Make sure the trunk of your car is empty," she instructed. When she opened her door to greet us, we saw her entry hall was filled with boxes. "These are some things I pulled out of the garage today," she said, beginning a lecture on home design. "Accessories are what make a house a home — interesting things to put on the coffee tables and hang on the walls. And those are the things you can't rent. I'm not using any of this stuff at the moment and thought it could help dress up your place. Mind you, I am not giving you these things, and I will not sell you these things. Just use and enjoy them until you get your own place. Anyway, that's why I wanted your trunk empty. So, let's go load up."

And with that, she grabbed a large basket and a picture and started for our car. We were dumbfounded, but recovered quickly and eagerly helped her load our car. There were antique wooden tools, French wire baskets, lovely bowls and trays, sculptures, a treasure trove of wonderful things that transformed our cold "rent-a-suite" into a warm and cozy home.

Anne Hamilton, an artist friend of ours, had painted one of the large works that had burned with our living room. It was a wonderful piece we had bought from her a couple of years earlier. Other paintings by Anne, in other people's homes, had also burned in the fire, and she knew other local artists in the same situation. They all wanted to help, so at church one Sunday they organized a gallery of paintings that the artists rented free of charge for one year to fire survivors. After that year, you could return the painting, buy it, or continue to rent it. We went home from that event with three excellent works to hang on the walls of our townhouse. When the year was up, we bought those three paintings, plus two more from those same artists. They not only look wonderful on our walls, but will always make us feel good when we think about the kindness of their creators.

Merchants were also generous. Auto dealers loaned cars for free to customers who had lost theirs, and/or gave discounts to help with replacements. Macy's offered personal shopper services, free alterations and delivery to fire survivors, beginning Thursday of the first week after the blaze. That morning, about 20 of us crowded into the Personal Shoppers' Office at the Union Square Macy's in San Francisco. It was obvious we were all fire survivors — we were all wearing sweat outfits. As we waited to register at the clerk's desk, we chatted among ourselves in a kind of desultory fashion. Nobody's heart was into shopping, but those of us who worked obviously needed to get something to wear besides sweats. Suddenly, the quiet murmuring in the room was shattered by a loud wail followed by convulsive sobbing. We all looked to the source of the crying and, as one, we all moved in to comfort a very distressed woman sitting at the registration desk.

The clerk facing her looked around at us helplessly. "I don't know what upset her. All I did was ask for her name and address ..." We all just frowned and shook our heads. We didn't have to say anything, but the clerk immediately realized that asking for an address was like pulling a trigger. "Oh, I'm sorry. Of course, now I understand. I am so very sorry. I just didn't think."

The personal shoppers were immensely helpful. I was due back at work the following Monday and needed a camera-ready wardrobe — suits, blouses, shoes, everything. The armful of clothes I had grabbed from my side of the closet on the day of the fire was practically useless — the couple of skirts didn't match anything else. I might have been able to put together one decent outfit, but my on-air job required a good-looking outfit every day.

My personal shopper was terrific. She took me on a quick walk through Macy's multitudinous women's departments so she could get a sense of what I liked and didn't like. Then she parked me in a spacious dressing room and, for the next two hours, ran back and forth through all those departments again, finding outfit after outfit for me to try on. I will thank her forever because I have always hated to shop, and when I do shop, I prefer small boutiques. Department stores like Macy's had always given me tension headaches, and usually I would leave them overwhelmed and empty-handed. But the personal shopper made those days not just bearable, but fun. I felt very good in all my new duds, which arrived two days later, with skirts hemmed and sleeves shortened at no extra charge — Macy's contribution to the recovery effort.

Craig and I were both surprised that reclaiming our normal lives was taking so much effort, time and money. We hadn't thought of ourselves as high-end consumers needing a lot of *things* to get us from one day to the next; our lives seemed simple to us. We worked hard five days a week and spent weekends with our friends and kids. But we quickly realized we really did depend on gadgets and machines, not only for our daily work but also for our comfort and hobbies. We took for granted, for example, that we could take a photograph whenever we wanted to. Suddenly, we were without a camera. For us, that was serious deprivation. Getting a new camera required market research because — for Craig — a camera is not just any old point-and-shoot. For him, a camera begins with a good body, to which you add good lenses, a sturdy tripod, adapter rings, filters and other accessories. Market research for all that takes a lot of time.

Then there was our home office. I was the only one who used a computer back then. As I write this, I still use one computer, but Craig now uses three. I do hope we only have to go through that recovery effort once in our lifetimes.

In the first couple of days after the Firestorm, we shopped for a new computer because we knew we were going to have to keep very good records, make a lot of lists and probably write many letters. We were still on the boat and weren't sure when we'd have an office again, so we bought a laptop. Sadly, replacing the software and data turned out to be easy; we didn't have much to log. Our personal address books had perished with the house and — worse

— so had my phone list for work, 20 years' accumulation of contacts, sources, home phone numbers of elected officials, political movers and shakers. I had taken my personal files home the week before the fire because my office was going to be painted while I was on vacation and I didn't want my stuff to get lost in the process. I could easily replace paper clips, pens and paper, but I would never be able to reconstruct my phone book of news sources. Developing stories and following up on tips would never be the same for me again. Information turned out to be one of my biggest losses in the fire, a handicap I lived with every day at work until I retired.

Craig hired a safecracker to open our safe, which was warped from the intense heat. When the safecracker finally opened the metal box, what we found was more ashes. There was a curved piece of black metal that was the barrel of Craig's .22. There were also a few coins. The boys collected them in a corner of the safe, but some scavengers stole them that night. Digging through those ashes was so painful I decided not to do it anymore. Letting go seemed more reasonable, more realistic and saner. Friends offered to help us dig through the ashes, but we didn't see any point in it. The lot itself told us there wasn't much to recover, maybe even nothing.

"We should have a ceremony," I suggested, "and say goodbye to our house. That might help us move on."

A couple of weeks after the fire, our family gathered in what had been our back garden — all the boys, and including my ex-husband who had also lived in the house for a dozen years. Craig poured champagne all around for a farewell toast, then handed a brand new Mason jar to each person. "I brought these," he said as he moved around the family circle, "so that each of us can take something from this place that sheltered us for so many years. Take your jar and walk to what were your favorite places in the house. Take some ashes from each place so you can keep alive memories of all the good times we had in this house. Dan, Mike, Steve, this is the only home you have ever known. You were born here and grew up here. All your childhood memories spring from this place. When we have finished with that, let's come back here to our circle."

Craig and I filled a jar together; I am looking in it as I write this. Our jar has a shard from a small bowl I had made in which I kept an Easter egg the boys and I had dyed with colors from the flowers in our garden. There is the blackened corpse of Craig's grandfather's gold pocket watch. There's the nozzle from one of my garden hoses — part of my futile attempt to save the house. There's a small magnifying glass from Craig's jewelry-making tools. There's a handle from our dresser drawer. There's the champagne cork from the celebration that day. And two inches of ashes to represent everything else we lost. An African good-luck charm a good friend gave us hangs outside the jar on the lid's metal clasp. So far it seems to have worked. We showed the others what we collected, and then listened as they talked about what they had picked up.

Dan went for the structure: He had a few nails that had held the house together and a few pieces of glass from the windows. He also took some old coins that had stuck together in an unruly pile. He picked up other coins melted around a dark green gemstone that had a white stripe running down its center. He also had his couple of inches of generalized ashes and topped the whole thing off with his house key.

Mike said he had gone to the area of his old room to fill his jar. Then he took out some notes and read, *"As my eyes open I see my brother, Dan, asleep across the bedroom. I know if I don't get up this second, I could fall back to sleep and possibly wet the bed. So I slide out onto the floor. My first step is met with the sound of crinkling paper and as I look down I see a floor covered with paper airplanes, remnants from the early evening activities. We discovered that if you fold one entire* newspaper into one airplane, it would yield tens of duplicate thinner airplanes. They now totally cover the green-blue rug in our bedroom. I wade through the sea of paper and out into the hallway where it is loud and bright. Because I'm squinting I almost step on a stray Lego, left there from one of many after-school Lego vehicle-crashing sessions. Lego cars were fun to build but they were no match for the destruction force of a speeding STP, neither was the closet door at the end of the hall. I flick on the bathroom light so fast that no monster could possibly grab my hand and push the door open. The door skids to a stop on the tile floor. Of course it does! Everyone in the family knows you have to lift up the door as you open it. The floor is cold, but not as cold as the rim of the toilet. I hurry and finish. The flushing seems so loud at night. When I enter the bedroom, I can't see a thing until my eyes adjust. I walk carefully to bed and go back to sleep, but not before taking one proud look at the sea of airplanes.

I wouldn't have these memories without my house, but now I have them and the house is gone, at least the building is gone. I can still see it and walk through it and I can see my family decorating a big tree in the living room, opening gifts, carving pumpkins, setting off fireworks, eating dinner with friends and just being there. And I see our pets: Benjamin, Kitty, Buffy, Sammy, Arbon, Ninja, Colours, Newt and countless fish. They all made it a home, the home I grew up in and it's who I am.

My house was the cup that held the waters of my youth. I have drunk and I will remember for as long as I live and be thankful."

Steve wrote a poem:

> One cannot discover
> The emptiness of things
> By denying them,
> But by embracing them
> And feeling the embrace.

A friend, Jean Gregory, wrote a poem about my having lost my grandmother's jewelry, and her poem made the same point that Dan had made when he brought me that wonderful picture of him and his brothers.

*"You are your grandmother's jewels:*
*You are! You are! You are!*
*And you are here.*
*And we are here.*
*. . .*
*We have each other.*
*We cling. We embrace. We comfort.*
*And we dance*
*The rhythm of life."*

After everyone had spoken, we put our arms around each other, bowed our heads and again thanked our house for having given us so many good memories. Then we said goodbye.

After that, Craig and I returned to the lot only for insurance or other business purposes. Seeing it was such a painful experience, we didn't want to do it unless we had to. The boys felt differently and visited a few more times to sift through the ashes, or just sit and remember. Mike now has a small collection of burned pottery, including one of his brother's clay handprints from kindergarten. It used to be glazed yellow — now it's black.

Steve found a bonanza. He turned the safe over and, although everything inside it had burned beyond recognition (except for the gun barrel and a few coins), the safe had fallen over and ended up protecting what it fell on — several pieces of Craig's grandmother's sterling silver and the pink flannel bag she kept them in, although it had burn holes in it. His prize though, was a scrapbook his father had made, consisting of pages from Craig's baby book, with snapshots and birthday letters his mother had written to him for his first five birthdays. The pages were soaking wet and the silver was blackened, but Steve bundled everything up and took it to the Zen Center on Page Street in San Francisco where he was living at the time.

Restoring something that belonged to Craig fit with Steve's efforts at the Zen Center, where he had gone looking for strength to help him in his battle against drugs. Craig had been Steve's favorite target for the previous 10 years whenever he needed something to sell so he could buy more marijuana or cocaine, and Craig had run out of patience with Steve long before the fire. The painstaking project of restoring Craig's photos and baby book was an act of contrition Steve hoped would help heal the relationship. He spread the burned pages on every surface in his room. During the time the pages were airing out, Steve says his room took on the smoky aroma of the fire. When the pages were dried, Steve ironed them smooth and remounted them in a new scrapbook that he gave Craig the first Christmas after the fire.

Every minute that Craig and I were not working, we focused on rebuilding our house. By the end of our first post-fire week, we had an architect and a general contractor. By mid-December, we had all the drawings and estimates State Farm told us it needed to rebuild our home. Basically, we wanted the same structure we had before; we thought our insurance company would appreciate the speed with which we had moved. We actually believed they would approve our plans and we would be under construction by spring. Silly us.

# CHAPTER 20

# THE SECOND DISASTER

## INSURANCE HARDBALL

Eventually, we realized that most of the insurance companies that covered houses lost in the Oakland Hills Firestorm really didn't *want* to settle with people quickly, but preferred dragging payments out — not just for months but for *years,* and apparently, the longer, the better. The way insurance companies settled claims seemed to have more to do with their own business interests than it did with helping their clients rebuild their lives. The promises of the insurance agents faded quickly in the heat of so many large claims.

But we didn't know that in December, 1991, when we called our adjuster to tell him we had figured out how much it would cost to replace our house the way it had been. We had done all our homework and had the numbers. "Let's set up a meeting. What's your schedule like?" I asked the adjuster assigned to our case. We were surprised at his response. "I am sorry, but I am leaving the area now. I've been reassigned elsewhere. You'll be dealing with someone else, so you might as well wait and set the meeting up with them."

We were disappointed to learn we would be switched to someone else. "Who will that be?" I asked, "can we set up a meeting with them right away? As you know, we hope to start building this spring."

"I don't think they've decided yet who will take over your case," the adjuster explained. "They'll let you know very soon though,

I'm sure." That was the last we heard from our first adjuster; he just went away.

Our second adjuster told us he needed time to acquaint himself with our claim. A month later, that adjuster left, and we got a third adjuster. We began to feel vaguely suspicious, but we kept working with the State Farm adjusters, giving them list after list of whatever information they asked for. After a couple more months, however, we saw a clear pattern: every month, we'd lose our adjuster and get a new one. The new adjusters never seemed to know anything about what the previous adjusters had agreed to do, or they said they "had to check with my supervisor." Every time we started over, we lost something we thought had already been settled. We began to feel like we were swimming in molasses — it was like a bad dream in which you try to run but can't make your legs move.

Later we realized that switching adjusters was merely one of a whole arsenal of delaying tactics most of the insurance companies were using to avoid settling the 3,000 claims that came out of the Firestorm. Claims to State Farm alone totaled more than a billion dollars. As the years and lawsuits piled up, and as internal company records were brought into the open, we learned that adjusters earned bonuses by delaying settlements so insurance companies could spread the payments over several years.

California State Insurance Commissioner John Garamendi even charged the insurance companies with "outrageous and despicable practices."

One year after the fire, only 35 homes out of the 3,000 that had burned were under construction, and the hills remained a vast wasteland. And then, a former insurance adjuster/turned consumer advocate rode in on her white charger. Ina DeLong had worked 23 years for State Farm in the Santa Cruz area, and apparently had liked what she did until 1989, when the Loma Prieta earthquake hit, and hundreds of damage claims flooded into the office. In the face of so many claims, Ina saw an entirely different response from her company. She told us the adjusters were instructed not to report all the damage they saw, and to hide structural damage that wasn't obvious in order to keep claims payments low. Ina felt this practice would betray everything she had ever believed in, so she left State Farm and became an advocate for homeowners. She knew State Farm's tactics from the inside, tactics many companies were now using in Oakland. She teamed up with Amy Bach, a lawyer who specialized in insurance claims. Together, they founded United Policyholders and organized homeowners into groups, according to insurance company. That way, clients of the same company could compare notes with each other. This was a first. Never before had so many homeowners shared information and organized to fight their insurance companies.

Ina and Amy gave homeowners a quick course in the intricacies of insurance policies. They introduced homeowners to Insurance Commissioner Garamendi, and after he heard their stories he took action and had enough clout to make the insurance companies change some of their ways.

One major issue was the temporary housing allowance. If your home becomes uninhabitable, most homeowners' policies provide rent for temporary housing for up to one year. But when that year runs out, you have to pay for your temporary housing out of your own pocket. At the end of the first year after the fire, with only 35 homes rebuilt, 2,965 families still needed temporary housing and housing allowances were expiring. Garamendi concluded that companies would use the expiration of the housing allowances to pressure homeowners into settling for less than they were entitled to. So he made the insurance companies extend temporary housing allowances for a second year.

By that time, Craig and I were dealing with our eighth or ninth adjuster and were in a state of cold fury about the lack of progress with our insurance settlement.

"We aren't getting anywhere, Craig," I complained one morning at breakfast. "The way things are going, either you or I have to quit work and devote full time to the insurance stuff or we're going to have nervous breakdowns."

Craig put down his coffee cup, gazed across the table at me for a long moment and then came up with a plan of action. "Let's look through all the literature we've received from companies claiming they can help us, like insurance lawyers and public adjusters. Then let's take a couple of days off this week to interview some and see who has the best deal. Let's get some professional help. We need it."

I had saved all the pamphlets and brochures we had gotten in the mail from businesses that specialize in disasters. We sorted through the pile, made appointments and arranged for a day off to see what kind of help there was out there for us.

After hearing proposals from several lawyers and public adjusters, we chose the Greenspan company, whose San Francisco manager agreed to take our case himself. For the next three years, Randy Goodman was our guide through the white waters of our insurance settlement. "Good morning, Betty Ann and Craig," he would chortle in what became our morning wake-up call. "Here's what I'm going to do for you today." Then he would list the calls or meetings he was going to make that day on our behalf.

After realizing, even with Randy on our team, that State Farm was going to bully us with their cruel settlement games for at least a couple more years, we decided not to rebuild our house. We simply were not willing to spend all that time and effort just to get our old address back. Our entire neighborhood was gone and would never be the same. A rebuilt house would never feel like our old house, because it would have different furniture, different paintings, different everythings. Nothing on our hill would ever be the same. We decided to move on, buy an existing house and get on with the rest of our lives.

While looking for houses to buy, we avoided Oakland because we didn't want to be anywhere near the site of our loss. We looked next door in Piedmont, but that city was still too close to the area destroyed in the Firestorm. We seriously looked on the island of Alameda, where we had been renting. There were some wonderful old houses in a section of town called The Gold Coast. We loved their style and their roomy yards, but we did not like their brick foundations, antique furnaces and teeny tiny closets, all of which would need serious upgrading.

One gorgeous Queen Anne, set on a corner lot and surrounded by a huge lawn, drew us back five times before we finally decided not to bid on it. That turned out to be a good thing because, a few months later, it burned to the ground, the victim of a gas line surge that set a dozen other homes on fire. We both agreed later that losing a second house in a year would have been too much to bear, and were grateful for even a little blessing.

But a couple families did suffer that grotesque experience. In one case, an arsonist set fire to a house that had just been finished. In the other case, some paint rags ignited and burned a house just before its owners were going to move back in. That was similar to what happened to Jack London's famous Wolf House in Glen Ellen, after workers left linseed oil-soaked rags on wooden timbers, which caused spontaneous combustion and destroyed his dream home.

Handling that kind of grief would have been a challenge, but insurance grief was bad enough, and I know a lot of families didn't survive it. Dozens of people had heart attacks and left grieving families to cope the best they could. Others, especially older people who didn't want to spend their remaining years locked in insurance anguish, just gave up and took whatever settlement their insurance companies offered them.

One elderly man we met at a cocktail party put it this way. "What I resent the most," he said, "is the theft of time. My insurance company has stolen all of my time these past three years. I have not been able to do any of the things I had planned to do. The fire, caused by nature, was the first disaster. The second, caused by the insurance companies, was the next disaster, and I resent it much more than I did the first."

The end of year two, after the fire, didn't see much improvement in the rebuilding effort, and the struggle between the insurance companies and homeowners intensified in 1993. By that time, I had retired from KTVU and was getting involved in the efforts to solve the insurance mess. In the process, I learned more than I had ever wanted to know about state insurance regulations. I learned that California's regulations did not protect homeowners, which was a disappointment but hardly a surprise. Our laws protected the insurance companies because the insurance lobby had written them. I had read about the power of big corporate lobbies, like the oil lobby, the timber lobby and the tobacco lobby. That was Poli Sci 101. But until the Firestorm, that knowledge was, for me, abstract and cerebral. It didn't get visceral until after the fire, when I learned first-hand how political power can translate into individual suffering.

Insurance policies, like the agents who sold them, always sounded good. "Like a Good Neighbor, State Farm is There." "You're in Good Hands with Allstate." They're good sales jingles, but they never mention that when you have a big loss and make a big claim, State Farm is not always there, and you're likely to feel the back of those Allstate hands.

As the months and years slowly ground by, Oakland's fire

survivors became more and more discouraged and, in many cases, threw up their hands and settled for much less than they were entitled to. That's what the companies wanted so they wouldn't have to pay out so much in claims. By the way, in the insurance industry's financial reports, money paid out in settlements is listed as "losses." That wording reveals a lot. One would think settling and paying claims is what insurance companies are in business to do. Isn't coverage what they *sold* us? Isn't money for settlements the same as their inventory, just like an auto dealer's cars? At least, that's what most customers believe.

But apparently, claims settlements really *aren't* what insurance companies are about. Truth is, they're about collecting premiums and using that money to make more money. It was all so obvious once we studied the industry's financial reports. *Of course* it was in their best interests to delay and stall on huge groups of claims like what followed after the Oakland Firestorm. State Farm alone was liable for more than one billion dollars in claims so, of course, they wanted to spread those payments over as many years as possible. And since they had written the state regulations, they could do exactly that.

Under state law, they could change adjusters as often as they wanted to. They could also put homeowners through lengthy hearings, during which they could probe any and all aspects of the homeowners' lives. At these hearings, homeowners were not allowed to be represented by lawyers, although company lawyers were allowed to be there. At these hearings, insurance companies could, and did, question homeowners about their personal lives, their friends, their house guests, even their sexuality, although God only knows what those things had to do with what had burned. What's more, if a homeowner refused to answer a question from the company, the company could, under state law, negate his entire claim.

The 3,000 homes that burned in the Firestorm were not being replaced quickly, because insurance companies could stretch the recovery over several years under cover of the laws they themselves had written.

In the first few years after the Firestorm, some survivors worked to underground power lines, others worked to build additional firehouses in the hills, others built a memorial garden or got involved in a dozen other post-fire tasks that needed doing. A few, including me, were drawn to the politics of insurance regulation. I became convinced that the laws were the main key to fairness for homeowners, and politics was something I enjoyed and knew a bit about.

My first phone call was to the Insurance Commissioner's office in San Francisco. They said they'd welcome a grassroots effort to press for insurance reform and immediately offered help and advice. The second anniversary of the fire was just a couple of months away, and, by the end of our conversation, we had agreed that holding a public hearing on insurance abuses would be an excellent way to celebrate the day. Local officials were also extremely cooperative, as were leaders from the state legislature. Two years after the Firestorm, they knew all about the problems people were having rebuilding their homes, and they seemed eager to correct the balance of power between insurance companies and homeowners.

The half dozen groups that Ina DeLong and Amy Bach had organized around the different insurance carriers became an obvious and excellent source for good and sympathetic speakers. At the hearing, their stories would fit together to form a mosaic that turned the image of the insurance industry on its head.

On October 20, 1993, half a dozen key officials sat in rapt attention as homeowners told their stories in a downtown Oakland auditorium. Hundreds of people filled the large hall to hear one witness after another tell of insurance terror. The press, happy to have something substantive to report for the second anniversary, covered our hearing and retold the stories for readers and listeners.

The testimony went on all day, with victims from every walk of life and age group — men and women, family people and singles, widows, everybody. By the end of the day it was obvious that insurance companies were getting away with murder. One family, in fact, made that accusation quite literally, and accused its insurance company of causing such depression in their mother, that she went to her burned-out lot and shot herself. Other people told about heart attacks from the pressure caused by the distress of endless meetings, and unreasonable demands for documentation to prove they actually owned what they claimed they had lost. Several elderly people said they felt that their companies were just waiting for them to die. Others said they had settled because they didn't want to spend their remaining years locked in battles over insurance.

When the hearing ended, the state officials who had attended pledged to work for insurance law reform. That pledge gave birth to Senate Bill 1355, which was introduced the following January, 1994. I spent the next 10 months helping that bill get through the state legislature. It was intense work that required every skill I had ever learned from both the League of Women Voters and my years at Channel 2. My computer and fax machines never stopped, our phone lines were in constant use. Our committee was small, but hardworking. We looked up every newspaper, television and radio station in Northern California, and personally talked to the reporters who were handling the Firestorm or insurance stories. We got their fax numbers and regularly sent out news releases. We visited every newspaper editorial board in the Bay Area and Sacramento. We became citizen lobbyists under the banner of Homeowners for Insurance Reform — maybe not a sexy title but it said who we were and what we wanted.

At one level, it was great fun. I met some terrific people who will be my friends for the rest of my life. During that year, a couple of major fires in Southern California added a few hundred more people to the ranks of homeowners who had fallen victim to the insurance industry's delaying tactics, so we had statewide representation at committee hearings in Sacramento. We were all mad as hell and on a crusade for justice.

In the eight months between January and August, when the legislative session ended, our group visited every state legislator, and every member of every committee that had anything to do with our proposed law. We were in Sacramento at least one day a week, sometimes two. We carpooled for the drive up, split into teams to call on offices, and rehearsed the spiels we would deliver to the lawmakers we were going to see that day.

By 3 or 4 in the afternoons, after finishing our office calls, we would meet in the insurance committee's office to assess our progress and plan what to do next. We even met several times with the insurance lobbyists. There were four or five full-time lobbyists in Sacramento, all very sophisticated, well financed and very well connected. They told us what they didn't like about our bill and, in some areas, we made compromises to soften their opposition. We got a lot of help in those sessions from the staff of the Senate Insurance Committee; they were our guides and teachers in the process.

It was all extremely interesting and, ultimately, a harsh lesson in the way government really works. Early in the year, during our first couple of visits to the Capitol, every legislator we talked to was totally sympathetic with us homeowners. As the year went along, however, more and more Republicans let us know that they had some reservations. "We have to keep in the provisions that will prevent fraud," they rationalized, as though homeowners were either arsonists or were out to cheat the companies. By the end of the session, in the State Assembly, the vote split straight down party lines with the Democrats *for* the bill, and the Republicans against it. But, because the Democrats had a clear majority, the bill passed and went to the governor for his approval. The governor, Pete Wilson, was a Republican, but we continued to believe that the righteousness of our cause would prevail over partisanship.

Throughout the year, we had had several meetings with Governor Wilson's insurance advisor and thought we had a good chance to get his support. After all, 1994 was an election year and there were unhappy homeowners all over the state. For the first time in history, homeowners' insurance had become a real issue. Governor Wilson's insurance secretary had been extremely cordial in all of our meetings, and gave us reason to be optimistic.

We had enjoyed great support in the press and had editorial support from every major newspaper in the state. We had even received a decent amount of coverage in the electronic press. But, it turned out, we had a distorted view of reality. One day, an industry lobbyist, in a single, blunt phrase, woke me up to the facts of life in the state capitol. It was the day the State Assembly approved our bill, the final vote before insurance reform went to the governor for his signature.

I had been in the assembly chamber, listening to the roll call, which, as I said, was right along party lines. That was good enough for me. I was happy as I left the chamber and feeling pretty good as I walked down the hall toward the elevator. One of the insurance lobbyists waved:

"Congratulations!" he said cheerfully. "Good work."

"Thank you," I answered, thinking maybe he wasn't such a bad sort after all.

"But it isn't going to do you any good, you know," he added with a grin. No, a leer would better describe his expression.

"Oh, why not? It's an election year. I think there's a lot of support for our legislation."

"Well," he paused and lifted his face just a bit to raise his eyebrows, so he was now looking down his nose at me, still grinning, "We" he said with emphasis, "have the governor." And with that, he laughed, turned and walked away, leaving me staring after him.

I suppressed the temptation to chase him and beat on him with my bare fists. Instead, I came home and, a couple of days later, got our team together and we wrote a letter to Governor Wilson which we printed in a full-page ad in the western edition of the *New York Times*. We thought it was pretty good. "Governor Wilson," the headline began, "Don't turn your back on California's homeowners. It's an election year!" And we enumerated all the reasons he should sign the reform bill.

Three weeks later, on a Friday afternoon, the very last day he had to act on our homeowners bill, Governor Wilson vetoed it. His timing was perfect from the insurance company point of view. Friday afternoons are called the "press graveyard" and not good times for coverage, so his veto didn't get much play in the news.

We did not get our reform legislation. Insurance companies could continue bullying homeowners, and the public wouldn't even know what it had missed. The only people who would know the truth would be homeowners who lose *their* homes in future firestorms — which are unfortunately now a predictable part of all our futures.

**Afterword**

One year after the fire, Craig and I were settled in a home we had bought across the Bay from Oakland. We had given up our initial hopes of rebuilding on our lot in Oakland after we realized State Farm's delaying tactics would mean that it would be four or five years before we could do that. We had wanted to stay in the East Bay but home prices drove us to high-priced Marin County. Here's why. After months of inexcusable and cruel delays by our insurance company, we hired a public adjuster and went to war with State Farm. Randy Goodman of the Greenspan Company educated us on the fine print of our insurance policy. We had been willing to settle for what our home would have sold for on the day before the fire (around $350K) but, Randy showed us how, according to the terms of our contract, it was worth far more because of two little words in the policy — guaranteed replacement. What that meant was that homes like ours and most others in the Oakland and Berkeley hills — older, built with lathe-and-plaster walls not sheetrock, with hardwood floors not laminate, with masonry fireplaces not inserts — would cost much much more to replace than they could have sold for the day before the fire. Guaranteed replacement was a phrase that sounded really good when insurance agents were selling the policies. No one expected thousands of policies to come home to roost at the same time, but that is precisely what happened with the Firestorm.

Craig and I decided we were going to get every dollar we could under guaranteed replacement in retaliation for the cruel and mean delaying tactics the company had used with us and other Firestorm survivors. We tried to find a home to buy in the East Bay but each time we wanted to bid on a nice little place, Randy would point out the terms in the policy that said — you had to spend all your guaranteed replacement dollars on your new house — otherwise the money would stay with the company. Our guaranteed replacement amount was almost three times what our home would have sold for the day before the fire and the only homes we could spend that kind of money on in the East Bay were huge mansions in Piedmont. We didn't want a huge mansion, so we went across the Bay to high-priced Marin County. We found a home the size of our Oakland home, with a breathtaking view of the bay. Then we settled in for a long war over money, but at least we could go on with our lives and that's really what was important to us.

After State Farm wrote a check for the price of the house in Marin, it was 2/3 of the money available to us under the guaranteed replacement clause of our insurance policy. It was spend it or lose it, so we remodeled the kitchen and the three bathrooms despite the fact the house was only five years old and didn't really need updating. Then we added a couple of rooms in the "dirt space" downstairs so Craig would have an office to do paperwork and another one to edit his videos. I got a potting room which doubled as an extra guest bedroom. But there were still a few thousand unused dollars under the terms of the policy so we sat in our new living room with our Interior Designer friend Bodo and Contractor Michael McCutcheon to think of what else we could do to spend the remaining money. Michael looked around and said, "Well, you could smooth the walls!" We didn't have a serious problem with the textured walls but decided that was the best option available to spend the money, so the following week two of his guys spent a couple of days replastering the walls in the living room, dining room, family room, and entry hall. That took it down to within just a few dollars of the guaranteed replacement money available, so we stopped remodeling and signed the final settlement with State Farm. It was 4 ½ years after the fire — about the same length of time it would have taken to rebuild our home on the lot in Oakland — but when we signed off with State Farm, we had already been living in our replacement home for four of those years.

The other long smoldering emotional ember that finally got settled was the relationship with my mother. By the time we bought the home in Marin County, several months had passed after the Firestorm. I was no longer as emotionally needy as I had been right after the fire and was able to return to the relationship with her that

I had worked out through some intensive therapy many years earlier. Once again I was able to accept what she was, no longer hoping she would turn into something she wasn't. I had managed to work it out when I was in my late 30s and for many years actually enjoyed my mother's company, but when I called her from that phone booth on that rainy Monday after the fire, I had forgotten it was better to have no expectations of her.

About a year after the Firestorm Craig decided it was time to see her so we drove to Costa Mesa in Southern California for our first visit with her since before the fire. As fortification against disappointment, we arrived with no expectations at all. We just wanted a cordial visit for a few days. And then, she did one of the nicest things she had ever done! We were chatting in her living room when she abruptly got up from her chair. "Wait there a moment, you two. I have something for you."

When she came back she was carrying what was probably her most cherished possession, an antique Hawaiian *tapa* wedding blanket. She had had it as long as I could remember. She kept it folded up in her sandalwood chest and even getting a look at it was a special occasion. Now she was giving it to me! "To replace all the things you lost in the fire," she said as she laid the *tapa* in my arms. This is the most precious thing I have from my tutu. Take it. Now it will be your Hawaiian legacy since you lost all your other things in the fire." It was the only time she ever brought up the subject of the fire. We thanked her the best way we knew how — by promising to take very good care of the *tapa* and to cherish it as much as she had.

As soon as we got back to San Rafael, I wrote to the Bishop Museum and asked for any special instructions to preserve it. They sent me a booklet on the care and framing of Hawaiian *tapa*. Keep it out of the sunlight; don't fold it; keep everything touching it chemically neutral. Then we found Bob Oscar, a framer who had done a lot of work for San Francisco's de Young Museum in his workspace in one of the warehouses on the City's waterfront.

When we showed him the *tapa*, he said he hadn't framed anything like it before but would like to try it, so we gave him the booklet from the Bishop Museum. We took the *tapa* back home and waited until Bob got all the special materials he needed for the job. A month later he phoned to say he was ready; he had cleared his studio of all other work so he could devote himself completely to the framing of the *tapa* blanket. "That sounds pretty scary, Craig," I said, suddenly realizing the cost was about to go through the ceiling. But what was the alternative? Putting the *tapa* back in the sandalwood chest for another 75 years?

The framing took Bob one week, during which he gave us daily updates on his progress — how he was going to hang the *tapa* from the acid-free dowel, how he would mount it on the acid-free board under the acid-free plastic "glass," and then how he was going to sweep the whole thing with an acid-free peacock feather just before he sealed it in the acid-free frame. Bob was totally caught up by the project and pretty emotional about it. If he had a frustrating day, he would phone and curse the moment he ever met us or complain he was sorry he had ever agreed to take on such an impossible task. But then he would follow that the next day by calling to thank us for choosing him to do this sacred duty with the *tapa*. Somehow we all managed to make it through that week and when he finished framing it, Bob phoned us again.

He laid out his plan for transporting the *tapa* to San Rafael and hanging it in our entry hall, the only place in our house with a ceiling high enough to accommodate the piece. "Bring a truck so we can lay it down while we drive it over there. We can't turn it on its side because the *tapa* is only hanging from the rod and is not attached any other place. And we have to move it before the sun comes up so it doesn't heat up and develop moisture inside the frame. Can you be over here tomorrow morning at 5:00?"

We set the alarm and threw some light rope and canvas in the back of our Nissan pickup so we'd be ready to go first thing the next day. Bob and his assistant were already there when we pulled up to the warehouse. It was still dark; the sun wouldn't be up for another hour or more. "First, we have to get it to the parking lot," said Bob, as he unlocked the door to his second-floor studio. "The freight elevator is large, but not large enough to take the *tapa* flat."

He put each of us on a side so we could carry the *tapa* like paramedics carry a litter. We positioned ourselves on the elevator platform, took a group deep breath, tilted the *tapa* and pushed the down button. I guess we beat gravity because the sheets of the blanket didn't slide from their places in the several seconds it took to reach the ground floor, and we were able to level out the frame again. We carefully tied it to the bed of truck, covered it with a tarp and headed for the Golden Gate Bridge, hoping that at 30 miles an hour we could make it home before sunrise.

Bob and his helper worked all morning hanging the *tapa* on the entry room wall. They fastened it on with four pairs of heavy-duty brackets so the frame would sit flat on the wall and not tilt from the top, which would eventually swing the bottom edge of the *tapa* in where it would hang against the glass. The whole thing was a gargantuan effort with the same-size price tag, but when it was done the *tapa* was majestic. I learned that Hawaiians had not made *tapa* since 1850 when the missionaries outlawed it and all other Hawaiian arts so, although I don't know exactly when ours was made, it has to be quite old. It consists of four thin sheets of the paper cloth stitched loosely together at the top with coarse twine. The three under-layers are the color of cornhusks, but the top layer is decorated with broad horizontal stripes of pinkish beiges and browns dyed with natural tinctures Hawaiians made from flowers, leaves and seeds. It's an ageless and universal design, elegant in its simplicity. It has become our great treasure. We thought it might be the lure to get my mother to visit us in San Rafael because she would want to see the *tapa* again, but she died three years after she gave it to us without ever coming to our new home.

Several years later, we decided to leave the big house in Marin County and move to a smaller home in a more rural community. House hunting was difficult; we found plenty of smaller homes we liked but if they didn't have a wall tall enough to hang the *tapa*, there was no deal! Eventually we found the perfect home on a quiet cul-de-sac in Sonoma with 8-foot ceilings in all the rooms except the living room where the ceiling slopes up from 8 feet to 12 feet, creating the ideal spot for the majestic *tapa* — a piece of timeless beauty from my Hawaiian ancestors.

Craig and I have had to deal with the threat of fire again here in Sonoma. A wildfire that became known as the Tubbs Fire would burn more than 5,600 homes before it was controlled. It was October 2017, and flames were raging on three sides of our valley when the advisory came for us to evacuate. Two friends offered their help and pickup trucks. Our son Steve was visiting us at the time, which was lucky, because he was able to think clearly about what we should take with us, and both Craig and I had sunk into a deep blank funk. Later we decided it was probably PTSD from the trauma of the Firestorm all those years ago, but we did manage to gather up paintings and Hawaiian artifacts. Steve kept going — opening closets and drawers and asking, "How about this ... How about that?" Eventually, we filled both pickups and both of our cars with stuff, and headed for Craig's brother's home in Novato to put everything into his garage for the duration.

We did better than I had done in Oakland that Sunday in October 1991, but I will never know what precious things we failed to take because, thank goodness, our home did not burn up and a week later we moved everything back and life went on as usual. It was just a little bump on the road, for *us*, but not for the more than 5,000 families that lost homes and loved ones in that mélange of fires.

It's now 2020. There have been countless devastating fires across the country in the nearly 30 years since *our* Firestorm of 1991. This year, California, Washington and Oregon have already lost more than five million acres to wildfires and, as I write this, we're just halfway through the wildfire season. As more droughts and more floods wreak havoc, apocalyptic is the word most often used to describe the level of devastation.

Homeowners find themselves caught in the terrible situation of wanting to stay where their jobs are, but too often finding they can't rebuild the homes they have lost. It's now standard for insurance to cover two years of temporary housing expense. Remember, that was imposed as an emergency measure by the California State Insurance Commissioner after the 1991 Firestorm, because the standard one year of housing assistance wasn't enough time. Now, two years isn't long enough, because rebuilding — if it happens at all — is even slower than it was then. Amy Bach, from United Policyholders, is still in there helping, and says the main problem today is that insurance rarely covers the cost of replacement. In some cases, strict new building codes drive up expenses. In other cases, prices of building materials have gone through the roof.

At the same time, insurance companies have increased premiums, cut back coverage, and have even pulled out of certain areas they consider too risky to cover. California responded to that ploy with a one-year moratorium banning insurers from dropping policies in areas of the state ravaged by wildfires. But the net effect is, homeowners can't rebuild. In nearby Santa Rosa, two years after the Tubbs Fire of 2017, not even 10 percent of the homes lost had been rebuilt. By year three, the fall of 2020, about 85 percent of homes destroyed in the Tubbs fire had been rebuilt, or were in various stages of the permitting or construction process. But tellingly, some 400 property owners had not even filed an application to rebuild.

I am no longer involved in the homeowners-insurance reform movement. But United Policyholders now works nationwide, fighting for homeowners dealing with stronger and more deadly floods, as well as fires, and it seems the basic game played by the insurance companies hasn't changed very much. There is talk that the companies will stop providing homeowners insurance, and leave it up to government — either state or federal — to provide protection to homeowners. Who knows how and when that will be settled? In the meantime, homeowners are still trying to catch the ball of fair play so they can rebuild and get on with their lives.

# COMING HOME

CHAPTER 21

## THE WHO IN THE HULA

# THE WHO IN THE HULA

Until my mid-twenties, I felt confused about my Hawaiian roots. In some ways, being part Hawaiian was quite wonderful. But I also felt insecure because I didn't know very much about the Hawaiian culture. My mother, born and raised in Hawai`i, was a native speaker, and although my brother and I were both born in the Islands, we grew up in California at a time when it was not cool to be ethnic. Mom protected us from her Island customs, making sure we knew all the Ps and Qs of my father's dominant *white* culture. While we lived in Hollywood, she taught us a couple of simple hulas, but that, and my Hawaiian name, was about as far as our Hawaiian upbringing went.

I so clearly remember the day my mother taught me how to spell that beautiful name — it was as big a day as the day I learned how to count to 100 by fives. I was probably six when I learned how to say *Ka i h i l a n i (Ka eehee lani)*, and that it meant "The Sacred Heavens." But she never called me by that name. No one did. It was just kind of a relic. The Hawaiian word my mother used for me was the nickname *Keko*. I didn't ask her what *Keko* meant, I suppose because it didn't occur to me to ask, any more than I would think to ask her what Betty Ann meant. But one day, when she was reading the *Tarzan* comics to me, she used the word "*Keko*" and I realized she was talking about Tarzan's chimpanzee. After that, I refused to answer whenever she called me *Keko*. I would just say that wasn't my name. But I didn't use or even think much about my beautiful

Hawaiian name until many, many years later.

In college, when new acquaintances asked me about my ethnic background, I would tense up and feel wary. It wasn't that I didn't *want* to be Hawaiian. I just didn't know how. As a child, and into young adulthood, I had thoroughly enjoyed knowing Auntie Berdie, a true, unabashed Hawaiian who celebrated and marketed her culture for a living. I loved my occasional visits with her because, when I was in her home, I felt I was in a Hawaiian home. Ditto with Auntie Maria and Uncle Tony in Hilo.

But a feeling of deficiency lingered, although maybe a better word is longing. My mother did what she thought was the right thing for my brother and me by repressing her own Hawaiian background and emphasized strong 'modern' ways. After all, America was a great melting pot, wasn't it? Yes, it was. If you were white, you could lose your heavy accent or thick brogue and melt right in. But if you had brown skin or almond shaped eyes, or kinky hair, you were more likely to be a lump in the nation's melting pot, never quite melting into the national cultural stew.

Twenty years after my dad died, Mom returned to her own roots and married a full-blooded Hawaiian named Noah Kalama. Their home was a Hawaiian home. They spoke Hawaiian to each other, and in her old age she became a much-revered *kupuna* (elder) in Southern California's Hawaiian community. That was wonderful for her, and by that time I had also found my own way to my Hawaiian roots.

The key for me was the hula, because I loved to dance. When I was 25, my first husband Russ and I were settling into Berkeley and I knew a lot of Hawaiians lived in the Bay Area. Where there are Hawaiians, I reasoned, there has to be hula. So I began my search in the Yellow Pages. There was no classification for 'Hula' in those days, so I looked up "Restaurants, Hawaiian" and found an ad for The

Beachcomber nightclub at Fisherman's Wharf in San Francisco. The ad promised "Live Hawaiian Floor Shows on Weekends." It was a start. If the dancers were good, I could ask them where they trained and go from there.

The floor show we saw was mediocre but, just when my hopes were fading, the announcer called a guest artist to come forward and dance. She hadn't done more than a couple of steps before I nudged my husband and announced, "She's the one! She's going to be my teacher!"

When she finished her bows, we rushed over to her table, introduced ourselves and, much to my delight, learned that she lived in Oakland, not far from our home in Berkeley, *and* gave hula lessons on Tuesday evenings. That was the beginning of a lifelong friendship with the woman whom I call my "Hawaiian Mom," Ida *Namanu`okawa`a* Wong Gonsalves.

For the next several years, I danced in her troupe nearly every weekend. In those days, Ida had the premiere Hawaiian troupe in the Bay Area, and was the first choice to entertain at luaus and Hawaiian parties. She was one of the most graceful dancers I have ever seen, and one of the sweetest, most giving people I will ever know. She became my ethnic guide, my teacher and my role model. She folded me into her family from the very first moment I walked into her home.

Ida's own mother had been a lei lady at the docks in Honolulu, one of those jobs surrounded by beauty and affluence, but that brings in very little money. Ida's family was poor, but that didn't stop her from learning hula from the best teachers in Honolulu. In the 1930s, Ida studied hula with two of the premier dancers and chanters of the day: Tom Hiona and Keaka Kanahele.

During the mid-20th century, the integrity of the hula was in great jeopardy, as were all things truly Hawaiian. *Haoles* were adopting the

Hawaiian culture and *changing* it for their own purposes. In some cases, they took it as a subject for comedy — ridiculing the Hawaiian people, their customs and their food. Consider, for example, songs like "The Cockeyed Mayor of Kaunakakai," and who hasn't heard the jokes about poi, dismissing the Hawaiian staple food as tasting like wallpaper paste?

Some composers took Hawaiian sentiment and Americanized it. Harry Owens composed *"Sweet Leilani"* as a loving tribute to his daughter, but then corrupted what had been a beautiful musical story about a lover's tryst and turned it into the *"Hawaiian War Chant."* Of course, the sword of assimilation cuts both ways, and Ida was trapped in the middle of it. She loved the traditional songs and chants of the hula, but she was faced with the practicalities of making a living, which meant giving white audiences what they wanted to see and hear.

When I met Ida in the mid '50s, she was living in East Oakland with her husband and two children, and she taught hula classes in her living room. The word *halau*, the Hawaiian term for hula school, was not used then, but would return to usage in the '70s and '80s as part of what is known as the Hawaiian Renaissance. We mainland students didn't even know what a *halau* was, nor were we taught the ancient dances and chants. I couldn't miss them because I didn't know about them. I was just grateful to have Ida as my teacher and eagerly absorbed her routines, her choreography and her *Hawaiian-ness*.

Every Tuesday evening, I boarded an AC Transit bus for the one-hour ride across two cities for an 8 o'clock hula lesson. In those days, East Oakland was a mostly Italian and Portuguese working-class neighborhood. When Ida found out how much I loved poi and other Hawaiian food, after every lesson she insisted I go in the kitchen and eat something. Poi was always accompanied by other good stuff: raw fish with *limu* and *kukui* nuts, *lomi* salmon, *laulau* and other delicacies of island cuisine. Whatever special Hawaiian treat Ida got from the Islands, she shared with me.

She was everything I had been looking for — a Chinese-Hawaiian who was comfortable in her own skin. She talked easily about her Chinese father and her Hawaiian mother and her growing-up years in Honolulu. My own mother — with the same racial mix — didn't like her heritage and had passed the discomfort on to me. Ida helped me thaw that chill. From the very first lesson, hula became my passion. I loved to dance and felt happy and beautiful doing it.

When Ida was a young woman studying the hula, she learned some of the ancient hulas, which were *kapu* (taboo) at the time, because they had originated as part of religious ceremonies very deep in the Hawaiian culture. One of the ancient chants embedded in that tradition was *The Kumulipo,* a 2,102 line epic poem about the creation of the universe. It describes the emergence of living things from darkness to mankind, and then becomes a genealogy of the royal family. It was part of the oral literature of Hawai`i, passed from one generation to the next by the priests, and was both sacred and political. Two priests took turns reciting the entire chant as part of a ceremony welcoming Captain James Cook in 1779, when he claimed to have "discovered" what he called the Sandwich Islands. A text of *The Kumulipo* was given to King Kalakaua in the mid 1800s, and his sister, Queen Lili`uokalani, translated it into English in the years following her overthrow and imprisonment by San Francisco's sugar barons.

Ida told me that while she was learning about the ancient chants, she had to live a very restricted life, both in the foods she could eat and in her interactions with other people. The hulas to these chants were performed only by very special people and only on very special occasions.

In the 1950s, when Ida was teaching hula, she told me the vows she had taken when she learned the *hula kapu* forbade her from teaching those dances to anyone. Once in a while, she would dance one for me, and I was in awe of the power of their rhythms and motions, but despaired because I was not allowed to learn them.

Twenty more years would pass before those forbidden hulas emerged from Hawaii's culturally-locked confines to become part of the regular curriculum in hula studios, or *halau* as they are once-again called. In the 1970s, Hawaiians realized if they were going to pass those ceremonial songs and dances along to future generations, they would have to loosen the restrictions and open up knowledge about them. They lifted the taboos and shared the old chants and choreography, and now those ancient hulas are performed and enjoyed everywhere. I still wish they had been available when I was younger and able to dance them, but at least I can watch them now and am proud to be part of the culture that produced them.

In my late twenties, I lived in two very separate worlds. My day job was in an office. Monday through Friday, I dressed up, wore gloves and high-heeled shoes, and pinned my waist-long hair up in a neat French roll. I drafted letters for my white male bosses to sign, shuffled papers to in-boxes, out-boxes and file cabinets, played bridge during the lunch hour, attended the lecture series at Sproul Hall on the UC campus, and watched foreign films at the Cinema Guild and Studio on Telegraph Avenue.

On Saturday evenings however, I would take the pins out of my hair, pack my sarongs and hula accessories into the car and drive to Ida's house to became part of her dance troupe, *The Hulamanu*. We performed dances from Hawaii, Samoa, Tahiti, New Zealand and the Philippines. I learned to play the ukulele and sing Hawaiian songs while dancing hula. I loved everything about it — the classes, practicing and performing.

That was the upside. I also discovered that being a Hawaiian dancer had a downside. Some of the people I met at the performances assumed I wasn't too bright because I was "just" a hula dancer, or that I had no interests beyond dancing. I also discovered that some of my new Hawaiian friends thought that, even though I was a good dancer, I was still a *haole* in my attitude. My sad conclusion, after years of immersing myself in the hula, was that I would *never really belong*. What could I do? How could I reconcile apparent contradictions in my background and interests? I was still being pigeonholed. People were still making incorrect assumptions about who and what I was, and I wasn't sure I even knew. So, I devised a way to find my own answers.

I made up a game called, "Who or what are you?" It went like this: I asked myself to describe me, then answered as quickly as I could, blurting out whatever first came to mind. My reasoning was that, if I talked fast enough, I would discover who I really was — or at least who I *thought* I was.

Each time I played the game, my first answer was always the same and had to do with my ability to learn and to think. The second word always related to gender — sometimes it was *female*, other times it was *woman*, but gender was consistent. Other descriptive words that followed changed from game to game — words like *musical, short, dark-skinned, graceful, shy, outgoing, nervous, energetic, high-strung*. But I always started out with *intelligent* and *female*. Eventually, I accepted the fact that being Hawaiian, or Chinese, or having dark skin were — despite my years of shame and self-loathing — not the most important things in my identity.

My little test told me what was important to me was that I had a fairly good brain, and I was female. These were my defining characteristics. By repeating that over and over again, I eventually came to peace with myself. Plus, I accepted that if other people asked questions about where I was *really* from, it was probably because they were curious, not hostile.

I continued dancing with Ida's *Hulamanu* even after I became pregnant with my first child. In fact, I kept dancing until I got so big that my point of balance changed. One weekend, Ida had a gig at a new Del Webb resort in Long Beach. Several of us flew down there for the show. I was five-or-six-months along and felt big as a barn. Ida always costumed us in fresh ti leaf skirts she made herself. Adjusting my skirt size to my girth was simply a matter of adding more leaves, and more leaves and more leaves. I looked like a chub, but as long as Ida thought I was okay, I kept dancing. On the beach that afternoon, she cautioned me not to stand facing the wind. I wore a *muumuu*, which disguised my pregnancy most of the time, but would have revealed all if I turned the wrong way. So I swiveled like a wind vane during that weekend so I wouldn't blow my cover.

In 1963, after my second son was born, I became more and more reluctant to spend Saturday evenings away from my family. Although I still continued going to Ida's house for Tuesday-night classes, I only danced in her major shows and left the weekend gigs to her other dancers.

The years passed and I followed another passion, politics, which eventually led to the job at KTVU-TV. Although I stayed in touch with Ida by phone, I rarely saw her except during the holidays or when she did a major show and asked me to help her. I found myself being her emcee instead of her dancer. I told myself that it was okay because I was still part of the production. I really missed dancing, but I figured any role was better than none.

More years passed and, as Ida got older, she became quite frail. After a bad fall one day she could hardly walk, much less dance, but she continued to teach her classes from a chair. She would tell me she wanted me to take over for her when she retired, but at that time I was deep into a demanding career as a TV news reporter. What little free time I had, I spent with my family that had now grown to three sons. I drifted away from all my friends in the Hawaiian community, because what had held me in it was the hula, and without the hula I found myself out of the loop.

One day, Ida's husband John called me to say that Ida didn't have much time left. I hadn't seen her for a while and when I got to her house I found the situation much worse than I had thought. Not only was Ida unable to get out of bed, but John was suffering from Alzheimer's and couldn't be much help to her. Their grandson Steve, whom they had raised, was busy with his own career and, although friends dropped in throughout the day, there was no one to make sure that Ida got adequate care or food on a consistent basis. The first day I visited, I searched their kitchen for Hawaiian goodies that would comfort her. I found some poi, fixed it for her and spooned it into her with some tiny bits of fish. Between bites, she murmured sounds of "Umm. *Ono, Ono*" (delicious, tasty).

It was 1996 and I had retired, so I was able to visit her every day. I drove there via Chinatown so I could pick up her favorite dishes and take them to her. The only other thing I felt I could do for her was to *lomi* (massage) her feet. Those feet had carried her for so many graceful years and now lay useless, the skin dried and cracked, and no matter how many creams and lotions I slathered on them, it was clear they would never carry her again. She was so weak and so very sick.

Ida died on the night of a full moon — Monday, November 25, 1996. I wrote a poem for her, the title of which, *Haina Pau Loa,* is the call a dancer gives to the musicians when she wants them to sing the last verse of the dance. I think of it as Ida's last call.

## Haina Pau Loa

*Monday*
*Moon Day*
*As November's night darkens Earth's valleys*
*The Moon brightens the hilltops*
*And casts a shimmering gangway to the water in the Bay*

*Invitation*
*Or Summons*
*Promise of Paradise*
*Dancer's nimble feet*
*Alight the golden moonbeam*
*Triple to the right*
*Triple to the left*
*Walk Forward — arms out*
*Na Manu*
*Na Manu o ka Waka*
*Promise of Paradise*

At her funeral, Ida's friends and former students danced one last time for her. The funeral home had probably never before held a scene quite like that one — dancing men, women and children filled the aisles. Others just stood and danced where they had been sitting. Everyone knew the words and the music. "Beyond the reef, where the sea is dark and cold, My love has gone, and my dreams grow old ..." Ida lay resplendent in a black-lace *holoku*, cradled in an elaborate cherry-wood casket, content beneath a perfumed mountain of fragrant pikake lei.

During the months that followed, John's Alzheimer's progressed to the point that it became impossible for him to stay at home alone. Steve found a nearby convalescent home where John would at least be safe and get regular meals. For the first few years, I would call Steve every few months to find out how he was doing, how his business was going and how John was getting along, and I would invite him to come and visit. But he would always say he was too busy and, after a while, our phone contact faded to an annual Christmas card.

In August 2008, however, all that changed. It was 12 years since Ida had died. I called Steve, issued my usual invitation to get together for lunch and, stunningly, got an invitation from him in reply. He said he had married and had a daughter and wanted me to come to the baby's christening the following week. That phone call would change the rest of my life and bring the hula back into it — big time.

I hadn't danced in a very long time and had lost touch with all my Hawaiian friends. Not only had I forgotten most of the routines I had once done so easily, but I no longer had costumes, music or choreography notes. All those things, along with everything else we owned, had burned up when our house was destroyed in the 1991 Oakland Hills Firestorm.

The funny thing is, when I called Steve, I had already begun thinking about dancing again, and had even managed to piece together one complete dance. A single hula, however, is a long way from being a repertoire, and I had no real prospects of learning any more. There was no hula in Sonoma where we were living. My Hawaiian stepsister, Naomi Kalama, had taught hula for many years, but she lived in Sacramento — too far away for me to go for weekly lessons. Steve's invitation to his daughter's baptism changed everything. It would be very nice to see Steve again and re-establish contact, and surely there would be some old family friends at the christening — maybe friends of Ida's who used to dance the hula.

As I sat in the church that morning, scanning the crowd for familiar faces, I recognized only two of the 60 or so guests. And yet, the event turned out to be a pivot point. At the luncheon following the ceremony, I sat at a table with Barbara Parkin and Jackie

Tompkins, the two other guests I had recognized as also having danced with Ida. We chatted happily, catching up on the 35 years that had passed since we had last seen each other.

Then Steve drew up a chair, poured himself a glass of wine, took a sip and announced, "I want to tell you why you are here — and why we're doing this party." Our forks froze midway between our plates and our mouths as we waited for him to go on. "Gramma told me to do all this."

"Gramma told you to ... what?"

He picked up a ham sandwich and held it to his mouth, "Crystal and I went to a psychic a couple of weeks ago and a few minutes into the session, the psychic announced that he had a message for me from Gramma." Steve stared hard at the sandwich before speaking again. "She said she wanted me to get closer to my roots, closer to the family. She said she was going to send a couple of old friends my way and that she wanted me to get together with them." He took a bite of the sandwich and chewed slowly, gazing at the three of us, one after another.

We just stared back at him — dumb with curiosity. He took another sip of wine. "The day after the psychic gave us that message, Barbara, you stopped by the house and rang the doorbell. And the day after that, Betty Ann, you called on the phone." He let his gaze move slowly around our little semi-circle again. "That's when Crystal and I decided, we'd better get everybody together. Ladies, you have my attention."

One year after that luncheon, two thick, loose-leaf notebooks were in residence on my desk. They are filled with copies of Ida's choreography, interspersed with a few dances from Uncle Joe Kahaulelio, a Kumu Hula who taught for a while with both Ida and Naomi. Those notebooks are the central reference points for what is now my life's core.

Barbara had lovingly scoured her files and sent me copies of everything she thought I would be interested in — and not just the dances. I now possess files full of hula trivia, including instructions about how to tie a sarong, how to make leis, lists of common Hawaiian phrases and much more. The spreadsheet in my computer now includes data on about 200 routines, and is still growing. Barbara had tape-recorded many of the classes she took when Ida and Uncle Joe chanted and danced together. Those recordings are now digitized and catalogued, and copies proudly sit on my library shelf.

The three of us began getting together once a month to dance all day in my kitchen/family room. Other days, I practiced hula alone every morning for about an hour. Ida taught me all of these dances years ago and she is with me every morning as I do them. I can still hear her 'instructor voice' in "Quarter turn left — palm up — Quarter turn Right — palm down." When I dance *Kawohikukapulani*, which was her signature dance, she is beside me, every step.

At about the same time as the christening party, Naomi invited me to teach her students the one hula I had reconstructed, a beautiful dance about the now-extinct Hawaiian ʻOʻo bird. She told me she thought it would be a good experience for her students because my hula style was "so sweet and so old fashioned." I could have reacted to that comment in any number of ways, but I was so excited about her wanting me to share my one hula that I just grinned with pleasure at the prospect. I also knew I would enjoy spending an afternoon with Naomi's dancers. It would be like returning to a Tuesday-evening class with Ida and the other young women of her A-Team.

The students liked my "sweet-and-so-old-fashioned" hula too, so Naomi invited me to perform it with them at their annual luau. Once more I was excited, but I also felt very nervous. I hadn't danced in public for decades and wasn't sure I would be able to do well. I actually was afraid I would lose my balance and topple over, or blank out and not remember the next step. On a more practical level, I didn't have a suitable costume. My one or two Hawaiian dresses were not nearly glamorous enough for a featured dancer in a number about the legendary bird, so Craig and a friend created a gorgeous black formal of brocade and lace, and I wore my grandmother's black and yellow feather lei. The hula, *Manu `O`o*, deserved no less.

The `O`o holds a unique place in Hawaiian history. It was a small honeyeater, black with distinct yellow feathers at its shoulders. Ancient Hawaiians used those yellow feathers, along with red feathers from other birds, to make helmets and capes for their royalty. Gathering the feathers was an honored skill. Bird-catchers would remove a few of the precious yellow feathers, then release the bird so it could grow new ones. Getting enough for a cape required monumental patience and skill. They say it took generations of bird-catchers to collect the nearly half million `O`o feathers to make King Kamehameha's floor length cloak. After Westerners came to the Islands and hunted `O`o — while introducing rats, weasels and mosquitos — native birds began dying off, and many species became extinct. Only a few survived into the 20th Century. The last `O`o song was heard in the late 1980s.

The night of the luau, my three sons and a dozen good friends made the trip to Sacramento to be there for moral support. I was in a nervous frenzy until the music started. But once I began to dance, all worry evaporated and only the music and my hula remained. I *became* the dance and the song. I was transported. It was almost an out-of-body experience.

Afterward, over a late-night snack at Naomi's house, some of her close friends were chatting about the highlights of the evening. A visiting *kumu* leaned over the kitchen counter toward me and confided that, when she saw *Manu `O`o* on the program, her first reaction was to block it out. That song, she said, had been written by her great-grandfather and stirred up bitter memories.

"My family recently discovered that my great-grandfather was not married to my great-grandmother," she began, as she moved closer so that others couldn't hear. "Our whole family had always thought they were married, and that he had written *Manu ʻOʻo* for her. It turned out that she was not his only wife. After he died, we learned that he had another wife and another family in Kahola, on the other side of the island. We were all devastated. We didn't know how to deal with that. It wasn't easy then, and it still isn't." She paused.

"When I saw that song on the program tonight, I closed my eyes when the musicians started to play, I didn't want to see it. Then I realized they were doing such a beautiful job, I was willing to listen. I still didn't want to see the dance, but when I opened my eyes and saw the way you were dancing, that you really felt the love and longing in it, I thought, yes, that's what it was all about, a deep romance, the love he felt for this woman. It was a relationship of long standing — they had children together, they had a life together, I had to accept that. You know, you did a beautiful job tonight, dancing that hula."

That was validation enough for me. I felt good, accepted. I had passed a test that I hadn't even realized I was taking. And what a story! That was October. By the end of the year, I had reviewed a number of dances and hula was becoming a bigger part of my life. I searched for a group or a class to join. I wanted to be able to do more of Ida's hulas and share them with others. Maybe I could share them by teaching them, though I didn't want a long-term job. A workshop might be the thing, but how should I go about it, and where? Who would be the students? Did I want to teach children? Teenagers? Or adults? As with so many things in life, once you clarify your intention to do something, doors begin to open.

At lunch one day with some friends, I mentioned the possibility of my teaching a workshop, maybe at the local teen center or the Boys and Girls Club. One of my friends at lunch had just finished a term as president of Vintage House, Sonoma's senior center, and before I could say *wiki-wiki* (quick), I was on the phone with the program director. Linda Gavron seemed very enthusiastic about offering a hula class because, as far as she knew, it hadn't been done in Sonoma before and it sounded like fun. We settled on a six-week, one-hour workshop on Fridays. In May, 2009, Hula Mai was born.

I had envisioned the class as all women, but one day Linda called with news. "Three men have signed up for the class," she said. "Is that okay?" After the slightest pause, she asked, "Do men do the hula?"

"Of course," I replied, instantly excited at the notion of a mixed class. And so, Hula Mai's first class consisted of 15 women and three men. Vintage House charged $30 for the six-class series, plus a $5 materials fee to cover class costs, including the choreography and the practice CD. That was a real departure from the way hula is taught elsewhere — and Naomi thought it was not a good idea.

"They won't appreciate it if you spoon feed them all the music and the choreography," warned my stepsister, who has taught hula for more than 40 years in Sacramento and is a strict traditionalist.

"It's different at the senior center, Naomi," I countered. "Primarily, my students will be retired adults who just want to have fun with the hula. And remember, I don't want a full-time job. This is a one-time workshop, and I need to maximize results in the short time span."

Then I explained, "I'm going to tell them in the first class that we're going to have a show after the last class, and the goal is for them to learn at least three hulas, and everything they need to get started is in the folders."

"Okay, Sis," she said, shaking her head, "go ahead, but I think you're crazy to think they're going to be able to do all that in only six lessons."

The gauntlet was down. The hula class became the buzz at Vintage House. Pretty soon, the receptionist was saying, "If you do a hula workshop again, I'm finding a way to take it. Everybody seems to be having so much fun. When they leave class, they're all smiling and laughing."

Five weeks into that first workshop, I dropped in to check with Linda about our upcoming program.

"Are you going back to see your students now?" she asked when we finished the items on my list.

My blank expression apparently made it clear I didn't know what she was talking about.

"There's a bunch of them practicing in one of the classrooms," she said. "They've been here every day this week. Didn't you know?"

I headed off down the hall to the classrooms. Some of the students had talked about getting together to practice for the show, but I hadn't heard any specific plans. I opened the classroom door and found eight Hula Mai students practicing *Lahaina Luna*, one of their three dances. One of them had appointed herself leader and was putting the others through their paces. The group squealed in surprise and froze in mid-motion.

"This is a sight to warm the cockles of any teacher's heart," I exclaimed, grinning. "Anybody got any questions?"

I stayed for about half an hour and helped them with the three dances they were going to do in the show. As I walked out to my car to drive home, I kept smiling at the pure joy of what Hula Mai was becoming.

As the fever built during the week leading up to the last class and show, Craig announced that he was taking his camera out of retirement and, for the first time since he had retired, my husband committed to a live shoot. I wouldn't have asked him to record it because, after more than 30 years of shooting news, he had been very clear that he was done. But I was thrilled that he cared enough about Hula Mai to document its first show.

Linda and the rest of the staff got caught up in the enthusiasm and told us that Vintage House would prepare a light *luau* lunch for the people who came to the show. One student brought in some huge crepe paper flowers and a couple of pink flamingos to decorate our venue. Craig ordered a couple of tropical backdrops to hang on the walls behind the dancers to create the effect of a stage. Somebody told me I could buy Hawaiian leis for each *graduate* at the Dollar Store.

"We all know it's more fun to get *leid* than it is to get a certificate!" I said, as part of my explanation to the class about plans for their show and celebration.

About 90 friends and family showed up for that show. I don't think anybody really expected it to be any good. After all, they all knew there had only been six classes. But I had invited several dancer friends to come in support of my new students, and to fill out the program. Naomi was the cherry on the cake. She gave the *pule* (blessing) to the class as they assembled for their first number, then, smacking her right fist into her left palm, cheered, "Now, go for it!"

What followed was enchanting. The students danced their three hulas better than they had *ever* done before. As I watched them moving in unison, all smiles and confident in their steps, I filled with pride. I had thought I might have to jump in from the side if they stumbled or got confused, but they just danced straight ahead and impressed the dickens out of their friends, themselves — and me.

The event was a triumph in every way, maybe best defined by a couple overheard in conversation heading home after the show.

The husband said to his wife, "After all these years of going to the Islands regularly, and after all the Hawaiian shows we've been to, this afternoon I finally got it."

"Got what," his wife asked.

"I finally got what the hula is all about," he said. "All these years I have always thought that the hula was something the Hawaiians did for us tourists. But today, I saw that it's really about family, about community, about friends and, as Betty Ann said when she quoted King Kalakaua in her introduction, the hula *is* the dance of the heart. Yeah, I saw that today."

When people *get* what the hula is really about, that's the best, as far as I am concerned. Ida would be so pleased.

Eleven years have now passed since that first hula workshop, and I marvel at what has happened to Hula Mai. I often describe Hula Mai as a hula rocket ship. We are now ready for liftoff at every show, seasoned entertainers with an extensive repertoire of modern and ancient songs, chants and dances. We perform fully produced, beautifully costumed, Hawaiian extravaganzas in Sonoma Plaza's amphitheater every June, and regularly entertain at Sonoma Valley's many retirement facilities and community organizations. And at every show I introduce myself as Betty Ann Ka`ihilani Bruno — proudly using the Hawaiian name that's been waiting in the background all these years.

Some of the dancers — without my having to be there — put on their own show every month at the local hospital, and cheer up wheelchair-bound patients at a skilled nursing facility by leading them in hula hand-and-arm motions to familiar Hawaiian songs like *Hukilau* and *Lahaina Luna*.

At our Hula Mai Christmas Party, the dancers presented me with a pair of sequined ruby slippers to "make all my dreams come true" and then gave me something they said they knew I had always wanted, an autographed photograph of Judy Garland. I suspect the signature was forged, but — well — I can pretend it's the real thing, can't I? After all, isn't that what *The Wizard of Oz* is all about?

Hula Mai has an active website full of pictures and videos (www. hulamai.org), with links to other Hawaiian resources and activities. We also have a small lending library of books and music for the dancers to use. And perhaps most important, Hula Mai has become a large, extended *ohana* (family) that strengthens, nourishes and enriches everyone who participates in it. The hula has helped us find ourselves and find each other, and we are all the better for it.

This year, as the cherry on the cake, the Fine Arts Commission of Sonoma named me as the city's Treasure Artist for 2020. The local tradition goes back decades and has honored dozens of outstanding painters, sculptors and designers. For me, the honor is profound. It is recognition of the beauty of the hula and the Hawaiian culture, and validation of a lifelong journey to an identity that I can now embrace without any reservation, hesitation or limitation.

Once, the hula was the way I found out who I was. Now, the hula is who I am. Mahalo, *Ida Namanu`okawa`a* Wong Gonsalves, for helping me find the "Who in the Hula."

# AND NOW *this* – JUST IN

A dear friend of ours, Uncle Bob Miyashiro, lost his home in the Glass Fire, one of the all-too-frequent wildfires currently plaguing California. It was September 28 when the fire that had been raging for one week in Calistoga and St. Helena suddenly roared into his neighborhood in northeast Santa Rosa. For 52 years Uncle Bob had lived on a quiet five-acre redwood and fern glade with a lovely stream running through it. But it wasn't quiet that night. Fire trucks with lights flashing and loudspeakers blaring were telling everyone to get out NOW. Uncle Bob grabbed a few pieces of his precious Hawaiian *hulu* (feather craft), ran outside and threw them into his car. He could see a huge wall of flames less than a mile away heading in his direction. He jumped into the car and barreled down the narrow country road to safety.

Although he was able to grab the *hulu* cape, helmet and a few leis he had made because they were in the living room, there wasn't time to get to the bedroom for the beautiful Hawaiian quilts he had also made. Since retiring from his career as Swim Coach at the local junior college, Uncle Bob had taught himself both of

*Mahi`ole*, helmet as worn by the *Ali`I* Hawaiian nobility. 20" tall, decorated with red and yellow feathers (2020).

these Hawaiian crafts and did them with such patience and skill that his creations were widely praised and valued. The fire devoured everything — all five acres of beautiful forest and woodland, the dock at the edge of the stream, his house and everything in it. The loss of the quilts is almost incalculable. He had made them in the "old way" — one stitch at a time, with literally millions of stitches in each quilt. Years and years of his life's work went up in flames.

Uncle Bob is also part of Hula Mai. He held a workshop for us in *hulu* and came to our monthly "Crafty Sundays" to help us both in *hulu* and in quilting, so of course we wanted to help him recover from his terrible loss. It's difficult because he's fiercely independent and claimed he didn't need anything, but some of the ladies insisted on sharing their family treasures with him. At an outdoor, socially distanced and masked get-together we had for him, among the treasures was a beautiful old Japanese scroll to hang on his new rental wall. One hula sister gave him a framed needlepoint picture she had made years ago, and another, a coffee-table book on Hawaiian quilts.

I couldn't think of anything to give him but asked if he would like to borrow my grandmother's quilt for a while — a quilt that had been on my parents' bed for years before it was on mine. He agreed, saying having a Hawaiian quilt on his bed would be colorful and bring him comfort. The quilt has been in a sandalwood chest that also housed the Hawaiian wedding *tapa* I write about in the Afterword to Firestorm. When I opened the chest to take out my grandmother's quilt, I saw another quilt I had forgotten about — an unfinished quilt project a cousin had given to me several years ago. At that time, he told me his mother and my mother had started it together but both of them had died before they could finish it. Since he didn't know anyone who could finish it, he insisted I take it. I have never quilted and have no plans to start so the unfinished quilt has remained in that sandalwood chest all this time.

As I was taking out my grandmother's quilt to loan to Uncle Bob and saw the unfinished quilt, an idea dawned on me. How about asking Uncle Bob if he would like to finish it and make it his own? He told us each quilt took about a year and a half to make, and he wasn't yet ready to undertake a project like that. But after showing it to him I asked, "How about this one?"

Showing the unfinished quilt project to Uncle Bob and Linda Bodwell (2015).

He looked at it, hesitated for a moment and then said "Yes, I think I would like to do that. Yes, I would like that." A few days later he told me he bought a needle, thread and hoop and had begun working on the quilt. While he was examining it he found a 10" thread dangling where my mother and Auntie Hattie had left off the last time they had worked on it. He said the thread was very fragile, but he was able to blend it into his new stitches and carry on right where they had stopped. "I'd like to know more about them," he said, "because now we are all in this quilt together."

Hawaiian style, when you make something, especially a quilt, you put part of yourself into it — your talent, power, spirit if you will. In sharing stories and photos about Auntie Hattie and my mother with

Uncle Bob, I renewed my connection with my mother — a positive one that that feels good.

My mother always had an artsy-craftsy project going — sewing, knitting, crocheting, embroidering. Always creating something. I remember her making lots of fun pillows for our home in Hemet when I was in high school — they were all decorated with colorful fish she had embroidered. She also painted an underwater scene for the little shower room in the bathroom downstairs that was originally a closet. It was always so much fun taking a shower there because the walls were covered with seaweed stems and fantasy seaweed flowers she had painted.

Lynda Morley-Mott listens as Uncle Bob teaches a *Hulu* (Hawaiian Feather Art) workshop for Hula Mai (2017).

I am so happy her quilt will now be finished after all these years of waiting. My mother and Auntie Hattie will be companions with Uncle Bob through the quilt, and he will have many pleasant evenings drawing his thread through the quilt while connecting to the past by the thread they left dangling for someone to find.

# ACKNOWLEDGEMENTS

Looking back over my life from the thin-air age of 89, I have to smile in wonder at the many unusual, rare, and perhaps even extraordinary things that have happened to me. Although I might not have appreciated it at times, I have been extremely lucky, and I would like to thank all the gods that be for the steady stream of talented, gifted, wacky, wise, troubled and generous people who have made some of my life's experiences worthy of telling.

Specifically, I would like to thank David Bolling, a brilliant editor who took my pile of somewhat disparate stories and molded them into a cohesive book with a beginning, a middle and an end.

Thanks to Kara Adanalian for her artist's eye and technical skill in making this book also a beauty to behold.

Many thanks to L. Frank Baum's great-grandson Robert Baum, for a lovely Foreword with an inside story about the origins of Oz.

To author Steve Cox for telling us some of his story about creating his book *The Munchkins Remember,* and sharing the story behind that memorable scene in the movie.

Endless thanks to Gail Ford, Sandra Hansen and Sheryl Leighton, not only for help in editing, but also for their support, friendship and patience throughout the birthing of this book.

To Walter Hansell, Roberta Cairney and Jay Schaefer for their boost in getting these stories out of my computer and into your hands.

To my former boss Fred Zehnder, who ran the KTVU newsroom with wisdom, fairness, and a sense of duty to truth and balance.

And to my hubby Craig Scheiner, for taking countless pictures to help us all remember where we've been and what we've done and, above all, for all the ways and all the things he helps with and gives forever.

Made in the USA
Middletown, DE
17 February 2021